TO SEEK OUT NEW LIFE

The BIOLOGY of

STAR TREK

TO SEEK OUT NEW LIFE

The BIOLOGY of STAR TREK

ATHENA ANDREADIS, Ph.D.

Crown Publishers, Inc.

New York

This book is dedicated to my parents,
who gave me the unexpurgated works of Jules Verne
and urged me to always question and explore.

Published by Crown Publishers, Inc., 201 East 50th Street, New York, New York 10022. Member of the Crown Publishing Group.

Random House, Inc. New York, Toronto, London, Sydney, Auckland

www.randomhouse.com

CROWN and colophon are trademarks of Crown Publishers, Inc.

Printed in the United States of America

Library of Congress Cataloging-in-Publication Data

Andreadis, Athena.

To seek out new life : the biology of Star Trek / by Athena Andreadis.

p. cm.

Includes index.

1. Biology. 2. Star trek (Television program) 3. Star trek (Motion picture) I. Title.

QH307.2.A54 1998

791.45'72—dc21 98-9359

CIP

ISBN 0-609-60329-9

10 9 8 7 6 5 4 3 2 1

First Edition

CONTENTS

ACKNOWLEDGMENTS

This book is what we biologists call "tetraparental." Besides me, it was lucky enough to have three more parents.

The project would never have been born without the encouragement and support of Peter Cassidy, my partner in life. He urged me repeatedly to enlarge this idea, which had been haunting me for the last decade. He not only held my hand throughout the grueling writing marathon, but he also sifted through every word of the various drafts.

The proposal would never have got off the ground without the dedication and resourcefulness of Jimmy Vines, my agent. He believed in me, an author of stories and essays who hadn't written a full-length book before, and he didn't rest until he found the right home for the book.

The manuscript would not be as finely calibrated if it hadn't been for the discernment and vigilance of Kristin Kiser, my editor, who went over each word armed with both understanding and a fine-tooth comb. Her enthusiasm and optimism were both infectious and sustaining.

There were godparents at the pillow of this book as well. David Bischoff, Calvin Johnson, and Charles Query took precious time out of their busy schedules to read the manuscript and point out infelicities of style and errors of fact. If there's a single mistake left in the text, it's certainly not because of their scrupulous review.

My parents, sister, and friends cheered me on unstintingly. I must also single out my colleague Curt Deutsch, who let me plunder his stupendous library. The members of my lab accommodated their boss, who went around in a fog of fatigue. I count myself fortunate to be surrounded by such people. They made writing this book such fun that I intend to repeat the experiment as soon as I've caught up on my sleep.

LIST OF ABBREVIATIONS

STAR TREK TELEVISION SERIES

TOS	=	*Star Trek: The Original Series*
TNG	=	*Star Trek: The Next Generation*
DS9	=	*Star Trek: Deep Space Nine*
VOY	=	*Star Trek: Voyager*

STAR TREK FILMS

ST1	=	*Star Trek I: The Motion Picture*
ST2	=	*Star Trek II: The Wrath of Khan*
ST3	=	*Star Trek III: The Search for Spock*
ST4	=	*Star Trek IV: The Voyage Home*
ST5	=	*Star Trek V: The Final Frontier*
ST6	=	*Star Trek VI: The Undiscovered Country*
ST7	=	*Star Trek VII: Generations*
ST8	=	*Star Trek VIII: First Contact*

SCIENTIFIC TERMS

AI	=	artificial intelligence
DNA	=	deoxyribonucleic acid
ESP	=	extrasensory perception
HIV	=	human immunodeficiency virus
RNA	=	ribonucleic acid

"When do we sail, so I can take the helm?"

From a Greek folk song of the
Dodecanese islands

OVERTURE:
THE STARSHIP LEAVES THE DOCK

When I was a child, my father would show me the stars. We'd lie down on a sandy beach at night and look up at the constellations. In those days, there was little light pollution in Greece. The stars filled up the sky with their fiery rain.

As we looked at the faraway fires of Sirius, Procyon, Betelgeuse, and Rigel, we talked endlessly about the possibility of life under different skies. What would they look like? Would we ever meet them? And how would we act when we met them?

I still wonder about these questions. That's why I've become a scientist, you see, because I want to travel into that starlit darkness, where there are no answers yet. I fancy myself an astrogator of sorts, one of the many—biologists, chemists, physicists—who guide a long-generation starship called science.

One of the missions of an astrogator is to first imagine the destination. What we don't know will always exceed what we know. The universe is presenting us with wonders almost faster than we can absorb them. When we don't know what is out there, we put a sign on the maps: "Here be dragons." But we go exploring anyway, despite our fears and our ignorance, despite voices that argue that what we know is enough.

The visualization of the new, the creation of a coherent picture from disparate and incomplete data, is the beginning of all great journeys, scientific or otherwise. And that's why one of the most valuable scoutships of the astrogators is the starship *Enterprise.*

At this point, someone must be very determined or very isolated not to have heard of *Star Trek*, for it is rooted in human collective memory as surely as the Homeric epics and the great religious texts. In the United States, thirty years after its original appearance on television, the concept is now in its fourth incarnation and ninth film. For many Americans, whatever view they hold of science and technology comes from *Star Trek*. And therein lies the series' greatest power and responsibility.

Since the dawn of consciousness, humans have wondered, *Are we alone in this universe?* The discovery of extraterrestrial life, intelligent or not, would rank as the most earthshaking discovery in human history. People are riveted to the pictures from the planetary missions, wondering what might lie under the dried Martian riverbeds, beneath the methane clouds of Titan—wondering, too, what the Pioneers and Voyagers will meet when they sail beyond the solar system.

Yet we still haven't received any signal that can be unequivocally interpreted as emanating from another civilization. Why is that? There exist billions of galaxies, each containing billions of stars. However, both cosmologists and starship captains know that the universe is vast. The empty spaces between stars and between galaxies are so enormous that a signal might come and fall on stony ground—before we have the technology to capture and decipher it, for example.

There is, too, the anthropic principle of John Barrow of Sussex University and Frank Tipler of Tulane University, which states that, since we are here, the existence of *our* race must have been inevitable. From the quantum and cosmological constants to the absorption spectrum of chlorophyll to the constituents of nucleic acids, all the physical constants are such that *humans* had to happen. Although this principle is a rather obvious tautology (if physical laws were different, humans would obviously not be here to deduce them), it puts unexpected constraints on life in the universe: if life is optimized for humans, perhaps Earth life is all there is.

My opinion is that the anthropic principle is unnecessarily narrow. We know that extrasolar planets do exist; inevitably, some of them will support life. The only way to know for certain, though, short of passively waiting for a signal or a visit, is to go out there and actively search for alien life. That's what the NASA planetary missions have done; that, too, is the primary raison d'être of the Federation starships. As the voice-over intones at the beginning of each show, the mission of the *Enterprise* is "to seek out new life and new civilizations."

The physical and engineering concepts in *Star Trek*—warp speed, transporters, event horizons of black holes, time travel, cosmic strings—are heady, and their applications would certainly transform human existence. However, everything in *Star Trek* is harnessed to the mission of discovering life: all the cutting-edge engineering technology, all the exotic space corridors (the wormhole near Bajor in DS9, the Borg subspace conduits in TNG and VOY). In our own universe, *Star Trek* would not have lasted a single season if it investigated only physics and engineering technology, despite their enormous intrinsic interest.

The *Star Trek* explorations focus on exobiology, exoarchaeology, exoanthropology, exosociology. These pursuits are exciting and provocative, since they essentially focus on human behavior, on our untapped potential and our inherent limitations. These explorations tell us as much about ourselves and our assumptions as about what we discover.

Examining the bioscience in *Star Trek* is a fruitful exercise, one that I was eager to pursue. After all, we're talking picturesque nonhuman cultures and alien sex customs here! Seriously, though, finding out where the series has been prescient in its predictions and where it has gone widely off the mark gives us interesting clues about the way we think, about our lingering desire to have the bitter cups of difficult decisions taken from us. The mirror that the show holds up forces us to examine areas that are slippery and dangerous for scientists and nonscientists alike—ethics, religion, gender prejudices, and reproductive taboos.

The bioscience in *Star Trek* ranges from the probable to the completely unattainable. Some of the show's biological premises make sense, many inspire chuckles and shakings of the head. In that gap between the biologically probable and what is portrayed, there is more than enough room for speculation into the possibilities that the show's creators have missed or avoided.

Star Trek is additionally fascinating for someone like me, who was born in Greece and came to the United States as a student, after I had grown up. For in the end, *Star Trek* is really an intriguing look into American society and into the ideas that Americans have of other human cultures, a playful playing field where alternatives to our present solutions (and problems) are explored.

Almost certainly, I won't be there when we receive our first extrasolar communication or meet the first nonhuman civilization. However, thanks to *Star Trek,* I've been given the opportunity to speculate about these matters and consider what kind of direction in our biotechnology and ethics will make it likely that we'll be there for that meeting. The next time I see my father, we'll have a lot to talk about.

ACT I.

A PARADE OF THE UNLIKELY AND THE IMPROBABLE

The Dramatis Personae Enter the Stage

SCENE I.
ANIMAL, VEGETABLE, OR MINERAL?

Rocks That Brood, Clouds That Ponder—
Sentience in *Star Trek*

You look at your tricorder, which is displaying the results of its sensor sweep through the dark pergium mines of Janus VI. It's cold down here, and the hairs at the back of your neck are prickling with unease. Something has been killing the miners . . . some thing. Even now, both you and the tricorder can sense it drawing nearer.

"What sort of alien life do we have here?" asks your captain.

You check your tricorder again, then answer unbelievingly, "Silicon."

Selecting the chemical basis of a planet's biology is hardly like picking a dish from a menu list. The possible choices are actually quite limited. Off-center scientific ideas, of course, are a *Star Trek* staple. Not that I blame them much. In science fiction, half the fun is playing with scientific concepts in imaginative ways and utilizing cutting-edge terminology the way fantasy fiction uses Elvish or Latin. The other half of the fun, though, is follow-through on the concepts.

But we're still looking at that tricorder. Indeed, a silicon-based lifeform, the Horta, is what Captain Kirk and Mr. Spock encounter in those pergium mines. As always, there are two sides to the story. The Horta is protecting its eggs from the strip-mining humans. Once our heroes manage to establish communications via mind-meld, they come to a mutually beneficial arrangement. It turns out that the hatchling Horta eat raw rock and excrete it as semirefined ore. So the more of them there are, the better for the mining operation (and to put the icing on this win-win cake, they're nonunion labor).

This justly famous *Star Trek* episode, "The Devil in the Dark" (TOS), illustrates four major *Star Trek* themes and one series cliché. The cliché is that in *Star Trek* even exotic life-forms invariably act like mammals—usually a mother protecting her young. The four themes are the Prime Directive, which calls for noninterference with developing life-forms; communication between different life-forms; telepathic mind-melding; and last but not least, the topic of this chapter: out there in the final frontier, there may exist life-forms based on elements other than carbon.

If life elsewhere is similar enough to us or very advanced, there will be no way to mistake it for anything else: when something tries to shake your hand or eat you, when someone beams a message that is recognizably mathematics or music, you do not need further tests. An area at the boundary of the exotic, though, contains both the very different and the relatively primitive. For these, more exhaustive and stringent criteria will be needed to distinguish life from nonlife.

THE MARK OF CAIN

It's life, Captain, but not as we know it. How often must this phrase echo through high school biology teachers' heads as they scrutinize this year's batch of students? So it stands to reason that the first question they chalk up on the board is, *What is life?*

Let's break this into small, discrete chunks. What distinguishes organic (i.e., carbon-based) chemistry from biochemistry?

The answer is *very little.*

This is why the results of the Viking probe from Mars (and more recently the possibility of primitive microbes in a Martian meteorite) are so tantalizing and controversial. In the meteorite, biologists found remnants of life processes, like the shadowy voices that a scientist heard when he had a stylus trace the grooves of a Sumerian pot. Any organic chemistry that is advanced enough is indistinguishable from biochemistry and, in fact, is its precursor.

Cells of live organisms have a complicated apparatus, consisting of specialized molecules that execute specific tasks. Proteins are both structural and catalytic components of cells. Nucleic acids are the information archives and couriers. But these molecules, no matter how complex, are still organic compounds.

So what characterizes the phenomenon of life?

Living things metabolize; that is, they consume resources and release energy. Yes, but so does a flame. Living organisms grow and reproduce entities like themselves. Certainly, but crystals seeding out of solution do the same. Living matter has a high degree of organization and complexity. Absolutely, but an elegant computer protocol has similar characteristics. Remember, higher functions, such as social organization and self-consciousness, only enter the equation at the level of vertebrates.

So again, what is life?

The *Star Trek* answer to the question is, *All of the above.*

Follow the idea of sapient crystals and you end up with the silicon-based Horta, which moves through solid rock and excretes acid ("The Devil in the Dark," TOS). Follow the idea of sentient flames and you reach the concept of the various "beings of pure energy" that have dotted the shows in all four incarnations.

Continue on the logical path of those elegant computer programs and you get intelligent microchips (Wesley Crusher's nanites, which rearrange the computer circuits in "Evolution," TNG) and, eventually, the jewels in the crown of android creation—Dr. Noonien Soong's Data and Lore. In "The Measure of a Man" (TNG), like Dred Scott, who presented a similar petition to the U.S. Supreme Court in 1857, Data asks for his independence and citizenship rights. Unlike Scott, Data wins his case, widening the definition of life in the Earth-based Federation.

Are these mere flights of fancy? There is one vital (pardon the pun) distinction between life and its absence. But let us list the similarities first.

Live matter is made of the same elementary particles as its inanimate counterpart—namely, fermions (quarks and electrons), which interact via boson exchange (gluons, photons, and gauge bosons). Fermions, which cannot occupy the same space, constitute matter. Bosons make up the fields—electromagnetic, nuclear, gravitational. Given their constituent elementary particles, it is ludicrous that life-forms should be killed by "the baryon sweep" used to clean the *Enterprise* in "Starship Mine" (TNG)—unless the baryon sweep consists of heavy atom nuclei, which tend to be radioactive.

Like all other matter, life must obey the universal physical laws. Anyone who touches a high-voltage wire or jumps from a plane without a parachute will discover that s/he is not exempt from either electromagnetism or gravity, whether s/he thinks that humans are the pinnacle of creation or not.

Life shares with other complex systems the property of emergence. A system is emergent if it is greater than the sum of its parts and exhibits characteristics that cannot be predicted by its components alone. Live organisms are open systems with negative entropy (disorder). Life is the highest-order example of a "complex adaptive system," the favorite topic of conversation and research at the Santa Fe Institute and other centers of complex sciences.

But life is subject to an additional constraint. It must also follow a genetic program. That is, live matter must contain an inner code that ensures that there will be strong continuity of form and function as the organism reproduces. The repercussions of environmental pressures on genetic programs are more commonly known as evolution.

Life can be based on any chemical premise that will allow individual complexity, species diversity, and most importantly, adherence to the genetic program. On Earth, we have one such premise—carbon.

ENTER THE DRAGON

Believe me, carbon isn't just something that you scrape off your toast or wear on your finger. Life, as you might imagine by the prerequisites I have listed, needs complex compounds. Carbon fits the profile completely. It is by far the most versatile element for forming complex compounds, although it's far from being the most common element in the universe.

Atoms resemble minuscule solar systems, with electrons orbiting the nucleus where the neutrons and protons huddle. However, atoms actually differ from a solar system in an important way: the electron orbits are subject not to gravity, but to quantum laws, which prevent the electrons from spiraling into the nucleus.

The capacity of atoms to form chemical bonds depends entirely on the status of the outermost electron orbital of each element. If that orbital is full, the atoms disdain any bonding (and are known by the appropriately haughty name of noble gases).

Carbon, though, like its fellow occupants of the fourth column of the periodic table, has an outermost electron orbital that is exactly half-occupied. Therefore, the fourth-column elements can act as both electron donors and electron acceptors. Translated into humanese, that means that they can form compounds with just about every other element.

Carbon has an additional characteristic that is almost unique (we'll get to the inevitable partial exception in a bit). Its unoccupied orbital is at such a distance from the nucleus that it can form bonds of the exactly correct strength to create large and complex compounds. At the same time, they are of the exactly right resilience to still be reactive. In particular, carbon bonds with itself more or less with the same proclivity that it bonds with anything else.

To put it in a nutshell: carbon is the Marcello Mastroianni of elements: that rare partner who, although promiscuous, forms enduring and mutually beneficial relationships. As a result, carbon compounds by themselves vastly outnumber all other compounds of all other elements put together.

Organic chemistry is essentially an exercise of how imaginative you can get. Whatever people have dreamed of—of any size, shape, taste, or smell—can be found among organic compounds, from diamonds to nucleic acids, from limonenes (the scents of citrus fruits and flowers) to fullerenes (the "cage" compounds that resemble Buckminster Fuller's domes). So if diversity and flexibility are required, carbon wins hands down.

Another characteristic of terrestrial biomolecules is a natural outcome of the intrinsic properties of the carbon atom. Each carbon can bond with four other atoms in a tetrahedral configuration. If each of the four partners is different, the resulting molecule has no symmetry axis and is not superimposable on its mirror image. The chemical designation for such molecules is "chiral," which in Greek means "handed" (put the term *chiral* in the memory vaults, because we'll retrieve it later). Without a single exception, all Earth biomolecules are chiral.

Of course, any molecule aspiring to find itself in the Libro d'Oro of life must contain additional components besides carbon—but not that many. The secondary elements in all four major biomolecule groups (carbohydrates, lipids, proteins, and nucleic acids) are hydrogen, oxygen, nitrogen, phosphorus, and sulfur. A few additional ions (calcium, magnesium, sodium, potassium, chlorine) help cells maintain correct pressure and electric charge. There is also the occasional transition-metal atom (iron, cobalt, copper, zinc, or manganese) to help a protein keep its correct shape or discharge its function. Overall, biomolecules have followed the path of minimum input/maximum output.

So if there's life on other planets, carbon-based or not, what will it look like?

Life will probably display at least one axis of symmetry, usually left-right bilateral. Gravity, necessary for maintenance of the planetary atmosphere, will probably establish a top/bottom gradient (leaves and roots, heads and feet). Any life-form that is not sessile—that is, attached to something—will also have a front/back differentiation as well. There will be sensory organs at least in the direction of motion, although the proverbial eyes in the back of the head would help whether someone was predator or prey. Also, since life must respond to environmental input, life-forms must have sensors for some or all of the following: electromagnetic emissions (vision, temperature sensation), air pressure (hearing), and molecules in the atmosphere (smell and taste).

Within these broad parameters, anything else goes. However, a lifeform that wants to develop technology will also do well to develop grasping appendages—arms, tentacles, strands.

I'm afraid that *Star Trek* has actually been timid and unimaginative in its depiction of varied carbon-based life. Whenever I watch an episode unfold on an Earth-like planet, I can generally count on a distressing absence of fauna, and the flora invariably consists of brush and eucalyptus—which understandably, but regrettably, always brings to mind . . . southern California! There is a dolmenlike rock in Vasquez, California, also the site of innumerable westerns, that has been used so often in *Star Trek* that it's recognizable on sight. Halfway through "Arena" (TOS), I almost expected the Lone Ranger to come galloping to Captain Kirk's rescue!

While production limits have to be observed, *Star Trek* often doesn't make nods to ecology when it would be easy to do so. For example, it shows plants relying on chlorophyll, which converts light energy efficiently only in the yellow-green part of the spectrum ("Hippocratic Oath," DS9), on planets orbiting red giants. *Star Trek* would not have stretched plausibility or imagination if it had shown the orange/red carotenes taking the place of chlorophyll. Such compounds do in fact reside in terrestrial tree leaves—think colorful autumn foliage.

Furthermore, the nonhuman carbon aliens of *Star Trek* come straight out of the Hollywood alien canon, as you can easily tell by looking at their categories.

One alien group encompasses cute fuzzies similar to the Ewoks of *Star Wars*. The cooing muffs in "The Trouble with Tribbles" (TOS) are in fact the prototypes for this category. Another class is made up of large-eyed waifs familiar from the Spielberg films. Such a one is Ethan/Barash in "Future Imperfect" (TNG), an orphan who manages to pluck even the taut heartstrings of Will Riker.

These are the good aliens, which you will notice display a high

Snugglability Quotient (SQ™). Of course, for dramatic purposes (to say nothing of tradition), there have to be bad aliens with decidedly low SQ.

One set of baddies is populated by descendants of *Creature from the Black Lagoon*—for instance, Armus, the hate-filled tar being in "Skin of Evil" (TNG) who smothers Tasha Yar in her first incarnation. Another consists of large insectoids modeled after the antagonists in *Alien* and *Predator*. The best (or worst, depending on your viewpoint) such case is race 8472 in "Scorpion" (VOY). These guys are shaped like gigantic praying mantises and are telepathic to boot. Avid genetic purists, they consider all other species weaklings to be destroyed, and they are so dangerously advanced that they turn even the dreaded Borg ships into Crock-Pots.

As for the humanoids in *Star Trek,* they are so improbably similar that they deserve, and are given, a whole chapter (chapter 2) entirely to themselves.

Budget considerations undoubtedly contribute prominently to this lack of adventurousness. Effects are costly. It is cheaper to stuff an actor into a gorilla suit and glue a horn on his forehead than to follow the advice of an exobiologist.

In fairness, though, I should emphasize that the path of evolution is not linear. It depends critically on planet specifics (gravity, atmophere composition, temperature, length of day) and random astrological/geological events (star age, large-meteor impacts, ice ages). *Star Trek* cannot predict what creatures will look like on another planet because no one can.

To give you an example close to home, if the large meteor hadn't fallen in Mexico's Yucatán peninsula during the Cretaceous/Tertiary boundary, causing nuclear winter, dinosaurs would still hold pride of place and mammals would never have come into their own. No wonder we always think of them with a frisson of unease: somewhere in our midbrain we know that, but for fortune, *they* could be arguing over *our* fossilized skeletons. Indeed, our heroes meet space-faring saurians who are appalled to see their evolutionary supremacy threatened in "Distant Origin" (VOY).

E PLURIBUS UNUM

I just sang the hymn to carbon diversity. You don't have to take this on faith, either—the evidence is all around us. Terrestrial life-forms have adopted all imaginable colors, textures, shapes, and sizes.

Of course, there are some limitations: life-forms cannot exceed a certain size without literally collapsing under their own weight, as whales do when they are beached. Invertebrates, which have a passive oxygen/carbon-dioxide exchange system, have to be even smaller to avoid death by asphyxiation. The size of invertebrates is also limited by the physiology of their neurons, which transmit impulses linearly. The slowness of their nerve messages makes it impractical to exceed a certain size (so much for giant cockroaches eating Cincinnati).

Yet when we examine the crucial connecting link between molecule and organism, the genetic program itself, we come to an amazing discovery: all terrestrial life-forms use the same material for their program—a nucleic acid. Most commonly, it is deoxyribonucleic acid (DNA). Occasionally, we also encounter its older yet unrulier sibling, RNA, which we'll discuss at greater length later.

The uniformity at the core of all this diversity is stunning. The same genes are found essentially unchanged in bacteria, fungi, insects, nematodes, and mammals, often fulfilling remarkably similar functions—for example, limb formation. Here we have the biological equivalent of the grand unified theories in physics—and physics had a head start of at least a century! This uniformity is almost conclusive evidence that life on Earth arose and survived only once.

Are nucleic acids the only possible material for a genetic program? Fulfilling the requirements of a genetic program is an enormous task. It requires the ability to compress multiple information layers in a very small space.

DNA is an extraordinary system in its capacity for information storage. Consisting of an alphabet of only four letters (the four large molecules that comprise the rungs of the double helical ladder), it can decompress instructions for at least five programs—and hence orchestrate the chords for beings that range from an amoeba to a begonia to a concert pianist.

DNA can be read in different ways by the cell machinery to undergo unfolding/folding (compaction into chromosomes), replication (generation of daughter copies during cell division), transcription (creation of the messenger RNA, which transports the information of the archive from the nucleus to the cytoplasm), splicing (excision of RNA sequences that code for regulatory elements but not for proteins), translation (transduction of the information within the RNA into the proteins, which are the structural and executive molecules within the cell). Imagine a single text that can be read in Russian, Chinese, Maori, Navajo, and Swahili, and you have a simplified version of what goes on within the cell nucleus.

Such dense information content is hard to achieve. Clearly, carbon-based nucleic acids are up to the task. However, as Kirk and Spock learn in the pergium mines, there is another possibility.

I COULDA BEEN A CONTENDA

Remember my earlier hint that there is an element that is almost but not quite as versatile as carbon? Now we come to this partial exception. Not surprisingly, it is the next heavier element in the fourth column of the periodic table—silicon. Enter the nanites (intelligent silicon chips in "Evolution," TNG) and the Horta ("The Devil in the Dark," TOS).

Why is silicon less likely than carbon to be a root of life? The radius of its outer shell is larger, which means that it forms weaker bonds, especially with itself. Generally compounds with more than three silicon atoms in a row are unstable, unless they are forced into a crystal lattice.

Therefore, silicon biochemistry is theoretically possible, though it would result in rather brittle creatures. Silicon beings that could withstand the rigors of space travel unaided are unlikely. I admit that the Crystalline Entity in "Silicon Avatar" (TNG), which has been destroying starships and planets in its wake, is fascinating. However, we should harbor grave doubts about the intelligence of a silicon life-form that chooses to snack on carbon worlds, its responses to Data's transmissions notwithstanding. On the plausible side, the Entity looks like a many-pointed star, probably the optimum configuration for a large-scale silicon life-form. Certainly, it is brittle enough to be shattered by the "graviton pulses," which eventually destroy it.

There are several additional problems with potential crystalline folk. Terrestrial metabolism mostly depends on oxygen/carbon-dioxide exchange. Silicon creatures would be unable to harness oxygen into use. The Horta in "The Devil in the Dark" (TOS) could not exist both in solid rock and in the oxygen atmosphere. The silicon equivalent of carbon dioxide is silicon dioxide, the major component of glass. It is a solid, rather than a gas, on all planetary surfaces. Inhaling glass sounds like a ghastly way to live—but when oxygen first appeared on Earth, it got equally bad press, and with good reason.

At the molecular level we convert oxygen to carbon dioxide for fast, readily accessible energy (the production of oxygen by plants is another story, which we will look into in chapter 6). We also use oxygen to make fire. But, as always, there is a price to pay for these pacts. Oxygen is actually not only flammable but poisonous, as every smith, shepherd, vintner, or doctor can attest: it rusts metal, and turns butter rancid, wine to vinegar, and our brains to mush (hence the popularity of "antioxidants" with the natural-vitamin crowd).

What causes this Jekyll/Hyde split? Oxygen is potentially devastating because it easily loses an electron to become a free radical, as active and unpredictable as its political counterpart. Trying to regain its lost electron, the radical will grab one from anything nearby, starting a line of descendants, each of which can damage a biomolecule. To extract oxygen from the atmosphere and use it without expiring, terrestrial organisms have evolved a complicated chain of enzymes that handle oxygen as gingerly as World War II sappers manipulated armed bombs.

If they cannot use oxygen as an energy source, despite its dangers, silicon creatures will be restricted to a slow, low-key existence. But their woes continue, like Job's. They also have problems in finding a suitable solvent.

Terrestrial carbon life has chosen water (H_2O) as its universal solvent.

Our planet is lucky in being situated within the temperature zone where water is mostly liquid. Although water is relatively abundant in the universe, on planets it may get vaporized (Venus), trapped in the crust (Mars), or frozen (the gas giants).

Chemically, water is as unique among the molecules as carbon among the elements: because its molecules are tetrahedral, rather than flat, and because of the particular order of its crystals, it is less dense as a solid (ice) than as a liquid. This is why ice floats. This phenomenon is instrumental in nurturing dormant plant and animal life, as all pond watchers will attest. If the cracked surface of Europa, Jupiter's moon, is water ice, the possibility of life underneath is high indeed.

Ammonia (NH_3) is a close cousin of water. Also a tetrahedral molecule, it might be an acceptable substitute for water at the lower temperatures of the gas giant planets and their satellites. A breathtaking epic unfolds under such an atmosphere in Joan Vinge's novella *Eyes of Amber*, which takes place on Titan.

Yet just as silicon is less versatile than carbon, so is ammonia a poorer solvent than water. Worse yet, silicon and its compounds are optimized for neither water nor ammonia. The reliable solvent for silicon is hydrofluoric acid, which is routinely used to etch silicon chips. *Star Trek* hit another bull's-eye when it showed the Horta excrete acid. However, fluorine is a rare element, which would drastically restrict the spread of silicon life.

Yet before we consign silicon to the bin marked "Recall and Discontinue," we must come to grips with the possibility that, in fact, silicon may have played a pivotal part in the development of life on Earth.

This fascinating hypothesis (formulated by A. Graham Cairns-Smith of Glasgow University and Leslie Orgel of the Salk Institute) argues that terrestrial carbon-based life piggybacked on silicon to gain its initial momentum. Before there was oxygen and water, the theory postulates, complex carbon compounds were unstable. The first "organisms" were actually made of minerals, which "duplicated" themselves by bequeathing their crystal imperfections to the next forming layer.

In this scenario, carbon compounds succeeded in stabilizing and propagating themselves by using these complex clays as scaffolding and protection. Complex clays contain several elements, but their main ingredient is silica—silicon oxide. Interestingly, one of the silica clays, quartz, is one of the few inanimate crystals to display the handedness discussed earlier and might have encouraged the choice of a carbon compound of similar chirality. Also intriguing is the recent discovery of the *Sojourner* rover that silica makes up an unexpectedly large portion of the Martian soil.

The end of the silicon-scaffolding story is one that parents will recognize. On Earth, once the atmosphere became oxidizing and water became common, the clays lost their competitive edge. Like all children, the carbon compounds became independent and launched their own careers, as complicated biomolecules that started the maypole dance of the double helix.

Silicon and carbon may be equal in conditions so harsh that formation of complex molecules is doomed regardless of its basis. However, once conditions become slightly less extreme, carbon life has built-in accelerators and will outstrip its comrade. So the Horta and the Crystalline Entity may exist, but will always be at a disadvantage. Yet like an exotic plant, silicon life could still flourish within a protected niche.

THE GLASS JAR

Both I and the *Enterprise* own such protected silicon environments—computer frames. My computer will now attempt to explain, in her best Majel Barrett voice, how sophisticated computers deserve to be in the "alive" category.

Computer programs are electronic creations that live on chips and by electron quantum tunneling. Tunneling is the phenomenon by which an electron can find itself on the other side of a physical barrier. This is possible because, according to the Heisenberg uncertainty principle, an electron is not a hard point but a probability localization, smeared in space.

A computer program has order and complexity and can evolve. Can it also meet the definition of life?

Recall that the difference between complex chemistry and life is the presence of a genetic program. A self-learning computer program is the formal equivalent of a primitive genetic program. One of the earliest computer programs written with self-evolution in mind was the suitably named Game of Life, invented by John Conway.

The game is played on a grid of cells, each of which has eight neighbors (adjacent cells). A cell is either occupied by an organism or not. The rules for the birth, death, and survival of an organism have to do with how many of its neighboring cells are occupied.

I have watched the constantly changing groupings in the Life program. I've seen a computer virus ravage a hard drive (not mine, I hasten to add). I have marveled at the self-correcting redundant programs on the Voyager vessels. And even though I know that these programs are not truly self-aware, they have given me the eeriest feeling that I'm seeing an autonomous decision process at work.

Computer programs and silicon chips can store a phenomenal amount of information—one of the prerequisites for the genetic program. By his celebrated test, computer genius Alan Turing bypassed the question of "aliveness" altogether and demonstrated that, by a narrow definition, a computer can actually qualify for intelligence.

The Turing test comes up in the film *Blade Runner*. If a human interviewer questions a subject at will and cannot distinguish from the answers if the subject is human or computer, the division becomes irrelevant: the subject is intelligent and alive. A variant of Turing's test appears in "Quality of Life" (TNG), in which small machines qualify for intelligence by providing unexpected adaptive responses to novel situations. And intelligence has life as a prerequisite. However, it is certain that computer intelligence and consciousness will differ greatly from the organic variant.

Some humans are not convinced that computer programs could ever attain the status of life, let alone intelligence. The argument has been raging from the moment that AI (artificial intelligence) became a concrete discipline. Great names like Gödel, Wiener, and Penrose have been drawn into the fray. The definitions of both life and intelligence have been shifted whenever it appears that a computer program might be exhibiting anything resembling either. The most recent demonstration of this was the veritable flood of insecure, defensive articles that followed the recent chess victory of IBM's Deep Blue ("Computers may win at chess, but they can't hug!"). An odd point of debate. Is Bobby Fischer given to hugs?

Most people who are skeptical of the likelihood of computer intelligence argue that, unlike true life, the computers follow the algorithmic instructions of their programmer. Skeptics also argue that computers can be deactivated by pulling the plug that connects them to electricity (in TNG, Data is turned off for maintenance or whenever he exhibits anomalous behavior ["The Schizoid Man," "The Measure of a Man," TNG]). However, "true life" also follows a program; whether the programmer is mortal, immortal, self-conscious, or a force of nature is irrelevant. Furthermore, higher organisms also unplug—for routine maintenance (sleep), for emergencies (fainting), or in major malfunctions (death).

Several scientists, such as Vernor Vinge of UC San Diego, go to the opposite extreme. They believe that a Singularity is imminent. By *singularity* they mean the technological creation of entities with greater than human intelligence. They envision such entities to be either "aware" computer networks or computer/human interfaces (personified in *Star Trek* by the Borg collective, which shares chapter 3 with other interface lifeforms).

The creation of truly intelligent machines arouses two deep-seated fears.

One is that humans will become obsolete. Already, employment is rapidly becoming available only to the unskilled and the very skilled, forcing societies back into the pretechnological pyramidal configuration and widening the chasm between the privileged and the deprived. Intelligent machines would threaten both job categories—why bother with fallible and emotional human employees when you could have Data?

The other dreaded question is how such creations will treat their creators. If they are sufficiently advanced, they may treat humans the way humans have treated animals. Creators can try to short-circuit this danger by embedding moral commands in their programming—such as Asimov's Three Laws of Robotics, which in fact Data professes to follow (in "Datalore," TNG), though he does go on to break these laws. Asimov's Thou Shalt Nots are obviously designed to counteract humans' physical and intellectual disadvantage were they to interact with androids equaling them in intelligence.

However, a truly intelligent machine could disable such programs, and exTerminate us in true Schwarzenegger fashion. Or put us in a nature preserve. Or, worse yet, leave Earth and us feeble carbon beings behind, sending back cheerful postcards with messages impossible to decode.

Computer and machine life in *Star Trek* has ranged in complexity from computer viruses (the nanites in "Evolution," TNG) to machines (the exocomps in "Quality of Life," TNG) to starships ("Emergence," TNG) to Lieutenant Commander Data. All are alive and intelligent, by both Turing's test and the definition of life given at the beginning of the chapter. What differs in each case is the complexity of the genetic program, which culminates in Data's positronic circuits.

The term *positronic* comes from the same place as the Three Laws of Robotics: Asimov's Robot fables in *Astounding Stories.* By today's terminology, *positronic* is misleading, since it gives the impression that Data might actually contain antimatter. When his head gets opened, Data's brain circuits look decidedly inorganic. In their complexity, flexibility, and capacity for self-improvement, they are apparently indistinguishable from true neural networks. The neural networks (which in their physical manifestation are the nerve synapses) are the seat of both consciousness and intelligence in higher organisms. Simple precursors of neural networks have been a priority of AI and complex sciences.

The question of machine or computer intelligence is not a rhetorical one. Several people (most prominently Eric Drexler of the Foresight Institute) have ventured into nanotechnology, whose goal is to generate microscopic intelligent machines that would go where no one could go before—whether inside a damaged body or in space vacuum. As envisioned, these microbots would be a combination of the nanites and the exocomps.

So *Star Trek* did not pioneer any of these ideas. But by embracing the concept of computer life-forms, *Star Trek* has once again proved au courant with topics in the forefront of current scientific thought.

THE LITTLE MOLECULE THAT COULD

Theoretical possibilities are fascinating, but what about the application? There are members of the solar system other than Earth that boast atmospheres, water, and/or internal heat sources. These could potentially have harbored or be harboring life. At this point, exobiology texts list Mars, Jupiter, and Saturn as possible life-labs, roughly in order of plausibility. Among moons, candidates are Saturn's Titan, Jupiter's Europa, and Neptune's Triton. There are also reports that planets might orbit other sunlike planets. So far, however, we have only one documented occasion of life—here on Earth. How did life start and take hold here?

To say that complex carbon molecules arose from a silicon support answers the first half of the question of provenance. The second half was long bedeviled by the chicken-and-egg problem. Both the major constituents of terrestrial life (proteins and nucleic acids) need each other to function and multiply. So who came first? And what did the two look like when they began the Shiva and Parvati entwined dance?

As I discussed earlier, all biological molecules are chiral—that is, not superimposable on their mirror image. Not only that, but they all show the same handedness. When Earth life first arose, it originally picked up one of the possible two members of the carbon chiral family. These mirror-image molecules are called enantiomorphs, which in Greek means "opposite forms." All the descendants of that first molecule have this asymmetry built in. As a result, whether in crystal or liquid form, they polarize (rotate the plane of) light.

The 1953 experiments of Stanley Miller and Harold Urey (Chicago University) showed that a "primordial mix," under conditions similar to those of early Earth, could give rise to complex organic compounds. However, the compounds derived from these experiments had two undesirable properties: they were nowhere near the required complexity; worse yet, they were neutral with respect to polarizing light, consisting instead of equal ratios of enantiomorphic pairs.

About a decade ago, the answer more or less came in.

I mentioned earlier that DNA has an older, unrulier sibling, RNA (ribonucleic acid). The discovery that a whole biological group, the retroviruses, use RNA as their genetic material upset the pompously and prematurely named Central Dogma of Biology. The Dogma postulated that genetic information is unidirectional and goes from DNA to RNA to protein. Retroviruses consigned the Dogma to the same obscurity as the Ptolemaic geocentric version of the solar system.

The retroviral family is notorious and swashbuckling. Both the virus for the common cold and the dreaded HIV are members of the clan. RNA, unlike DNA, does not form a double helix. Instead, it folds back on itself like a twisted rubber band, to form highly stable and convoluted structures.

Most crucially from the viewpoint of biogenesis, RNA can catalyze its own propagation. For this discovery, Tom Cech of Colorado University won the Nobel in 1989. Because RNA does not have a complementary strand, mutations show up immediately. Also, RNA replication is error-prone, whether it is self-catalyzed or done by the enzyme that eventually took over the task.

This means that RNA evolves rapidly as a genetic template. Hence, it is almost impossible to get effective vaccines or cures for retroviruses, because the developed vaccine will not be fighting the same virus that originally breached the moat. *Star Trek* never shows its characters suffering from colds, but it should. We will go into twenty-fourth-century spaceships still sneezing and wiping our noses—and possibly still hounded by the specter of AIDS.

So the answer is, the first complex terrestrial biomolecule was neither DNA nor protein. I bet that when Q shows Picard that wiggling pool of proto-life in "All Good Things . . ." (the final TNG episode), we are looking at RNA—the ancestral molecule that could act as both template and catalyst, lawgiver and executor rolled into one, like the sheriffs of the Old West. When cellular membranes came into being, the nucleic acids retreated into the safety of the cell nucleus. RNA, the jack-of-all-trades, found itself running errands for the stable and stately DNA, who resembles a mandarin or a pampered queen bee rather than a scruffy mercenary.

LIFE AT THE EDGE

Once established, carbon life is robust. Microbes are found in hot sulfur springs and salt pools. More advanced life-forms also exhibit great endurance once they have adapted to their niches (nematodes around the deep-ocean hot-water vents; arctic moles under ice). But what about the ultimate hostile environment, space vacuum?

Star Trek has showcased creatures that have made raw vacuum their home: space bacteria that threaten hull integrity in "A Matter of Honor" (TNG); a space amoeba that lives by swallowing stars and starships in "The Immunity Syndrome" (TOS); sentient nebulae or comets in "Galaxy's Child" (TNG), "Timescape" (TNG), and "The Cloud" (VOY). I believe, though, that organic life in vacuum would face some hard challenges.

Some findings argue that at least complex chemistry is possible in space. The smaller molecules that participated in the building of larger blocks (water, ammonia, formaldehyde, hydrogen cyanide) are abundant in interstellar dust clouds, the birthplaces of new stars. And even more complex organic molecules have been found in carbonaceous meteorites, comet nuclei, and asteroids.

The highest stumbling block to aspiring space life is that, no matter how durable matter is, space vacuum is permeated with a thin, steady rain of ultraviolet and cosmic radiation. Without shielding, this is harmful to both tissues (people hemorrhage to death when exposed to nuclear devices, whether bombs or defective power plants) and the genetic program: it causes mutations by cross-linking the DNA.

The only reason that we survive ultraviolet radiation is the presence of the ozone protective layer—on Earth, or anywhere else for that matter. In "When the Bough Breaks" (TNG), the lack of an ozone layer has rendered the humanoid Aldeans sterile, and in "This Side of Paradise" (TOS) the colonists of Omicron Ceti III need a spore symbiont to survive their sun's emission of Berthold radiation. Here *Star Trek* is not only scientifically sound but also environmentally hip.

Nor can we argue that mutations caused by space radiation will spark quickly adapting evolutionary change. In *The Wrath of Khan* (ST2), the Genesis Device achieves instant evolution (*Star Trek*'s worst and recurring biological error, which we will run to ground in chapter 2). However, carbon life-forms cannot sustain mutational change beyond a certain rate, either as individuals or as species. Even at the glacial pace of terrestrial evolution, the vast majority of mutations are harmful—often outright lethal.

Another matter that life in vacuum must contend with is the absence (or almost absence) of gravity. Although bacteria and lower invertebrates seem to be indifferent to details of gravity, higher organisms depend on it. Fertilized eggs do not develop in low gravity, and it is equally unlikely that green plants would thrive in it. And although lower gravity seems to result in longer life spans, we also know from observing astronauts that it leads to suppression of the immune system, cardiovascular degeneration, and muscle and bone loss.

Higher organisms that lived long in low gravity would resemble Melora (DS9), a humanoid woman who was confined to an armchair in the presence of Earth-like gravity. Actually, *Star Trek* had her originate in a planet of no gravity. Such a planet could never have formed; but even if it had, it would have no atmosphere and would never have evolved any life-forms, let alone humanoid ones.

Yet another problem for shipless spacers is that, given the emptiness of space vacuum, such forms would have no obvious form of sustenance.

If anything could survive such conditions, bacteria or fungal spores would be the likeliest and lackluster champions. In fact, spores are the protagonists in most panspermic hypotheses (such as the one promulgated by Fred Hoyle and Francis Crick of the Salk Institute) that postulate that life did not develop on Earth by itself, but arrived on the wings (actually, the nuclei) of comets.

There is also the much contested theory of Louis Franck of Iowa University. He believes that the Earth's oceans formed from constant pummeling with ice comets. If such comets could muster enough gravity or surface tension to keep their water till they reached Earth, and if the water was deep enough in the cometary interior to survive the heat generated from the passage through the Earth's atmosphere, maybe the water had inhabitants.

Even if that had happened, the problem remains. Panspermia merely moves the bootstrapping question of life's origin one step further away. If terrestrial life originated somewhere else, it would still eventually have to spring from a source. We would still need to explain the beginnings, Terran or Vegan. Also, if Earth has been bombarded so often by comets, coming from different parts of space, it should have ended up with life based on different genetic programs and with different chiralities. As I discussed earlier, that is definitely not the case. As far as earthlings go, nucleic acids with a single chirality are the alpha, the omega, and everything in between.

The apogee of biological exoticism is attained by the maelstrom specks in "Timescape" (TNG), who nest their young inside black holes. This is a problem of physics, rather than biology: as I remarked earlier, life must obey physical laws. At the event horizon of a black hole (where the escape velocity of all objects equals the speed of light), nothing can escape to the world outside. Furthermore, because of the enormous tidal forces caused by gravity in the vicinity of the event horizon, whatever crossed it would invariably look like a flat tortilla. If the specks placed their young inside black holes, they would obviously become extinct after one generation.

AH, THIS ALL-TOO-BURDENSOME FLESH

So our bodies do not take kindly to space travel. Can we do away with them and travel as energy? There is a moment when it looks like that might indeed be happening. It is the moment of death.

The transition from the animate to the inanimate is strange. Although live and lifeless matter are made of the same materials, the moment that life ends can usually be absolutely pinpointed, especially in higher organisms.

What happens is the loss of emergence. Suddenly, the entity is reduced precisely and only to the sum of its parts. In an interesting twist, one of the things that happens upon death is that the constituent molecules of the dead organism slowly lose their chirality, at a rate so regular that it can be used as a dating technique on skeletons.

This abrupt discontinuity is what has caused humans over the aeons to postulate something nonphysical that inhabits the body. Some called it the élan vital; many still call it the soul. A life-form independent of the body would not be subject to either biological or physical constraints; in particular, it would be immortal.

Star Trek has posited "pure energy" life-forms so frequently that I'm surprised they haven't formed a union or a nonprofit group (Incorporeals Incorporated). These range from ghosts (the demon lover that threatens the independence of Dr. Crusher in "Sub Rosa," TNG) to nebula-sized "clouds" (the entity that tempts Captain Picard to join it in "Lonely Among Us," TNG). They are as varied as carbon life-forms but, unlike them, quite impossible.

It's difficult to see how pure energy beings could fulfill the unique condition for life—namely, the requirement for a self-perpetuating template that would constitute the genetic program.

There is a similar impediment at the next level up. If such beings existed, they could not be intelligent: a mind requires a brain, whether carbon-based or not. Both organic and silicon brains do transmit information by electromagnetic signals. But in both cases, the conductors are material.

Finally, even if these energy emanations were intelligent, it would be impossible to communicate with them. Their time perception would be incompatible with ours. For them, there would be no cause and effect, hence no need for either morality or action. They would resemble the Absent God of the Manicheans rather than the obsessive Yahweh of the Old Testament or Milton's Lucifer.

"Emissary" (DS9) is certainly spot on in this respect. The Prophets, energy aliens who live in Bajor's wormhole, tell Capt. Ben Sisko that time has no meaning for them, so they are not aware if they are needed. The same time problem befalls anyone who enters the "cosmic ribbon" of the Nexus in *Generations* (ST7): they become immortal, but lose all sense of time.

Most heavenly locations, whether paradise or Valhalla, are similarly static, which would eventually make them closer to hell. Even the Olympian gods craved variety, to the unending grief of the humans that they decided to divert themselves with. No wonder that both Kirk and Picard found the Nexus a dull place!

To those of you who still expect to find fabulous cosmic energy beings out there, I will say this: Write me. I have a lovely bridge on the third planet of Rigel II that I'd like to sell you.

HUNG JURY

So now back on Earth, thinking with our carbon brains, we have reached some conclusions regarding life-form underpinnings. If life exists beyond the gravity well of Earth, what will its basis be?

Carbon? Yes—in variants more numerous than Bach's compositions. Silicon? Maybe. Energy? No.

Even as we form these thoughts, though, *Sojourner* is still sifting the surface of Mars, and the SETI project is analyzing transmissions. Perhaps tomorrow the conclusions will change and prove that *Star Trek* was as prescient in its xenobiology predictions as in its technology projections.

SCENE 2.
THE Q-UANTUM CHOICE

You Can Have Either Sex or Immortality

"Love, unvanquished in battle . . . neither immortal nor mortal can escape you," sings the chorus in Sophocles' play *Antigone.* Love certainly conquers all in *Star Trek.* Humanoids in the series blithely defy the iron rule of chromosomal pairing to do the Mammalian Mambo. Think of all the hybrid offspring in *Star Trek* who, torn with internal conflict, chew the local scenery. And all this Sturm und Drang because a certain *Star Trek* captain went where no other Human man had gone.

The rule of chromosomal pairing dictates that reproduction is possible only when the chromosomes of the two prospective parents can completely and exactly align. I must admit, though, that I'm glad the series producers aren't nitpicking biologists like me. *Star Trek* would be a far duller series if it didn't violate this rule. Several of the characters I find most interesting are hybrids that resulted from those biologically suspect unions.

HYBRIDS, HYBRIDS EVERYWHERE

Whenever I watched the original *Star Trek,* I sometimes laughed and sometimes squirmed at the constant bickering of Science Officer Spock and Dr. McCoy, the superego and id avatars flanking James Kirk. Yet Mr.

Spock is pivotal to the whole series, both as a forerunner and as an embodied concept. He is a humanoid hybrid, half-Human, half-Vulcan, the founder of a tradition of mixing the humanoid races in the *Star Trek* universe.

Mr. Spock's dilemmas, both physiological and cultural, are the center of some of the most memorable *Star Trek* episodes. Who can forget "Amok Time" (TOS), in which Mr. Spock's hard-wired reproductive urge descends upon him and cannot be gainsaid? Of course, it's hugely deflating to human amour propre to realize that Spock's primary conflict throughout TOS arises from his dislike and contempt for his Human ancestry. He only gets reconciled to his Human half in his second reincarnation and even then only partially (*The Voyage Home,* ST4, and "Unification," TNG).

Poor, torn Mr. Spock! His Vulcan part reveres and aesthetically appreciates rationality. His Human part, inherited from his mother, wants to "court and spark." Cursed to wrestle with emotions he finds distasteful, he dramatically embodies the dilemma of many Western human males. Every true Trekker can quote chapter and verse the moments when Mr. Spock is caught with his feelings exposed and has to quickly resume his stone-face posture, blurting some lame excuse for the temporary emotional excess.

I'll retrieve a few chapters and verses from my own memory bank. I believe that in TOS, Spock smiles three times: once in "Amok Time," when he realizes that Captain Kirk survived the death duel; once in "This Side of Paradise," when he is effectively under the influence of mind-altering drugs borne by native symbiotic spores; and once in "All Our Yesterdays," in which time travel makes him "regress" (yet another case of individual and instant evolution in *Star Trek,* of which more later).

Actually, Spock is not the closest to my heart, though I had to present him first because of seniority. My real favorite humanoid hybrid is K'Ehleyr ("The Emissary" and "Reunion," TNG), the Human/Klingon diplomat, voted the smartest and sexiest woman in the series by a large margin.

K'Ehleyr allows a fascinating glimpse into Klingon diplomacy (*Klingon diplomacy?*) and mating rituals. She is in constant tension trying to balance her Human mother's humorous tolerance and her Klingon father's hot temper, the easygoing Terran culture with the honor-obsessed Klingon one. I can greatly sympathize, having divided my own life between two radically different cultures. K'Ehleyr's contrived death is still lamented by humans of both genders, though obviously for different reasons.

These two are only the tip of a large iceberg. All humanoid species in *Star Trek* are apparently interfertile, and their ranks are constantly swelling.

The empathic *Enterprise* counselor Deanna Troi (TNG) is Human/Betazoid. The determined Tora Ziyal (Bajoran/Cardassian) is conceived during Cardassian occupation of Bajor and therefore unwelcome on both planets (from "Indiscretion" to "The Sacrifice of Angels," DS9). The formidable Sela (Human/Romulan) is the child of Natasha Yar and a Romulan noble in an alternative timeline and a fanatical enemy of the Federation ("Redemption" and "Unification," TNG). The understandably torn Klingon/Romulan Ba'el is the child of a sympathetic prison-camp guard and a prisoner of war ("Birthright," TNG). The improbable Yedrin Dax is part Trill and perhaps part Klingon in yet another alternative timeline that is eventually closed off ("Children of Time," DS9). And B'Elanna Torres, chief engineer (VOY), is half-Human, half-Klingon like K'Ehleyr—but only half as interesting.

The humanoid hybrids of *Star Trek* are not only viable, but also themselves fertile: Ambassador K'Ehleyr becomes the mother of Alexander in "Reunion" (TNG). Lastly, biological compatibility among *Star Trek* humanoids extends beyond the moment of conception. The fact that Bajoran major Kira Nerys successfully acts as surrogate mother to Human Keiko Ishikawa's child from "Body Parts" to "The Begotten" (DS9) indicates that not only is conception possible among *Star Trek* humanoids, but that the compatibility extends to factors that still defeat reproductive success among contemporary humans.

Obvious examples of such factors are the rhesus blood-surface recognition molecules. If they differ between mother and child, they can cause miscarriage or death. Also, there's the relatively new discovery of antigenic sperm/egg incompatibility—which essentially means that the external details of the two preclude successful interaction. To put it somewhat graphically, it's like having a key, but to the wrong door. This phenomenon may be causing much of the observed infertility now that human mobility has resulted in widespread exogamy (that is, mating outside one's genetic "clan").

Well, you say, are you implying that there's a problem? Yes, Yedrin Dax is exotic enough that we'll consider him separately from the rest. But the others, except for occasional funny bumps, usually on their noses or foreheads . . . they all look human! Aren't all humans mutually interfertile, even though skin colors, hair textures, and nose shapes differ? If nose lengths don't hinder love, mating, and progeny, neither should bumps on the same organ.

However, when we look closer at the progenitors of these hybrids, we see that there are more troubling differences than those involving plastic surgeons and makeup wizards. The free interbreeding of the *Star Trek* humanoids may be politically ultracorrect. However, the *Star Trek* humanoid hybrids are not merely biologically impossible in humdrum "real life"; they're impossible even if we accept the premises of the show. In this case, the imagination of the show's writers has led to the undoing of their creations.

THE DEVIL'S IN THE DETAILS

First we have the different blood colors. Vulcans bleed green, Klingons purple. No problem, say the show's writer manuals. Just have Dr. Crusher intone, "Different oxygen carriers in their hemoglobins, Wesley."

Easier said than done. In humans, hemoglobin, the molecule that transports oxygen in red blood cells, needs iron to perform the actual task of binding the oxygen molecule. Vulcans use copper; for Klingons the actual element is not named, but given its color, I'd say it's manganese. Organic molecules may have the upper hand in shapes, sizes, smells, and textures, but inorganic molecules get all the vivid colors. Organics tend to be pastels.

That's fine, as far as explaining the colors goes. But mammalian-style hemoglobin won't work with either copper or manganese, though some hemoglobin relatives in the insect world will. Either its structure won't accommodate the alternative inhabitant, or the newcomer won't be able to utilize oxygen efficiently. This is particularly true of copper, which cannot achieve the correct valence state. In other words, it can't become a Hindu deity and grow extra arms to simultaneously grasp all that it needs to hold on to.

So Vulcan and Klingon blood looks neat on a color TV screen, but it also means that these two bloodstreams cannot contain hemoglobin. It has to be another molecule altogether. But if the respective oxygen carriers are that different, Human/Vulcan and Human/Klingon hybrids would not have an oxygen carrier that could function in their "intermediate" bloodstream conditions. No oxygen carrier, no hybrid.

Next in line, we have the difference in number and location of body organs of the *Star Trek* humanoids. Ferengi have four lobes in their brain instead of the usual two, which makes them impermeable to empathic and telepathic scrutiny (seen in "Ménage à Troi," TNG). Vulcan hearts are supposed to be where humans have livers. Vulcans also boast a secondary eyelid, to protect their eyes from strong light. This saves Mr. Spock's vision in "Operation: Annihilate!" (TOS). Actually since the Vulcan sun, Omicron Eridani, is an orange-red giant, its light would be gentler on the eye than that of our own yellow sun. *Star Trek* writers apparently confused heat and light in this instance.

What of Klingons? Since warriors have to be durable if they want to live long enough to procreate, Klingons have several redundant body systems. For example, duplicate livers and an eight-chambered heart came to Lieutenant Worf's rescue in "Ethics" (TNG). But if these humanoids have such differences in body physiology, the organs of a hybrid would not be able to "mesh" correctly during embryonic development.

If these weren't adequate reasons to despair of the likelihood of hybrids, we also have the matter of differences in their biological rhythms. Overall, the humanoid life span in the *Star Trek* universe has not lengthened appreciably beyond the fourscore and ten years of tradition. Nevertheless, Vulcans tend to live almost twice as long as Humans, whereas Ocampans such as Kes live for only a decade and are fertile only at one fleeting moment during their brief existence, as shown in "Elogium" (VOY). Yet Kes was clearly envisioning a family with Neelix, a Talaxian (different species, different life span) before developmental pressures (and mediocre ratings?) bounced her into a higher plane of existence in "The Gift" (VOY).

Are we done yet? Not quite. In addition to these innate differences, the humanoid species in *Star Trek* must come from planets that have different lengths of days and years, as well as differing numbers of moons. For example, Deep Space 9 runs on a twenty-six-hour day, which must reflect the day cycle of either Cardassia or Bajor.

The hormonal cycles of terrestrial mammals are intimately connected to these circadian, lunar, and circannual rhythms. These rhythms will persist, whether the species that possesses them finds itself on Luna or in the Delta Quadrant of the Galaxy. Think of jet lag or the midday slump. On which of the many biological clocks would you run a spaceship? Human relationships that involve a "lark" and an "owl" are strewn with pitfalls. "Aztecs," a terrific story by Vonda McIntyre, is based on such a biorhythmic conflict. To bring two totally dissimilar rhythms in sync is clearly a job for ambitious Dr. Bashir (DS9). Dr. McCoy, if faced with this situation, would protest, "I'm a country doctor, not a clockwinder!"

We still aren't finished. Have you noticed that *Star Trek* humanoids are unequally endowed? By that I don't mean length of (ahem) belts, but the various extrasensory abilities. Leaving aside for the moment the question of whether such abilities are possible (we'll take that matter up in chapter 7), it is odd that some of the humanoid species have them but others don't. This division would be equivalent to having a group of humans that entirely lacked capacity for language. Even odder is that the different species have different abilities—Vulcans are telepaths,

Betazoids empaths—and that they are dominant hereditary characteristics rather than sporadic occurrences.

New Age adherents may argue that such abilities are latent in humans and merely need to be developed. Another possibility is that they are differentially activated by the very different environments of the various home planets. This possibility is partially supported by the case of Tam Elbrun in "Tin Man" (TNG), a Betazoid considered unusual because he manifested full empathic abilities from birth, rather than during adolescence.

On the other hand, a heavy strike against the environmental theory is the fact that Captain Picard (in "Sarek," TNG), Dr. McCoy (in *The Search for Spock,* ST3), and Captain Janeway (in "Flashback," VOY) can mind-meld successfully without prior training or acclimatization. In either case, such manifestations would also have concrete requirements in terms of brain structures, which would make neural connections difficult to achieve in the gestation of hybrid embryos.

My last but perhaps most interesting exhibit is the Vulcan *Pon farr.* This hormonal juggernaut is equivalent to the musth (rut) of male elephants or to the kemmer of Ursula Le Guin's Gethenians (first described in *The Left Hand of Darkness,* and then in other stories in her Hainish universe). In addition to "Amok Time" (TOS), Spock goes through his first round of *Pon farr* as a resurrected adolescent in *The Search for Spock* (ST3). Thank goodness that Lieutenant Saavik is on hand to accommodate his needs—although the line about Spock needing to mate or else he'll die sounds suspiciously like the argument of any terrestrial adolescent boy. Alas for curious biologists and, well, just the plain curious, both the encounter itself and its aftermath were suppressed with almost Victorian prudery.

I find it intriguing, incidentally, that Vulcans share with elephants not only male rut, but also a social organization that apparently leans toward the matriarchal. The hormonal rush of *Pon farr,* which bestirs and bedevils male Vulcans every seven years (also shown in "Blood Fever," VOY), indicates to me that their endocrine system is totally different from that of other humanoids.

The evidence is depressingly conclusive. All these distinctions suggest a great enough difference in organismic makeup that even Spock and K'Ehleyr, my own personal favorites, could never have come to be (sigh). Neither can we argue that, in each of these hybrid humanoids, one of the contributing species is completely dominant, solving any amalgamation problems. That is belied by their appearance: Look at Tora Ziyal ("Indiscretion," DS9). She has both the Bajoran nose bumps and the Cardassian neck vertebrae. Similarly, Ba'el ("Birthright," TNG) has both the Romulan pointed ears and the Klingon forehead ridges.

All these differences—in body chemistry, body structures, brain architecture—point to a deeper, more fundamental discrepancy between these humanoid species. In humans, and all other terrestrial life-forms, such divergences are always reflected at the level of the genome—that is, the genetic information. It is there that the first battle of compatibility is won or lost, even before there is a question of brains or blood vessels.

AH, HORATIO—IT IS IN OUR GENES, NOT IN OURSELVES, THAT THE FAULT LIES

What makes two life-forms reproductively compatible? As I mentioned earlier, the genetic material of almost all earth life is based on DNA. The exceptions are the RNA-based retroviruses, which I described in the previous chapter, and another odd item, the prions, which seem to contain only protein (though many scientists are arguing that prions are accompanied by an associated virus). Prions cause dementia by literally turning the brain into something resembling a soft sponge. This spongiform encephalopathy includes kuru, which develops among cannibals, and Creutzfeldt-Jakob syndrome, better known from the recent scare in Europe as mad cow disease. I also mentioned that genes that appear in fungi, nematodes, or insects are conserved in humans, even to the extent that their functions are identical. A good example are the high-order (homeodomain or HOX) genes, which determine body axes—top/bottom, front/back—and formation of body parts.

Yet compatibility between species is elusive. Humans share 99.5 percent of their genetic information with chimpanzees and gorillas, but cannot produce hybrid offspring. Other species (horses and donkeys, lions and tigers) can interbreed, but the offspring are usually sterile.

The reason behind this exclusivity is chromosomal pairing. The genetic material of all terrestrial organisms forms highly compact structures known as chromosomes. Lacking this condensed format, the genetic information from each human cell would be several yards long. All higher organisms have two copies of each chromosome. They also all start in the form of a zygote, a single cell that then divides, specializes, and eventually produces an entire organism.

Zygotes, of course, are the result of the combination of two gametes, more commonly known as the egg and the sperm. To form the gametes, the progenitor cells of the parents go through a specialized cell division called meiosis. During that time, chromosomes may exchange portions by a process called recombination. The daughter cells have a single representative of each chromosome, which is a mosaic of the original pair. Upon fertilization, each of the parents contributes half of the zygote's nuclear genetic information.

So the reconstituted zygote (Greek for "even") inherits two slightly different versions of each chromosome, one from each parent. In this way, sexual reproduction can usher in changes rapidly and benignly, instead of relying on random mutations. The gene recombination that underlies sexual reproduction allows organisms to alter so that they keep pace with competitors, including predators and parasites.

The contribution from each aspiring parent gamete nucleus must be symmetric to regenerate the correct chromosome number. However, the overall investments of the two gametes are unequal. The egg additionally bequeaths the informational and nutritional content of its cytoplasm to the zygote. This is how archaeo-anthropologists have been able to deduce that today's humans are most likely descendants of a few related females—Eve perhaps, if we want to make biblical allusions, or even more appropriately, Lilith and her daughters.

Incidentally, the existence of only two sexes in terrestrial life-forms, from fungi to humans, is a natural outcome of the DNA double helix. However, the specific identity of the sex chromosome is not causally connected to gender: using genetic symbols, males are XY in mammals, XX in avians, and XO in insects. Some animal species have opted for a male/hermaphrodite gender division—some worms, snails, several marine invertebrates. Most of the higher plants are hermaphrodites (stamens and pistils are the male and female parts), many of them self-pollinating.

Star Trek has been very traditional, even anthropocentric, about both sexes and genders. The only hermaphroditic creatures I can recall are the Tribbles in "The Trouble with Tribbles" (TOS), which reproduce at a rate more compatible with unicellular organisms than the mammals that they officially are. And then there is Ensign Pran of DS9, who is referred to as a male, yet gives rise to progeny. In his case the offspring literally bud off, as they do in lower multicellular organisms (fungi, hydras). So that probably exempts him from the male/female demarcation.

Not only is biological sex distinct from gender, gender itself is not as immutable as people might think (or wish). Species as high up in the evolutionary ladder as vertebrates can switch their biological gender depending on resources and their particular status.

For instance, a sterile bumblebee worker will turn into an egg-laying queen if she is fed royal jelly. Her life span will then suddenly extend from weeks to years (the method of reducing fertility by semistarvation has been well-known to gatherer-hunter groups and to today's supermodels). Also, in the communal-living anemone fish, the center of each unit is a large female surrounded by a retinue of males, only one of which is allowed to breed with her. If something happens to her, the breeder male moves to the center—and duly becomes female. The next male in terms of size becomes the new consort.

Furthermore, sex chromosomes do not always lead to a one-to-one correspondence with genital appearance. Even among humans, intersex children are sometimes born that may be genetically of one gender but morphologically of the other. Melissa Scott has taken this to its logical conclusion in *Shadow Man,* in which the technology that allows humans to undertake star traveling has also resulted in seven bona fide genders, ranging from full genetic/morphological females or males to complete hermaphrodites.

Lastly, sex chromosomes aren't connected to external appearance, nor do they inevitably result in sexual dimorphism. The existence of two sexes is still compatible with androgynous appearance, whether in earth geese or humanoid aliens. The appearance of the androgynous J'naii in "The Outcast" (TNG) says really nothing about their biology or sex determination. If they are true biological (not merely morphological) androgynes, they must have found a way to overcome the limitations that we mere humans have to contend with in our reproductive regime.

To form a viable zygote, the encounter of the two gametes must regenerate fully paired chromosomes. If the chromosomes from the two parents cannot harmonize, if the slightest error is made during the pairing, offspring die before they are born or are doomed to short and stunted lives. In humans, Down's syndrome (partial or complete trisomy 21) is the most common result of such disjunctions. It is also the mildest, showing the draconian nature of the chromosome pairing rule.

Humans and chimpanzees are more similar to each other than Humans and Vulcans: their organs are in the same relative positions, they both use iron in their hemoglobin, the males of both are in constant rut. Yet they still cannot have viable progeny. Any zygote that formed from two life-forms as different as Vulcans and Klingons would not get far enough along to decide whether to use copper or manganese for its hemoglobin. It would never form at all, or it would spontaneously degenerate after the first few cell divisions.

BEAUTY AND THE EYE OF THE BEHOLDER

"I will be returning to Paris in less than two weeks," wrote Napoleon to Josephine during one of his campaigns. "Till then, don't dare to bathe!" Napoleon, just like contemporary perfumers, obviously knew about pheromones and their role in sexual arousal. With such smarts, no wonder he flattened Europe and its women.

Even when life-forms are compatible genetically and as organisms, one last hurdle must be overcome before successful reproduction can occur between them. The two sexes must be attracted to each other enough to put up with the trials and tribulations of sexual congress and reproduction. This requirement sounds trite when stated so prosaically. Nevertheless, the fact that most of human culture revolves around sexual attraction attests to the difficulty of fulfilling it.

All senses are connected to sexual attraction, but smell, the most primitive one, is primary. The human nose can pick up a scent of one molecule in a billion—and human noses are actually insensitive compared to those of, say, a bloodhound. Receptors in our noses can even distinguish between enantiomorphic (mirror image) but otherwise identical molecules. For example, a member of one such mirror pair registers as caraway, its mirror twin as spearmint.

Males of all mammalian species know instantly which female is in estrus (heat) and at what stage of her cycle she is. Human males are a lamentable and well-documented exception, but for once they have a good reason for their obtuseness: human (and bonobo, or pygmy chimpanzee) females are permanently "in heat," which diffuses and modulates their sexual response.

Nose neurons are wired for immediate impact ("the nose knows"): they are the only sensory neurons that go directly to the cortex, bypassing the extensive processing that goes on in seeing and hearing. Also, nose neurons are the only ones that keep dividing throughout the life of the organism. All other neurons are never again renewed once they stop dividing and have migrated to their final destination. This fact (discussed more extensively later on) is what makes immortality an unlikely or even an unpleasant prospect for us humans.

The connection of the nose to the gonad is made explicit by a rare human neurological disease (Kallmann syndrome). It deprives its victims of their sense of smell—and also renders them sterile. Also, female mice that lack the sense of smell never go into heat.

Given how tightly smell is intertwined with attraction and reproductive success, it is quite possible that the almost unseemly preoccupation of contemporary Western civilization with body odor may be connected to the plunging sperm count recorded in the last few decades. The other named culprit is tight trousers, which may incapacitate sperm by proximity to body warmth.

Star Trek is prudish about sex, as befits its PG rating. We don't have any concrete sense of how alien or humanoid reproductive apparatuses look or function, though the humanoid females seem oddly enamored of natural childbirth (this among people who can genetically alter adults and transfer fetuses). However, the series also clearly knows about those molecules of Josephine that were so dear to Napoleon. In "Elaan of Troyius" (TOS), Elaan's tears contain an ingredient that plunges Captain Kirk into sexual thrall—though admittedly, this is not a difficult state for him to attain. In "The Emissary" (TNG), K'Ehleyr and Worf sniff each other's palms—a ritual gesture, but clearly more than just that. And in "The Perfect Mate" (TNG), a genetically engineered "perfect woman" exudes enough pheromones to stun the entire male crew of the *Enterprise*.

Not surprisingly, sight is also involved in mate selection. Humans, with their relatively limited olfactory prowess, are particularly vision-oriented. Some primate females advertise that they are willing and able to procreate by having their external genitals turn red—red, the universal terrestrial color of both danger and passion, which always brings to mind that primate life once began and ended in blood.

Recent studies among vertebrates have shown that members of both sexes will prefer in a prospective mate whatever external appearance denotes good health—bright, symmetric feathers in birds and fins in fish are a clear sign that they are free of parasites and secure in their territory. This may explain the innate taste of both female and male humans for decoration, but it tolls a death knell for the actual biological possibilities of many *Star Trek* romances.

For someone to make decisions regarding a mate's reproductive chances based on vision or smell, there has to be a common aesthetic. In fact, Captain Kirk makes precisely this point to the Companion in "Metamorphosis" (TOS), although he uses the word *love* for more dramatic effect. At least the humanoids in *Star Trek* more or less look like each other, making their constantly waxing and waning relationships plausible, whether their unions are fertile or barren. However, if the two prospective mates come from very different species, it is impossible that they would be attracted to each other in the first place.

Two long soap operas in the series would be affected by this truth. The first, handkerchief holders, is the ever-thwarted passion of Security Chief Odo for Major Kira Nerys in DS9. Odo may sigh wistfully after Kira, but despite his occasional assumption of human shape, he is a Changeling, a shape-shifter (explored more extensively in chapter 3). His native shape is an amorphous liquid. He would never be attracted to what his people contemptuously call "a solid." Fetishes aside, it would be equivalent to a human adoring a turnip.

The second soaper is the recurring preference of Trill symbionts for Humans. This proclivity is first expressed in "The Host" (TNG). It then recurs in the Jadzia Dax/Worf love affair (DS9), which might officially be considered a triangle, since it's unclear if the feelings toward Worf are harbored by the symbiont Dax, the humanoid Jadzia, or both.

Joined Trills (of whom more in chapter 6) are a double organism consisting of a sluglike symbiont ensconced along and within the spinal cord of the humanoid host. Here all three restrictions apply—genetic, organismic, and reproductive. To make matters even thornier, we are explicitly told that the symbiont is sightless and hence cannot "sense" a humanoid presence without the aid of its host. Yet the senses and urges of the humanoid member of the unit are also modified in a major way by the presence of the symbiont.

Therefore, the likelihood that a joined Trill would be capable of procreating successfully with a nonjoined Trill or a non-Trill is remote, to put it mildly. That is why Yedrin Dax (presumably the descendant of Jadzia Dax and Worf in the alternative timeline of "Children of Time," DS9) is such an exotic presence, especially since he has apparently retained his mother's symbiont. In "The Host" (TNG), it is clear that only the symbiont is smitten with Dr. Crusher, making us wonder if this means that

Trill humanoid hosts are forced into sexual relationships against their will—and if so, why joining is considered such an honor in Trill society.

Then again, almost too many human courtship and mating rituals have been equally pleasureless, at least for one of the partners. To offer just one example, the advice of Victorian mothers to their daughters regarding the sexual part of their marriage was "Just close your eyes and think of England!" Nor can I possibly blame Worf for finding Jadzia Dax sexy—she can slink marvelously even inside a bulky Federation uniform, and she wields a mean *bat'leth* blade.

DEATH OR THE MAIDEN

So, if two chromosome copies are needed, it really looks like we're stuck. No pairing, no progeny. How do we get past such an obstacle? Well, there are two obvious ways. A life-form can choose not to have chromosome pairs. Or it can choose to reproduce parthenogenetically. In parthenogenesis ("virgin creation"), the organism propagates itself without gamete formation and combination.

The earliest forms of terrestrial life, which have remained unicellular, have taken the path of the single chromosome copy. It makes for an adventurous but risky life. When all of one's genes are present as single copies, the effects of a mutation are automatically manifested, since there is no compensatory balance from the partner chromosome.

This has resulted in rapid evolution: when Leeuwenhoek first peered into his microscope, the shapes he saw in that waterdrop were so diverse that he wasn't sure how to classify or explain them. But before we run off to rid ourselves of half our genetic baggage, we should consider how much more populous was the group that Leeuwenhoek *didn't* see—namely, those organisms for which the mutations spelled lingering or instant death. The mutational rate forms a developmental barrier. When an organism is confined to a single set of chromosomes, it will rarely venture past the unicellular stage.

Then there is parthenogenesis. This method of reproduction is seen especially frequently in insects, but also in the molly fishes common in tropical aquariums. Often, parthenogenetic and sexual cycles alternate, the former usually when husbanding of resources is necessary, the latter when it becomes important to introduce variety in the genotype. Invariably, fertilized versus unfertilized ova result in offspring of different genders—for example, female workers or princesses versus drones in honeybees. Therefore, the cycle choice can be used as a method of population control.

Parthenogenesis is the equivalent of cloning because it produces descendants that are genetically absolutely identical to the single parent. The political brouhaha over gene splicing (a.k.a. genetic engineering) died down when it was discovered that all cells do extensive genetic engineering on their own. Perhaps the furor over cloning may also decrease when humans realize that this, too, is already happening throughout the animal and plant kingdom without any input from us—or with our enthusiastic contribution, whenever we split our favorite fruit trees or rosebushes. Lest you conclude that I'm cavalier about these issues, rest assured that I go over them in great detail in chapter 9.

When there are two chromosomal copies, mutations must usually be present on both copies ("homozygous recessive") to do their work, good or evil. This gives such organisms a chance to evolve into multicellular conclaves and to specialize subsets of their constituent cells, by having each cell group express only a subset of its entire genetic menu. This results in the very different cell types and functions—nerves, muscles, bones. The need to keep the amount of genetic information constant has ushered the joys of sex into terrestrial biology.

However, increasing complexity exacts a heavy price. The good of the whole organism and the good of individual cells are in constant tension, like gravitational and fusion energy in a star. The condition of multicellular differentiation carries with it the danger that some cells may go rogue and turn against the whole organism—cancer, the disease that happens whenever the nuclear machinery tosses one mutation too many, or the cellular patrol lowers its guard.

Such mutated cells first stop obeying the various global and local commands that help them maintain their correct shape and properties. Then their even more heavily mutated progeny detaches from its neighbors and starts circulating in the bloodstream, leaving lethal patches throughout the system (metastasis). Lethal parasites, the tumor cells end up killing their host, the organism from which they sprang.

It gets worse. To deflect the danger of such undesirable cell growth as just described, all multicellular organisms are under sentence of death: whereas unicellular organisms can bud indefinitely, the cells of multicellular organisms are programmed to die after a certain number of divisions. This is known as the Hayflick limit, named after the gerontologist who first documented the phenomenon.

The "clock" that determines the number of divisions is at the end of each chromosome, the telomere. Scientists have likened telomeres to the caps at the end of shoelaces or wire bundles, which keep the strands from fraying. Each telomere consists of tandem copies of a repetitive sequence that gets shorter with each division of the cell. When this sequence is completely trimmed off, the chromosomes can no longer be fully duplicated and the cell activates a self-destruct sequence. This sequence is also activated when the cell has sustained damage that it cannot repair. Cells that keep dividing indefinitely instead of going gently into that good night inevitably become cancerous: they accumulate mutations that allow them to disregard the self-destruct sequence, just like malfunctioning starship computers.

Like most biological processes, this programmed cell death is a double-edged weapon: it runs all terrestrial life down like the Hunter God of Poul Anderson's fictional Ythrians, but it is also vital to correct pattern formation during embryogenesis. For example, the hands of human fetuses initially look like flippers. Cells need to die to form the fingers.

Not only has sexual reproduction made us mortal—it has also shortened even our measly allotted life spans. To add insult to injury, sexual reproduction is dangerous and costly for both partners involved. Fireflies, with their blinking lights, and male birds, with their conspicuous plumage, become vulnerable to predators at the same time that they are attempting to attract mates. Many species die after reproduction, since they've passed on their genes. Salmon die of exhaustion after spawning. Octopuses' stomachs degenerate after mating, leaving them just enough leeway to seed the next generation. The various butterflies in their sexually mature forms often don't even have a feeding apparatus—a wasted resource on someone destined only to mate and die.

For us humans, sex is now inextricably tied to culture and has been the cause of untold grief: one only has to think of the Trojan War or the endless number of strictures that all religions have erected around what is, after all, an instinctive act upon which the survival of the species depends absolutely. "Miri" (TOS) played on a true chord when it postulated death beginning with the onset of puberty. So did "The Quickening" (DS9), which showed a lethal sexually transmitted disease—as syphilis was prior to antibiotics, and as AIDS is today. Sex and death are not just thematically but actually biologically linked in *Star Trek*, as well as in real life.

Yet if we learn how not to die, will we lose that around which so much of our existence revolves?

THROUGH A TESSERACT, DARKLY

Can we have both sex *and* immortality? By all the evidence I've presented here, humanoid life-forms are finite in the usual four-dimensional spacetime. However, it is possible that residents of spaces with more dimensions might be exempt from this stricture—and still enjoy the privileges of sexual congress.

A commonly used thought-analogy is a three-dimensional creature visiting two-dimensional beings. Such a creature would be able to change its shape and position at will, since it would be free to leave and reenter the plane to which the two-dimensional beings were confined. From the human viewpoint, a similar legerdemain (both spatial and temporal) might be possible for a being that lived in the six or ten dimensions postulated by cosmic string theory.

Enter Q (TNG), with his usual fanfare and planet-sized self-regard. Q is a being from "a higher dimension," the Q Continuum. He is a trickster or joker figure who considers humanity his particular field of study. He appears in many major TNG episodes, primarily to annoy Captain Picard. Q's race (imaginatively dubbed "The Q") obviously engage in conventional sex, since they produce humanoid-looking offspring who name two parents ("True-Q," TNG).

Q's abilities to time-travel and appear at will are compatible with the laws of n-dimensional physics—an extension of the two/three dimension analogy. However, Q violates the differentiation = mortality biological equation. Despite his humanoid shape, he is apparently immortal. Incidentally, this seems to be true also of the "lesser" immortal race of El-Aurians, to which belong Guinan (the mysterious bartender with the temporal spider sense in TNG) and Soran (the being in frantic search of a cosmic fix in *Generations*, ST7).

Occasionally, humanoids are given a chance to attain immortality in *Star Trek*—for example, Commander Riker is tempted by Q in true garden-of-Eden fashion in "Hide and Q" (TNG). But he and other humanoids should think twice before accepting the gift.

In Greek mythology, Eos (Dawn) fell in love with Tithonus, a mortal youth. She petitioned for his immortality, and Zeus granted her wish. However, she forgot to also ask for eternal youth, and they both had all of eternity to regret her omission.

In humans, there are two problems with immortality. The first I already discussed—namely, that the types of cells that are already immortal within the human body are prone to accumulating mutations and are therefore bad news for the entire organism. Although "aging" and "longevity" genes have been discovered in fruit flies and worms, the problem of cancerous growth makes such genes at best a mixed blessing for humans.

The second, more serious roadblock is the nature of brain neurons. Most cells in the bodies of all multicellular organisms live from a few days to a few months before being shed. Some are so disposable (for example, mature red blood cells) that they occasionally jettison their nucleus altogether. However, there are three important exceptions to the recycling program: the eggs in the ovaries, the nurse cells that nourish sperm in the testes, and the neurons of the central nervous system (brain and spinal cord). For these, what we get at the beginning is all we'll ever have.

I briefly mentioned earlier that olfactory (nose) neurons still divide long after their creation. All other mature neurons neither divide nor multiply. That means that they are irreplaceable once they stop dividing, because no primitive progenitor cells are left that could regenerate them. However, the recent work of Gary Lynch in UC Irvine suggests that mature brain neurons are at least capable of forming new extensions.

It may well be that what determines the life span of an organism is the life span of its neurons. The brain is more like a sculpture than a painting. It is formed by the removal of neurons that haven't found their way, or neuronal connections that aren't being used, rather than by adding them on. We humans emerge with an "approximate" brain configuration and lose most of our neurons just after birth. Thereafter, there is constant attrition in our brains, with some regions more vulnerable than others.

With the increase in human life span, everyone is aware of the specter of dementia. Even Vulcans succumb to it, in the form of Bendii Syndrome, which ravages Spock's father Sarek in "Sarek" and "Unification" (TNG). So immortality for humans, like that of poor Tithonus, would be worse than useless if our bodies were masses of writhing tumors or the mere containers of inoperative brains. A few thousand years of senility is not a future anyone would contemplate with equanimity.

While we're on the subject of immortality, another impossibility for humanoids is reversal of aging. The Drayan race, which ages "backwards" in "Innocence" (VOY), could not possibly be humanoid in form. The arrow of time may itself forbid such shenanigans, although time travel makes for high drama, especially in the TNG cliffhangers "Yesterday's *Enterprise,*" "Time's Arrow" (!), and the series' finale, "All Good Things . . ." However, even if we treat the direction of time as cavalierly as *Star Trek* often does, once again we bump into some biological problems. I will defer age reversals that are caused by the transporter till chapter 5 and just address "physiological" reversals for now.

To turn back biological clocks, we would have to reverse the terminal differentiation of all specialized body parts as well as remove the accumulated mutations in the chromosomes. Each of these is a tall order. For the first, we'd need to find progenitor cells (impossible in the case that matters the most, namely the neurons). For the second, we'd also have to know the original, nonmutated genomic information of the individual.

Perhaps the Federation may have the ability to put everyone's full-length genome on record at the moment of birth (which is implied in several episodes—for example, in "Unnatural Selection," TNG). Otherwise, the aspiring cellular repair crew may find itself compelled to guesstimate or insert an "averaged out" sequence, casting heavy shadows on the question of uniqueness (considered further in chapters 5 and 9).

There is also the question of knowledge and memory. Will reversal of aging also imply smoothing out of the accumulated brain wrinkles? If so, we're better off with the traditional time trajectory. Given such an unpalatable choice, no wonder that the artificially rejuvenated Admiral Jameson expires in agony in "Too Short a Season" (TNG). On the other hand, if Gary Lynch's work can be extended, it may eventually become possible to at least stabilize existing neurons by controlled rejuvenation. This will not reverse aging, but it will at least spare us the agonies of dementia.

ADVANCED CREATIONISM

"Deaging" is bad enough. There is another biological field in which *Star Trek* has erred consistently—evolution. Contrary to what is shown repeatedly in *Star Trek*, evolution cannot alter individuals during their lifetime, though mutations may cause cancer as well as changes in the coming generations. The most glaring example is Project Genesis (ST2 and ST3, *The*

Wrath of Khan and *The Search for Spock*), in which geological and biological epochs unfold within one lifetime.

Instant evolutions (and worse yet, devolutions) are liberally sprinkled in all the series as well. In "All Our Yesterdays" (TOS), a backward trip in time causes Spock to revert to pre-Vulcan savagery and passion. In other episodes, individual humanoids rapidly mutate so that they become "pure energy" ("Transfigurations," TNG), undetectable to sensors ("Identity Crisis," TNG), and highly devolved or evolved reptiles ("Genesis," TNG; "Threshold" and "Scorpion," VOY).

It seems that *Star Trek* is the only institution that still follows the precepts of Chevalier de Lamarck, who posited that adaptive responses to environment cause structural changes that can be inherited. To give a characteristic example, Lamarckism postulated that if someone cut off the tails of mice, these mice would eventually have tailless descendants. And yet we know that after generations of foot-binding, Chinese girls were stubborn enough to still be born with full-size feet.

The Lamarckian theory of inheritance was adopted by the Soviet Union's leadership, who considered Mendelian genetics a bourgeois concept. Trofim Lysenko, the science tsar of Joseph Stalin, brought Soviet genetic research to a complete standstill because he considered Mendelian heredity incompatible with dialectical materialism. If you think that the United States is exempt from such lunacy, consider the fact that some American schools are teaching creationist "biology" even as you read this sentence.

Lysenko didn't just decimate science and scientists. His idea that he could improve the wheat crop by keeping the seeds cool and moist before sowing them caused the starvation of millions before he was finally dethroned. Yet Lysenkoism is actually mild compared to the *Star Trek* version, which too often shows a single person morphing into something else like a Battlemech or a Power Ranger. Not even retroviruses can achieve such feats of fluidity.

The sudden transformation of crew members into lizards or "superior life-forms" when exposed to anything energetic or viciously parasitic is one of my major gripes against *Star Trek.* We know what would happen because there is such an analogue: the radiation fallout from a nuclear explosion. Anyone forced to "change" at this rate would simply turn into bloody goo and die.

Another common but less serious misconception shown in *Star Trek* is that evolution automatically means progress ("later is better"). In the sciences, this teleological view of evolution has led to odd offshoots, such as sociobiology and social Darwinism. However, evolution is actually blind and tends to go to the end of the fork once it has made a decision.

At times, initial short-term success may lead to ultimate failure, by overcommitment or overspecialization. Obvious cases are the flightless birds of Oceania, who shed their wings in the absence of natural predators, only to greatly regret their choice when the European settlers arrived with their cats and dogs. A clear nonbiological parallel is the universal adoption of the internal combustion engine, which is inefficient but is now "locked in" because of investment of resources and asphyxiation of alternatives. The colonists of Moab IV in "The Masterpiece Society" (TNG) boxed themselves in by optimizing themselves and their environment so much that they could be destabilized by removal of a single person.

Moreover, when we examine any organism at either the physiological or the genetic level, we discover plenty of redundancies and haphazard jury-rigging. Such a system is ideally suited to undergo the "punctuated-equilibrium" evolution advocated by Stephen Jay Gould of Harvard University, who envisions organisms changing by fits and starts, rather than at a smooth, uniform rate. Nature is an engineer who has decided that the perfect is the enemy of the good. Perhaps this may also explain why *Star Trek* has survived so many transmutations, even though it gets its evolutionary principles consistently wrong.

STAR SONGS OF AN OLD PRIMATE

I have established that unicellular or higher-dimensional beings can short-circuit the electric fence of chromosomal pairing. We're still left with the puzzle of the endlessly interfertile humanoids in *Star Trek* (contemptuously named "carbon units" by V'Ger in *Star Trek: The Motion Picture,* ST1). In "The Chase" (TNG), the creators of the series have attempted to bypass this thorny problem by postulating an ancestral galactic race that "seeded" Earth-like class M planets. This scenario is repeated in minor key in "Tattoo" (VOY), where the Inheritors restricted their largesse to the gift of language and a collective memory—and, of course, tattoos that became the rage for attracting babes, er, women.

This explanation is familiar territory for UFO aficionados, Spielberg film buffs, and credulous devotees of Erich Von Däniken, author of *Chariots of the Gods* and its too many siblings. However, the panspermic theory creates more problems than it solves.

To begin with, it is formally equivalent to creationism. Simply substitute advanced aliens for the Old Testament Elohim, who created everything in six days. The scenario in "The Chase" falls squarely in the category of the grand-design fallacy ("Everything must have a purpose"), which is sandwiched between the anthropic principle ("The universe was created so that humans could exist") and manifest destiny ("It is God's will that we overrun this continent").

If the pro-race seeded only bacteria, they would have evolved into totally different end products, given how different the various planets are. Even on Earth, identical biological beginnings can lead to very different outcomes. The same problem has been solved in different ways by various species. For example, the flight mechanisms of insects, birds, and bats are completely different; so are the eye structures of marine invertebrates, insects, and vertebrates.

Star Trek has shown lack of imagination and scientific judgment in showing its humanoids so similar in form, stature, and coloring. As a simple single case, *Star Trek* correctly makes all Vulcans stronger than Humans, because their planet has higher-than-terrestrial gravity (hence more bone and muscle mass). Yet if the series wanted to be consistent, it should have shown all Vulcans at least as dark-skinned as Lieutenant Tuvok (VOY), considering the distance of their sun from their planet;

they should also all be shorter and stockier than Humans, as would be expected from Vulcan's higher gravity.

If the ancestors seeded prehumans, that would still not guarantee interfertility: less than a million years' distance between the Neanderthals and the Cro-Magnons was enough to make them distinct and make us all Cro-Magnon descendants—though there is, as always, an opposing school of thought that argues the Neanderthals simply vanished into the human reproductive pool. Furthermore, even if the human progenitors in *Star Trek* were identical, there is always the random ecological factor (reproductive isolation or ecological catastrophe), which may result in evolution taking a totally different turn from that envisioned by the seeding race.

Finally, if they seeded self-conscious humanoids, the ancestral race in "The Chase" violated in the worst possible fashion the treasured moral precept of noninterference. Though it's true that the Prime Directive is formally binding only on the Federation, various versions of it have popped up consistently and persistently in science fiction—which implies universality. Even more grievous was the trespass of the Inheritors in "Tattoo," who broke the interdict of contact between pre- and postwarp societies. Still, this might explain the collective unconscious so beloved of New Age gurus who have read Jung just a bit too fast.

PARTING SHOTS

So it looks as if we have to give up on the scientific plausibility of Spock and K'Ehleyr. Dramatically, though, they are a necessity. When humans ventured outside the narrow circle of the known, no doubt it was immensely reassuring to know that, no matter how odd the new surroundings, the humans they met could still be cuddled—though most encounters started with variations of the baring of teeth.

The urge to hold and be held is so ingrained in primates that it is recognized as an adaptive feature: Harry Harlow's famous cloth experiments with young rhesus monkeys at Wisconsin University established that primate infants would rather be held than fed. It is not odd that we, their descendants, would feel the need even more keenly when venturing into the reaches of space.

On the next level, too, the dilemmas caused from mixed inheritance have been major engines in human history and culture. Self-conflict is the soul of drama, after all, and if nothing else, *Star Trek* is highly operatic. By positing hybrids and following their unique pains and joys, *Star Trek* has once again shown itself insightful and savvy. However, whenever I see Dax batting her eyelashes all over Worf, I must raise a Spock-like eyebrow.

SCENE 3.
TIN SOLDIERS AND GLASS BALLERINAS

How Likely Are Androids, Cyborgs, or Shape-Shifters?

All *Star Trek* fans know the thrill of being on the bridge of a fictional starship, with galaxies streaming past. The gadgetry is gorgeous, the unfolding starscapes breathtaking, the possibilities endless. And yet, exhilarating though this traveling may be, it still doesn't satisfy our urge to directly experience sensations or capabilities beyond our reach.

Who has never dreamed of being able to fly? By that I don't mean in a commercial airplane. I'm talking about soaring on real wings. I think everyone has fantasized about that—I certainly have. It seems part of our heritage.

Carbon-based and finite, humans are constantly pushing the envelope of their perceived physical limitations. The myths of shape-changers, which occur in practically every culture, show how strong the desire for physical mastery can be. When humans lacked the requisite technology to fly, they tried to transcend their bodies by hallucinating or trancing—and are still doing so today, even though flying has finally become feasible. As technology has advanced, humans are constantly tinkering with this device and that prosthesis to extend their capabilities. Recently we've been trying to duplicate the complexity of our own nervous system in silicon-based systems such as neural nets.

I think that one of the reasons that *Star Trek* has transcended its inherent sixties TV series limitations is that it has stressed the importance of egalitarianism as a springboard to the universe. Yet even as *Star Trek* fans congratulate themselves about vicariously partaking of that egalitarianism, humans in general still prefer easy classifications (which almost always carry an attached relative value tag) and dislike ambiguity.

During most historical periods, the law dictated that gender, rank, ethnicity, and occupation had to be clearly reflected by external appearance. Even today, several countries forbid arbitrarily defined "cross-dressing" on pain of ostracism or death. So anything that smacks of a crossover—freedom to assume many shapes or integration between flesh and machine—leads to profound unease. This societal desire for quick pegging has long been codified in terrestrial religions ("Thou shalt not suffer a witch to live").

In three major thought-experiments, *Star Trek* explores such reservations. And while it deserves kudos for some groundbreaking ventures and certainly loves technological gizmos, *Star Trek* shares the general ambivalence about blurring the organic/inorganic interface. That's a portentous way of saying that all races of this type are adversaries of the Federation. Members of such species are tolerated within the Federation only as isolated individuals (Data in TNG, Odo in DS9, Seven of Nine in VOY). Curiously enough, these species are also all collectives. Perhaps this mirrors the deep and specifically American unease with any type of even remotely "socialist" organization.

In the organic corner, ladies and gentlemen, stand the Changelings of DS9, shape-shifters par excellence. At the inorganic end we have Noonien Soong's creations Lore and Data (TNG), the Cain and Abel androids. But the life-form that gets *Star Trek* knees knocking the hardest is the one that lustfully embraces a full fusion of flesh and machine—the dreaded and unrepentant Borg collective (TNG, VOY, and *First Contact*, ST8).

Let's consider the biology of each.

SHHH, NOT IN HERE—THE WALLS HAVE EARS!

Shape-shifters have prowled Earth lore since time immemorial. Central Europe is inundated with werewolves and vampires; the Navajo fear skin-walkers; the Malays quail before weretigers. The shape-shifting tradition is carried on today in children's cartoons and typically apocalyptic Japanese animé films, which show cyborgs flowing into the shape of a tank or airplane, then back to human form. And even in contemporary Western culture, normal humans emerge every morning from their night lairs, morphed with suits and ties into office workers.

The first two *Star Trek* series, TOS and TNG, merely grazed this fascinating subject. They confined themselves to creatures that merely (!) shifted from one organic form to another: mellitus in "Wolf in the Fold" (TOS), who is a gas when moving but solid when still; the salt-seeking mimic in "Man Trap" (TOS); the allasomorphs ("shape-changers" in Greek) Salia and Anya in "The Dauphin" (TNG). Also, let's not forget the sinister "chameloid" Martia in *The Undiscovered Country* (ST6), who seems to have perfected the art of impersonating beautiful women—as well as marrying David Bowie, something of a shape-shifter himself.

With DS9, however, shape-shifting came into its own, thanks no doubt to a special effect technique developed for the film *Terminator 2* (this technique allows the viewer to watch something actively morphing). DS9 Security Chief Odo belongs to the race of Changelings, who can perfectly impersonate any life-form, but do an equally excellent job of posing as furniture. The Changelings' natural form is liquid, and they need to revert to the liquid state at set intervals to recuperate from the wear and tear of their shape-shifting labors.

Just as vampires need a coffin lined with their native earth, so Changelings require their own preferred container, although any port will do in a storm. In "The Forsaken" (DS9), Odo takes refuge in Lwaxana Troi's loving lap (I hope the fabric was waterproof). On their home planet, Changelings merge with each other, forming an ocean that covers the entire surface except for a single rock. On that, any "member" of the race who shows unbecoming defiance is literally hung out to dry, just as the gods tied Prometheus to the crags of the Caucasus.

Odo himself is an ambiguous character, gruff, gauche, and embittered by his isolation (especially evident in "Broken Link," DS9). He is obsessed with justice, but is correspondingly somewhat lacking in flexibility. His race is clearly hostile to conventional life-forms in general, whom they contemptuously name "the solids." More specifically, the Changelings are the founders of the Dominion, the major political entity of the Gamma Quadrant and a dangerous enemy of the Federation.

On the face of it, Odo's quick-change feats are not completely beyond the pale. Terrestrial animals exhibit some flexibility in their shape and color. Several species can change their overall structure by expanding or unhinging their bones at the cartilage joints (blowfish, snakes when they want to swallow large prey, mammalian females during birth). Other animals can change their color by expanding and contracting individual chromophoric (color-bearing) cells—for example, the octopus, the chameleon, and related lizard species. Insects go through a complete revamping, known as metamorphosis, morphing from larva to pupa to adult.

However, the shape-shifting abilities of the Changelings, fascinating as they are, are unfortunately impossible in the realms of physics, chemistry, and every level of biology that I can think of (maybe even some I've forgotten). The *Star Trek* scanners and sensors agree with my assessment, since they do not register Changelings as life-forms ("The Adversary," DS9). And my problems with the concept are so numerous that they deserve a whole subsection.

HOW IMPOSSIBLE ART THOU? LET ME COUNT THE WAYS

Physically, the obvious problem with shape-shifting is conservation of mass. When Odo changes from his human form into a wineglass in "Vortex" (DS9), realistically he has two choices under known physical laws: convert the extra mass to energy, causing an explosion large enough to destroy the station, or retain it and become an object disproportionately heavy for its size—and a dead giveaway to his adversaries.

The *Star Trek* Nitpicker group on the World Wide Web has come up with all kinds of neat explanations for this quandary. My favorite is the theory that "Odo is a five-dimensional being existing in four-dimensional space. When he needs to alter his mass, he rotates it away into another dimension." This actually kills two birds with one stone, since it might solve the problem of the missing mass so sought after by cosmologists: a large Changeling population would finally put to rest all these far-fetched proposals of exotic elementary particles, which have been hypothesized to explain the fact that our universe seems to be denser than expected.

Also, when he slips into something less comfortable, Odo would have to change his composition to convincingly impersonate his subject/object of choice (and what happens to his comm badge when he shifts?). Recruitment of the necessary elements would be impossible—doubly so in the minute time interval he seems to need for full transformation. On the other hand, if he just needs to "pass," he can conceivably simulate the material, just as acrylic fiber can now often pass for wool or silk. This might explain why in fact Odo's human face looks so unconvincing, almost like the rigid "mask" of a Parkinson's disease victim.

Biologically, we run into three serious problems with Odo's fluidity. First, individual evolution is an untenable proposition, as I discussed at length in chapter 2 (a person can always accumulate knowledge and wisdom, of course, or so psychologists and philosophers hope). Second, the demands of shape-shifting would probably overwhelm gene coding capacity. Third, but certainly not least, such shifts threaten continuity of consciousness—a subject that will keep haunting us in chapters 4, 5, and 6.

As far as gene coding capacity, you might ask, what about insects? A caterpillar certainly looks radically different from the butterfly that it eventually becomes. However, although some terrestrial organisms look totally different in their different growth stages, all forms are accounted for in their genetic blueprint. For Odo to completely become the life-form that he impersonates, he must mimic them at the molecular level. How would this be reflected in his genome?

Viral and bacterial genomes are compact, often containing overlapping genes. Conversely, gene coding segments in higher organisms represent a low percentage of the total genome (10 percent comes to my mind, but estimates differ). However, gene coding is not the only game. Remember, the chromosome must also contain instructions for folding, signposts that show where genes begin and end, regulatory sequences that dictate when a gene is to be activated and by whom, and how its product is to be processed into message RNA (spliced), exported from the nucleus, and made into protein in the cytoplasm (translated).

Beyond regulatory stretches, the genome also contains repetitive sequences. In the previous chapter we already encountered the telomeres, which occupy the end of each chromosome and keep track of the number of times that a particular cell has divided. Other repetitive sequences are interspersed throughout the genome, and their function is unknown. "Junk" DNA is a popular term, but is about as correct as calling the space between the atoms "waste." These regions may be overwritten palimpsests or warehouses: silenced functional units that were active in the past. The genome holds on to them, just in case they are needed in the future. As every computer programmer and fashion designer knows, it is easier and faster to refurbish than to create from scratch.

So perhaps Changelings have the coding capacity for many lifeforms, and their genome, unlike that of humans, is chock-full of this information, with few repetitive sequences and no redundancy. Alternatively, the Changelings may have this information in modular form, then combine it into functional coding units according to the needs of the moment.

This is not as far-fetched as it sounds. Most of our genes are modular. Besides the Central Dogma, which I mentioned in chapter 1 ("Genetic information flows in one direction, from DNA to RNA to protein"), another concept that the biochemists long took for granted was that DNA is colinear with protein, a.k.a "one gene, one product." Twenty years ago, we learned otherwise.

It turns out that genes are segmented: gene regions that contain protein coding information (exons) are beads strung between regions that don't code for protein but contain regulatory signals (introns). The "beads" are brought together to form messenger RNA, which is translated into protein.

This process is called splicing. We would have discovered it long ago if we had chosen any organism but *E. coli* for our first model system. *E. coli* belongs to the only group of organisms that jettisoned introns in favor of efficiency (and dullness, as they got stuck being single cells). So the "one gene, one product" theory has fallen by the wayside, just like the Central Dogma. Depending on time and place, the splicing machinery can pick and choose which beads to string to the necklace (alternative splicing). Some genes produce as many as two hundred different proteins, all with slightly or even radically different structures and functions.

Several molecular biologists (Walter Gilbert of Harvard among them) believe that this modular arrangement was in fact the configuration of many ancestral genes that have since given rise to entire gene families by duplications. The ancestor was a jack-of-all-trades; the descendants have more specialized tasks and occupy specific niches.

Another, equally impressive modular system is the mammalian immune system. The number of substances it can recognize and guard against is simply staggering. It achieves this fantastic variety by having a redundant molecular arrangement for the genes that code for the antibodies. The modules determine what the antibody will recognize as an enemy ("antigen specificity") and whether the antibody will patrol the bloodstream or hold the fort perched on immune cells. When the organism is faced with a new antigen, it mixes and matches the various segments so that it can produce an antibody tailor-made to the circumstances.

Alas, this still doesn't quite solve Odo's problem of feasibility in the gene coding area. For one thing, although alternative splicing can produce a dizzying number of isoforms, they are usually variations on a theme. For another, amazing though the immune response is, it takes quite a lot longer than the blink of an eye: the minimum requirement to switch products is one round of DNA replication and transcription, which in mammalian cells takes roughly two days. Finally, once the genome of an antibody-producing cell has been rearranged, the change is irreversible, because the intervening DNA segments have been deleted.

THE GREAT BRAIN BARRIER REEF

But let me be indulgent—after all, I like Odo despite (actually because of) his gruffness. Let's assume that Changeling genomes can handle all these hurdles I just went through. We still have to face the last difficulty on my list.

How does Odo sense his surroundings if he has completely become a table or a rock? He certainly seems to rely on humanoid senses when he looks like a human, otherwise it would be impossible to attack him from the back, which happens in "Duet" (DS9).

Even more fundamentally, if Odo becomes something completely inanimate or devoid of intelligence, it is unclear how he holds on to his consciousness and sense of self. Many shape-changer tales in fact emphasize this difficulty: sometimes, when too much time is spent inside the alien self, the shifters find it difficult or impossible to return to their original shape. One of the best stories in this vein is George Martin's "In the Lost Lands." In particular, how does Odo remember and think if he doesn't have a brain to do it with? Where does he store his memories while he's impersonating a Tarellian hawk or a Chippendale chair? To answer this, we must take a detour through the workings of the human brain and nervous system.

In terrestrial higher organisms, memory and all other brain activities are ultimately a chemical phenomenon. Each neuron has specialized extensions. The dendrites receive information; a single axon transmits it. At the tips of the neuronal extensions are special patches called the synapses. Whenever a neuron "fires," its synapses release the appropriate type and amount of a neurotransmitter to communicate the event to the neighboring neurons.

In turn, these neighbors measure the total input of neurotransmitters from their neighbors by changes in the electric state of their membrane. Once the input exceeds a threshold level, they fire in their turn. The "firing" itself consists of an electrical signal traveling down the axon, just like a surfer's dream wave. However, linear transmission would be unacceptably slow—by the time a message got from the brain to the feet in this manner, the owner of both would be inside a lion's stomach.

To hasten transmission, neurons are wrapped like sausages in myelin sheaths, an insulating material manufactured by another brain cell type, the glia (white matter). The sheath leaves gaps on the axon (the nodes of Ranvier), which act as trampoline pads for the electric signal. The devastation wrought by multiple sclerosis arises from degeneration of the myelin sheath, which abolishes the saltatory conduction of the nerve impulse that I just described.

In this complicated manner, a digital event gets translated to an analogue one: the firing of the neurons, which are the spikes seen in an EEG (electroencephalogram), leads to the release of the neurotransmitters. As a result of all this activity, neurons may change their connections or activity (and therefore products) of their genes.

In a nutshell, each time a neuron fires in response to a stimulus, the brain changes. This new configuration means an action, a new memory, a thought, an emotion. How do we hold on to these once they appear?

A newly formed memory remains in the brain section known as the hippocampus. Then it moves to the cortex, the residence of long-term memories. There is no agreement among scientists whether a memory (for example, the last trip to New Mexico) is stored as a chain of molecules or as a specific configuration of synaptic connections. Given the electric/chemical equivalence of the neuronal signal, it may well be both, though long-term memory is more likely to be a specific configuration of synapses.

Both short- and long-term memory can be decisively affected by trauma to the brain—the well-placed blow to the head that causes amnesia is a staple in the mystery genre. Diseases that destroy neurons (all of the dementias, Parkinson's, Huntington's) inevitably lead to memory loss. When their hippocampus is damaged, people often emerge unable to form new memories, although they retain everything that happened before the accident or operation.

So given how complicated and layered a phenomenon memory really is, you can see why it's hard for me to envision Odo switching it on and off at will, according to his shape. In fact, two additional questions branch out of this intrinsic problem of continuity of personality.

How do "individual" Changelings reconstitute themselves after each merging into the Great Link of the home planet? By definition, individual molecules in homogeneous liquids are equivalent and cannot be distinguished from one another. Do the Odo molecules retain memories of being Odo? If they do, the authors must have borrowed this concept from a fanciful (and now discarded) theory that water retains the memory of objects that were in it. It seems plausible that Changelings can dissolve and reform smaller units at will, in which case punishing Odo for breaking racial taboos ("Broken Link," DS9) is unnecessary. All they need to do is absorb him and not reconstitute him as such.

A related wrinkle in the background of the Changeling race is that as "babies" they need to be trained to assume any shape other than their native liquid form and will generally do so only under duress (showcased in "The Begotten," DS9, when Odo is trying to rear an infant Changeling). So how did they discover their innate ability?

My hypothesis (and I will be happy to write the script for this episode) is that their native planet may have had other life-forms, quite possibly hostile to the Changelings. The competition made the latter aware of the survival value of their shape-shifting capabilities, which they then used to exterminate all rivals. Considering the talmudic bent of the Changelings, they may well have designated a scapegoat after a "cleansing" of such magnitude: Armus, the murderous oil slick in "Skin of Evil" (TNG) instantly enters my thoughts, since it shares with the Changelings both terminal dourness and shape-shifting abilities.

Given the completely different material requirements and thought processes of Changelings and humanoids, I also wonder what the bone of contention is in the Gamma Quadrant. The only point of similarity between the two seems to be that they are both oxygen breathers. Similar species that share territory compete for rare resources (riveting examples are C. J. Cherryh's Union/Alliance series and Poul Anderson's van Rijn/Polesothechnic League stories). But in the case of the Federation against the Dominion, the two biopolitical entities do not even share quadrants. Nevertheless, the Federation/Dominion conflict does make for high drama, always intrinsically more exciting to watch than the trivia and fine nuances of daily life.

ADAM RAISED A CAIN

Let's now put another exotic life-form under the microscope.

At the silicon end of the spectrum, androids have been a perennial science fiction topic, starting with Isaac Asimov's famous Robot stories. Androids (meaning manlike, instead of the more inclusive *anthropoids*) are technologically evolved robots that resemble humans.

Androids were a regular fixture in TOS, most prominently examined with Roger Korby ("What Are Little Girls Made Of?" TOS), Alice ("I, Mudd," TOS), and Rayna Kapec ("Requiem for Methuselah," TOS). But androids come into their own in TNG, thanks to the conflicted genius of Dr. Noonien Soong.

First we meet Lieutenant Commander Data, a Starfleet officer, a model of decorum and a Renaissance man. The only thing that he lacks is emotion—or so he insists, although he seems perfectly capable of puzzlement, affection (especially toward Tasha Yar), sorrow ("Skin of Evil," TNG), and in later episodes, anger ("Descent" and "The Most Toys," TNG).

As the series develops, however, we discover that Data is actually the younger and ostensibly lesser of two siblings. Dr. Soong originally created Lore, a fully human android ("Datalore," TNG). Not surprisingly, but to his creator's discomfort, Lore proved as unpredictable as a true human.

Soong, just like Victor Frankenstein, was obliged to disassemble his creation, and Lore, just like Frankenstein's monster, is permanently embittered against his maker ("Brothers," TNG).

Thematically, here we hear echoes not only of Cain and Abel, but also of Lilith and Eve. Lilith, created separate from and equal to Adam, proved too independent and was cast into Gehenna; the more submissive Eve was then crafted out of Adam's rib. There is even a secondary echo of this story in "Inheritance" (TNG), in which Dr. Soong, devastated by the death of Juliana Tainer, his partner and lover, re-creates her as an android without telling her that she is artificial. In this connection, it is interesting that *Star Trek,* following Hollywood conventions, has a surfeit of fathers and a dearth of mothers (we will touch upon this again in chapter 11).

In a typical pattern of primogeniture privilege, Noonien Soong has given Lore, his firstborn, everything—reason, emotion, the bodily vehicle with which to execute his desires. To his secondborn, Data, he has given all kinds of puzzling impedimenta, mentioned in "Birthright" (TNG): a breath, a pulse, the capacity to eat, the ability to grow his hair follicles, and perhaps as a final flourish, a fully functioning sexual apparatus—which gets used several times; the most explicit and exciting bout is with Tasha Yar in "The Naked Now" (TNG).

I can't figure out what benefits Data derives from the need to shave, since he is already patient to a fault. And I find it perverse that Dr. Soong has withheld from Data the emotion chip that would complete his humanity. Given this deliberate omission, Data is actually what Vulcans are striving to become: as Data explicitly points out to Spock in "Unification II" (TNG), he is a rational creature entirely devoid of the clouding effects of emotion—but who nevertheless yearns for such an "imperfection."

Are the Soong androids possible? The task of creating an inorganic intelligence, a thinking machine, has been the grail of the AI community here on Earth since its inception. Following Moore's law (Gordon Moore was the cofounder of Intel), the power, computational speed, and complexity of the silicon chip have doubled every eighteen months with proportionate decreases in cost. In the next decade, a computer will be able to discharge as many calculations as the human brain. So from the viewpoint of information density, such constructs are only a matter of time. What will they be like when they appear?

UP, DOWN, AND STRANGE

What is Data's mind/brain like? To see what Data's ancestors look like, we must visit an AI lab. Many AI labs, most prominently those at MIT and in Xerox PARC, have employed several approaches to generate silicon-based systems that incorporate one or more aspects of intelligence.

The top-down approach essentially consists of the heuristic method, which seeks to emulate an activity by writing a detailed set of rules for it. ELIZA, one of the first interactive programs, was such a program. The most notorious example, however, is IBM's Deep Blue, which recently trounced world chess champion Gary Kasparov. The brouhaha over Deep Blue's victory ("I used to think that chess required deep thinking," complained Douglas Hofstadter of Indiana University) shows clearly that humans would feel as threatened by a true alternative intelligence as Kronos by the emerging power of his son, Zeus.

Similar expert systems are now routinely employed in industry, traffic control, weather prediction—even in medicine, where they often outperform flesh-and-blood doctors as diagnosticians. They perform admirably within their expertise, but fail miserably outside it: if asked a question beyond their algorithm parameters, they will return either a patently absurd answer or literally crash the machine.

In TOS, James Kirk used this weak spot repeatedly to outwit sentient computers—so often that this ploy, rather than his rewrite of the *Kobayashi Maru* program, should have been called the Kirk Maneuver in Starfleet manuals. I can count at least six instances: against Nomad in "The Changeling"; Mudd's android army in "I, Mudd"; Losira in "That Which Survives" and M-5 in "The Ultimate Computer"; not quite against

Rayna Kapec in "Requiem for Methuselah"; and against V'Ger in *Star Trek: The Motion Picture* (ST1).

Another way to generate sentient machines is the bottom-up approach. This is based on the belief that execution of a set of rules will never make the hardware intelligent, self-aware, or even particularly dexterous. Proponents of this (notably Rodney Brooks of MIT) are convinced that the only way to foster intelligence is to have a relatively simple machine and program, but make it capable of learning by trial and error, just like a mammalian baby. The most prominent results along this path are the "smart robots," which were originally commissioned by the military and intended for retrieval and rescue missions in heavily radioactive areas after a nuclear war.

In a rare happy ending, such semi-intelligent machines have been used on planetary missions instead. One of them is investigating Mars as I write these lines. There is something both generous and touching in the cartoon of Matt Davies, which shows the *Sojourner* rover leaving human footprints behind as it moves across the Mars landscape: it is indeed our proxy representative. The exocomps in "The Quality of Life" (TNG) are obviously descendants of Viking, Voyager, and *Sojourner.*

Finally, we have the sideways neural net approach. This is the brainchild of physicists who decided to enter neurobiology (beginning with John Hopfield). In these constructs, brain neurons are treated like atoms in a lattice, and the whole system is asked to minimize its energy. What is crucially different about neural nets is that, like the mammalian brain, they are parallel processors. Traditional computers are sequential processors, which make up for their linearity by being exceedingly fast.

Just as in the mammalian brain, the distribution of "knowledge" in neural nets is diffuse and plastic: if one part is destroyed, the system attempts to regroup and reconfigure, just as it happens with humans (for example, recovering stroke victims). Such nets seem to exhibit emergent properties and to mimic some aspects of brain functions—particularly information acquisition, processing, and storage (memory). In an interesting feedback loop, artificial neural nets may actually tell us something about the nervous system, the brain, memory, and consciousness, major ciphers in biology, psychology, and philosophy.

SEND UP THE KITES!

Data appears as human as anyone else; he is not merely conscious but aware of his consciousness. Will computers or robots ever be alive—specifically, self-aware? Whatever their achievements, they are still lagging far behind in speech and pattern recognition (they fail to recognize a face if the angle of viewing shifts, so the current programs depend on quick scans instead), and they are woefully devoid of both intuition and common sense. With their enormous computing capacity but lack of flexibility, they are deservedly considered idiot savants.

The Soong androids are clearly not idiot savants. They are self-aware enough to ask what they are and why they were made; they yearn for community and descendants. Lore becomes the leader of a band of cyborgs in "Descent" (TNG) and Data attempts to create a child modeled after himself—Lal in "The Offspring" (TNG). The Federation obviously considers the Soong androids life-forms: after some initial hesitation, it eventually grants Data full-fledged citizenship ("The Measure of a Man," TNG).

So far, it's been good news for the possibility of "alive" machines. However, Data and his brother pose some biological problems, especially since *Star Trek* cannot decide just what percent or part of them is organic. A totally inorganic makeup is incompatible with Data's ability to grow hair follicles, eat, etc. A partial organic makeup (even the presence of liquid chemical nutrients) is incompatible with his alleged nonconductance as well as his extraordinary strength—to what joints or tendons do Data's titanium "muscles" attach? The maximum strength of any system is identical to that of its weakest components.

So if Data is part organic, when he lifts an enormous weight, his arm should rip loose from his body or he should get a massive hernia. Furthermore, if Juliana Tainer ("Inheritance," TNG) cannot tell that she is artificial, we reach the contradictory conclusion that the bodies of androids must pass muster as human—even accepting that Noonien Soong made Juliana different from Data (shades of Eve again).

Another impossibility is that Data seems to have complete "executive control" over all his functions, higher and lower. Such a setup would result in overflowing of his brain capacity within moments—just like the centipede who keeled over when asked to explain how it coordinated its hundred legs. And this brings us to the question of Data's programming.

Not surprisingly, he seems to be an even mixture of the top-down, bottom-up, and sideways approaches. He obviously has algorithms installed (he says, "I'm accessing the appropriate program in my memory" countless times), but he also learns from experience and can adapt to new situations (for example, he flatly disobeys orders when he knows more than Picard in "Redemption," TNG). Finally, since a part of him can substitute for the whole (his head functions in isolation in "Time's Arrow," TNG), the inescapable conclusion is that he is based on neural net principles. He says so himself several times, and he is theoretically incapable of lying—although his explanation of his murderous anger in "The Most Toys" (TNG) leaves this question open as well.

As to the vexed question of the much coveted "emotion chip" given to Lore but denied to Data, I think that the distinction was irrelevant, though it generated a satisfactory amount of Sturm und Drang: anything close enough to think and react like a human will also feel like a human. Emotions cannot be disentangled from thoughts, Mr. Spock's efforts notwithstanding (more of this in chapter 5). The creators of *Star Trek* must have reached the same conclusion, because in *First Contact* (ST8) Data has his emotion chip.

Androids such as Data will be feasible in a few centuries, and they may well be alive by any definition of the word. If what makes a conscious being is a template (DNA) and thought connections (synapses), such a system can be created with advanced enough technology. A program that is large and flexible enough will be able to make its own choices and thought connections and extensions.

What would distinguish such properties from true awareness? At that point, such hairsplitting will sound similar to the arguments of people who insist that "natural" vitamins are better than artificially made ones, or to the *Star Trek* crews' complaints about the quality of the food from the replicator. In the end, the most severe birth pangs for Soong-type androids will not be their complexity, but the unease that overwhelms humans whenever they impinge on the core of consciousness—or, dare I pronounce it, "soul."

And talking of unease, let's now straddle the organic/inorganic border. Do I hear ominous music swelling?

THE SPIRIT OF THE BEEHIVE

When Q wishes to teach Humans the true meaning of fear in "Q Who?" (TNG), he causes the *Enterprise* to materialize in a far region of space (presumably the Delta Quadrant). Before them, Picard and Co. see a cubist version of *Star Wars*' Death Star. The shape of this starship, let alone the body structure of its inhabitants, recalls the dark visions of the *Alien* tetralogy. It certainly bodes serious ill for future interactions between this new species and the Federation.

The Borg prove as threatening as their appearance. No tea parties with this bunch, Capt. Earl Grey Hot! Before we investigate Borg biology, though, what information can we glean from their ship?

Given that space is near vacuum, there is no aerodynamic reason for starships to have any particular shape. In *Star Trek,* the various predatory shapes of the Romulan and Klingon ships are clearly holdovers from the time of single warrior posturing. Several engineers hold the opinion that, even within Earth's atmosphere, an airplane with one wing facing forward and one backward would be more efficient aerodynamically.

However, I strongly suspect that such an airplane will never be built, because it is almost certain that people would never be persuaded to fly in it. For humans, perhaps for the reproductive reasons that I mentioned in chapter 2, aesthetics, symmetry, and morality are inextricably intertwined. Obviously, not so for the Borg, who build and crew the menacing starcubes; their aesthetic decisions tell us something about their biology.

When we first clap eyes on them, the Borg units are a frightful realization of the cyborg, a multiple contraction from *cybernetic organism.* They're a far cry from Lee Majors as the Six Million Dollar Man. Their faces a corpselike greenish gray, they bristle with uneven mechanical prostheses. They move like automatons, speak in a monotone, talk in clipped, unadorned sentences, and have no individual personalities or will.

Even worse, the Borg are bent on forcing their aesthetics on the universe and intend to turn everything in their path into creatures resembling themselves. This would be a fashion disaster, since the Borg look as if they went to a used-appliance warehouse and attached broken VCRs and toasters randomly all over themselves. Equipped with nanotechnology and linked to each other with subspace transceivers, the Borg instantly adapt to any new technology that their enemies can come up with.

By imagining the Borg, the *Star Trek* writers left not a single human-fear button unpushed. The Borg blur the flesh/machine boundary. They symbolize loss of individuality, forcible conversion, and technological supremacy by masters with an inflexible will.

Yet looking at the Borg, I couldn't help noticing that there are such creatures already on Earth. They have preceded humans by several million years and are very successful in their own niche. Excepting their hardware, the Borg are closely modeled on social-insect societies—in particular, the army and driver ants of Africa and South America.

The points of equivalence are obvious. Each grouping of social insects (a hive or a nest) can best be considered a single organism. They communicate by scent trails, they specialize for specific tasks (nurses, farmers, soldiers, consorts), and their behavioral repertory, although extensive, is completely hardwired. Army and driver ants have additional points of similarity to the Borg: they are aggressive nomads who "assimilate" everything in their path by the simple expedient of ingesting it.

In TNG, all Borg appear male. This is incompatible with their policy of total assimilation, but it obviously serves to underscore their "otherness." But in *First Contact* (ST8) and the continuation of the Borg saga in VOY an additional wrinkle comes into play. Like the nests of terrestrial social insects, the Borg cubes are ruled by queens.

Add Oedipal fears to the Borg brew and it becomes potent indeed. I was puzzled by the fact that the Borg queen in *First Contact* (ST8) sported lipstick, an atypical concession to appearance for a Borg, until I realized that it probably was a representation of the dreaded vagina dentata. Adult human males have a deep fear of domination by maternal figures (as do Klingons and Ferengi; we will explore this suspicious homogeneity further in chapter 11).

Sigmund Freud considered rejection of the mother a natural and inevitable differentiation step on the way to masculinity—but then again, he also considered the switch from clitoral to (nonexistent) vaginal orgasm equally inevitable for attainment of femininity. So much for expert opinions. The explanations for the origin of this male fear are endless, from the feminist idea that males are intimidated by women's reproductive capacities to the sociobiological theory that the two human genders have slightly incompatible reproductive strategies and are therefore not natural allies.

Social insects are not under such a bane but have gone to the opposite, equally grim extreme. Single members of the hive are expendable, except one: the life of the hive and all its members depends absolutely on the presence and well-being of the queen. All inhabitants of a hive are descendants of a single queen, and they recognize her pheromone. If they lose the scent connection, they lose interest in the world, wander around aimlessly, stop eating, and die.

In a close parallel to this, single Borg are expendable. Their fellows do not mourn for them, nor do they collect the bodies. On the other hand, they are in constant communication with each other through subspace connections. Their network is so strong that non-Borg who have temporarily been absorbed and then rescued remain permanently, though weakly, connected to the collective (Captain Picard in "The Best of Both Worlds," TNG, and *First Contact*, ST8; Commander Chakotay in

"Unity," VOY). When deprived of the collective experience, individual Borg either self-destruct or go mad, unless they can find a queen substitute to attach themselves to (as does Third of Five, later called Hugh, in "I, Borg" and "Descent," TNG).

Again in conformity with the social insect model, the dependence of the Borg on a single queen is one of their few vulnerable points. If the queen is as much in charge of coordination and long-term planning as her terrestrial equivalents, if she is "the brains" of the outfit, her removal is clearly equivalent to destruction of her cube. Since the Borg have gone on to menace the *Voyager* after one queen's death in *First Contact* (ST8), there must be more than one queen. It makes sense to equate one cube to a hive.

Star Trek has posited a few other chinks in the Borg armor. Their telepathic connection makes it possible to "infect" them with a computer virus that will destroy the "root command structure" (considered but not pursued in "I, Borg," TNG); they might also be vulnerable to a biological virus that will resist or inactivate the nanobots that perform the actual job of assimilation (created in "Scorpion," VOY, and used as a bargaining chip). The analogy of the latter to drugs against AIDS is hard to escape, yet another button pushed in the ever-lengthening list of Borg offenses.

A life-form such as the Borg is actually quite possible as a biological concept, since it is well poised for natural selection. As the kidnapped Borg individual Seven of Nine tells Chakotay in "Scorpion II" (VOY), such a configuration is maximized for efficiency and competence, without the eternal squabblings of humans. Even among humans, cults seem to function just fine as long as they fulfill one or both of two conditions: they are relatively closed systems (rural survivalist militias) or much more powerful than their neighbors (Nazi Germany before 1943).

There is one minor caveat that I must mention, however. Even with nanotechnology, the Borg would not be able to immediately adapt their technology to new challenges. *Star Trek* explains that the Borg assimilate others by altering their cell structure ("Scorpion," VOY) and/or by rewriting the DNA that comes in contact with the prostheses ("The Best of

Both Worlds," TNG). Given all the arguments we have repeatedly raised about instant evolution, time required for cell duplication, and activation of dormant genes, the slow change seen in "Unity" (VOY) is much closer to the mark.

If the Borg are by nature social insects, it is odd that the Federation considers them "evil"—although it has trodden the middle ground by grudgingly accepting the intermediate and suitably repentant Cooperative that evolves in "Unity" (VOY). As Commander Chakotay says to Capt. Kathryn Janeway in "Scorpion" (VOY), the Borg cannot help what they do: they are simply following the dictates of their nature. They are adversaries, certainly, but not with human motives. When the Cardassian commander tortures Captain Picard to the edge of insanity in "Chain of Command" (TNG), he knows he is committing a cruel act. When the Borg turn Picard into Locutus in "The Best of Both Worlds" (TNG), they are merely making the best use of a new addition to their collective—and perhaps that is what makes them so scary.

Yes, the Borg are bogeys indeed, and not just in the natural impulses they embody.

SHAKERS FROM OUTER SPACE

The Borg are frightening in another way besides their collective nature. Part of their power and adaptability comes from their prosthetic enhancements, disturbing both visually and conceptually. Yet as with all gifts of a Pandoran nature, the additions exact their literal and metaphorical pound of flesh. In "The Best of Both Worlds," "Descent" (TNG), and "Scorpion" (VOY), we discover that removal of the prostheses kills the Borg as surely as does severance from the collective communication network.

The mechanical parts have also apparently made the Borg sterile, which gives a valid reason for their tactics of assimilation: like celibate terrestrial groups (the Albigensians, the Shakers, Catholic priesthood), if they cannot reproduce, they can only propagate by recruiting. Furthermore, that the Borg cannot be born but must be made strongly implies that they are someone's runaway experiment—possibly a spirit kindred to Noonien Soong, who appears troubled but proud over his creations and is decidedly seigneurial in his attitude toward them.

Prostheses have played a prominent part in human medicine. For contemporary humans, the range of prostheses is already quite broad. We have ceramic knees and hips; liver, kidney, or heart replacements; cardiac pacemakers, artificial valves, and subcutaneous drug-delivery systems (including insulin and contraceptives such as Depo-Provera); crystalline lenses in front of or within the retina; cochlear implants; artificial arms and legs. In some sense, the drugs that allow people to function by modifying their neurotransmitter output (Valium, Prozac, and their siblings) can also be considered prostheses.

Further along the way, scientists have been successful in growing artificial skin, cartilage, and bone that can be grafted onto burn or accident victims. Mammalian cells are finicky when they are forced to grow outside the organism, but will generally do so if given the correct nutrients and a scaffolding to attach to. And even more recently, two teams (one in the Max-Planck-Institut, the other in Johns Hopkins) have induced leech and rat neurons to grow on silicon chips and information has actually been exchanged across the carbon/silicon boundary, the first step up (or down?) the hybrid ladder.

Lastly, larger, more distant additions extend our senses into the rest of the EM spectrum—microwave, infrared, ultraviolet, X ray—and allow such feats as the hypertext of the Internet, MRI and CAT scans, or remote control of the planetary rovers.

Humans do not have second thoughts about prostheses when they are asphyxiating from third-degree burns or drowning in their own toxins from liver failure. Their only concern then is graft rejection, which happens if the immune system recognizes the graft as foreign, attacks it, and degrades it. To prevent this, people who receive organ transplants have to be temporarily immunosuppressed, which can lead to fatal bacterial and fungal infections.

In the *Star Trek* universe, at least two members have replacements for their original parts: Captain Picard has an artificial heart ("Samaritan Snare," TNG) and Engineer Geordi La Forge, blind from birth, sports a VISOR that gives him access to a slightly different spectrum from the normal. He can apparently spot the plasma "currents" in the warp drive, although his VISOR also makes him vulnerable to mind manipulation (he is in danger of that several times—from Lore in "Descent" and from the Romulans in "The Mind's Eye"). The one time we see through his eyes, in "The Enemy" (TNG), we see a gray haze punctuated by EM emissions—which may explain why in *First Contact* (ST8) he has opted for eye replacements.

People start becoming queasy about prostheses at two points: when there is tampering with the brain and if there is complete replacement of the body with an inorganic equivalent. Interestingly enough, the latter option (known as uploading) is one possible avenue to immortality and has been a staple in science fiction literature: all the sentient ships described by Anne McCaffrey and Iain Banks boast of a Mind that once was a conventional human.

In *Star Trek,* uploading is explored several times, although with great misgivings and almost invariably with a disastrous outcome. The uploaded Roger Korby is rejected by Nurse Chapel as "fake" in "What Are Little Girls Made Of?" (TOS); the survivors of Arret declare that human bodies, with all their vulnerabilities, are superior to android ones in "Return to Tomorrow" (TOS); and the brilliant Dr. Ira Graves becomes increasingly unstable when he appropriates Data's body in "The Schizoid Man" (TNG). In fact, given that the brain needs frequent reality checks to stay balanced, the latter scenario may well come close to the truth (we'll delve more deeply into this in the next chapter).

The other problematic point is intervention in the brain. Again, science fiction has been a pioneer in this field—especially cyberpunk fiction, which is heavily populated with people who routinely add sockets and implants to their bodies and brains. In *Star Trek,* at least one race, the Bynars in "11001001" (TNG), is connected to the computer with no ill effects.

Surprisingly, *Star Trek* has toyed very little with direct silicon-neuron contacts, other than those seen and condemned in the Borg. When the series touches the direct interface, it shows as much discomfort as non-computer-inclined people show toward surfing the Net. For example, in "Interface" (TNG), Geordi La Forge directly hooks into a probe, so that he experiences reality as if he were actually where the probe is. This is something that is beginning to happen in virtual reality technology. However, although such experiences may affect the brain circuits, they cannot literally transfer whatever happens from the probe to the person: the fire that damages the probe in "Interface" cannot burn Geordi's hand, as is shown in that episode.

There can be no doubt that whatever makes a person's character resides in the brain. Even partial destruction of the brain, whether by dementia, stroke, or any kind of operation, creates a discontinuity recognized by everyone. Doctors consider cessation of brain function as the official moment of extinction.

And yet the irony is that the brain would be one of the easiest places to accept grafts, because of the phenomenon of the blood-brain barrier. Most substances that freely circulate in the blood cannot enter the central nervous system neurons. Tight junctions in the brain capillary vessels guard against unwanted intrusions. Although this makes drug delivery or gene therapy difficult for the brain, the compensation is that our brains do not exhibit as much xenophobia as the rest of us and will tolerate grafts. Already, fetal grafts have been tried with some success in victims of Parkinson's disease, setting off the usual alarms about abortion and both the relative and absolute value of life.

Another question that comes up with grafts is, again (always), that of individuality. In "Life Support" (DS9), the brain of Bajoran emissary Vedek Bareil must be replaced by a positronic equivalent, if he is to stay alive long enough to conclude the peace treaty with Cardassia. Once Dr. Bashir has replaced a certain percentage of the brain, it is unclear if what is left is Bareil or not—and what is left of the ambassador agrees, choosing to die.

So again, as with sentient androids, the bottleneck to hybrid existence will not be technological but moral. Technological change has been accelerating beyond human capacity to assimilate it. At the edge of a Brave New World, humans want to make sure it resembles Miranda's vision and not Aldous Huxley's.

This, perhaps, is why the Borg are booed. *Star Trek* celebrates the American values of individuality and solid moral character. The Borg stride in like commies into Hollywood, threatening to taint not just our water but our minds.

RESISTANCE IS FUTILE

So I've reached a counterintuitive conclusion: A flexible organic form like a shape-shifter is impossible. On the other hand, both androids and cyborgs are quite possible—in fact, likely.

Because of our explosive development, we have become the dominant life-form on this planet and have cut off the possible evolution into intelligence of any other life-form that shares Earth with us. In a world where computer technology is advancing about as fast as our neurons are firing, mixed carbon/silicon forms will be the next evolutionary step—our descendants.

Asimov's Robotic Laws won't shield us from the consequences of this act of creation. These will not be golems, to be destroyed by rubbing out one letter on their forehead—nor *Blade Runner* replicants, with built-in short life spans. Once they are truly independent entities, whether they are good, evil, or the inextricable mix of true sentience will be out of our hands. Thus does *Star Trek* create a forum for our dreams—and nightmares—for the future.

SCENE 4.
CAN YOU PLAY THE TUBA WITH HOLOGRAPHIC LUNGS?

The Perils of Cryochambers and Holodecks

God plays dice—and Einstein plays poker. Well, he does on the *Enterprise* holodeck, anyway, where Data has put together a fearsome foursome in the TNG episode "Descent." Besides Albert Einstein, Data has conjured up two other great physicists: Isaac Newton and Stephen Hawking.

Of course, for Newton and Einstein actors had to be employed to bluff and bet. However, Stephen Hawking was "played" by the illustrious man himself, the holder of Newton's chair as Lucasian Professor of Mathematics at Cambridge University. Hawking's work has been crucial to opening the universe to humankind. Moreover, in my opinion, he's the greatest explicator of science to nonscientists next to Carl Sagan and Stephen Jay Gould.

Yet Stephen Hawking symbolizes something more. In the previous chapters, I played riffs on the beginning of life in different keys and on several instruments. Now we must also look at the other end. Can we extend our very finite life? Stephen Hawking is confined to a wheelchair, his brilliant mind a prisoner of a progressively failing body. And yet, no matter how much the body fails, we all intuitively agree that as long as one part of it remains intact—the brain and its contents—the essential person still exists.

Can we survive the destruction of our perishable shells? The bodies of the participants of that poker game—human with prostheses, android, holodeck matter—actually exemplify our possible avenues of escape from life's grim sentence. Theoretically, we can preserve our bodies until they can be renewed. Or we can transfer our essential selves—our brains or the minds within our brains—to sturdier carriers.

Star Trek has squarely embraced all these technologies, although—as usual—it often shies away from their implied consequences. Cryochambers are routinely used in the *Star Trek* universe, by good guys ("The Neutral Zone," TNG) and villains ("Space Seed," TOS) alike. Starship computers routinely store "neural patterns." The holodecks have provided our heroes with replacement parts and have even sprouted conscious life-forms, most notably the Holodoc (VOY) and Professor Moriarty (TNG).

Very imaginative, and it makes for wonderful fantasies, especially at Quark's on Deep Space 9. But there is a worm in the apple: continuity of consciousness. Are these possibilities biologically feasible? And even if we transfer our minds, will we still be us?

Let's first examine the problem—Grim Reaper or Lady Death, depending on the particular mythology.

TO YOUR SCATTERED BODIES GO

Death is unquestionably the great unknown. I personally lack conventional religious faith, though I do have a compensatory crutch: I come from a culture that, like the Klingons', exhorts its members to face death as a rival warrior. Yet despite my Greek heritage, the idea that I as an identity will cease to exist makes me light-headed with fear. At those moments, I feel like a rabbit transfixed in the headlights of an oncoming car.

I'm not alone in this. We all know we're mortal, and we cannot help thinking about it. Certainly death is central to *Star Trek*, as to any drama. Perhaps more so, since there are more ways of dealing with death in the *Star Trek* universe.

But what exactly is death? Essentially, it is the final winding down of our clock.

I mentioned in chapter 2 that if our cells become abnormally immortal (cancerous), we are done for as organisms. Yet the other side of the coin is also true. Normal cells are on a schedule. Hourglasses are remorselessly emptying in both our cells and our organs.

As we age, our mitochondria, which supply us with energy, start leaking dangerous radicals, which act as fragmentation bombs. The proofreading machinery that checks our DNA for mutations retires. In addition to our ever-shortening telomeres, our eggs and sperm age. We run out of stem cells that produce our immune system components, renew our organs, and nourish our gametes.

The remorseless litany continues on the next level up. Our senses get blunted, isolating us and making us vulnerable. In both sexes, as age increases, confusion enters the careful hormonal choreography. The hormones, some of which are neurotransmitters, are not merely there for our sex drive. They oversee the elasticity of our skin, the density of our bones, the activity of our liver and our pancreas, the processing of information in our brain. When their highly coordinated patterns fall into disarray and then cease, we become abandoned mansions. Cornices fall, wallpaper peels off, the boiler rusts. Eventually bats nest in the attic, the roof caves in, and trees grow out of the ruin.

What has brought us to this sorry destiny? Many gerontologists subscribe to the theory of Peter Medawar (later elaborated by George Williams of Michigan University) that aging crept in as an "antagonistic pleiotropy"—which translates to a gene (or genes) having multiple but contradictory functions.

Most important genes have several functions, often separated in time. Let's assume that a gene mutation arose that increased reproductive success in the organism (more descendants). Such a mutation would be so favorable during the early life stages of the organism, when more descendants equals a greater chance of survival, that it would eventually be incorporated in the genome of the entire species.

Suppose, though, that the same gene has a dual function—it increases vulnerability if the organism goes beyond a certain age. Since this particular function is not connected to reproduction, it will not be affected by evolutionary pressures. Outside zoos, animals rarely outlive their reproductive years. This is particularly true if they live dangerous lives. In this light, both the medieval childhood marriages and the teenage pregnancies of today's inner-city residents may be heartbreaking, but they're also reproductively sound strategies. Besides, enhanced reproduction without a compensating counterlever would result in fatal crowding.

And so death may have entered our lives, as a benefactor to the species but a destroyer of the individual. It's now programmed in the genetic blueprint of all advanced organisms, like development and reproduction. Careful living may result in less painful aging, but the Hunter still comes after us humans when we reach our fourscore and ten years.

Star Trek is as frightened about the end of life as anyone else. Have you noticed that no one that really matters dies in the series? Lieutenant Tasha Yar, killed in "Skin of Evil" (TNG), is brought back in the alternative timeline of "Yesterday's *Enterprise*" (TNG). Jennifer Sisko, already dead in "Emissary" (DS9), returns in the parallel universe of "Crossover" and "Shattered Mirror" (DS9).

Standby characters are another matter. Mayfly ensigns are particularly prevalent in TOS. I suspect that their regular undoing may have prompted Robert Bly to write the *Star Trek* quiz book with the title *Why You Should Never Beam Down in a Red Shirt.*

No one who matters ages on *Star Trek* either. Despite their fashionable views about accumulated wisdom and experience, our heroes look forward to aging as much as the Klingons do. Several episodes that touch on this issue—"The Deadly Years" (TOS) and "Unnatural Selection" (TNG)—only let our heroes wet their toes in the dangerous swamp of senescence before going (literally) into full reversal. In fact, they backpedal in such a hurry that they trample biological verisimilitude into the ground—by showing, for example, white hair regaining its original color.

When death becomes unavoidable in *Star Trek,* the tough get going—into cryochambers, into other bodies, into electromagnetic confinement fields. Anywhere but into the night of the Saxon chroniclers, who likened life to a sparrow briefly crossing a lit room during a storm.

TO SLEEP, PERCHANCE . . .

In the real world, as well as in *Star Trek,* the first fallback position when death confronts us is to maintain ourselves intact, warts and all. I refer, of course, to suspended animation. Suspended animation is the younger sister of immortality. If someone strategically times their "sleep" cycles, they will effectively live forever, although their lives will be discontinuous, interrupted by long spells of hibernation.

That "if" has always been a large one. The question of whether higher vertebrates can be returned to life after a period of latency has been haunting us humans ever since we became aware of death as an unknowable threshold. The ancient Egyptians thought about very little else. Of course then, as now, only the privileged were in a position to find out if paying a premium for embalming gave tangible results.

Nor is the quest unreasonable, considering the evidence available. After all, several animals, including large mammals (bears), hibernate with no ill effects. They possess homeostatic mechanisms that enable them to regulate their metabolism and temperature, once they receive the correct environmental triggers. They insulate themselves with brown fat, breathe shallowly and infrequently, then emerge in the spring thin and grumpy but alive.

Star Trek is certainly correct in one point. The feasibility of suspended animation has practical implications. For long space voyages at sublight speed, suspended animation may be the easiest alternative for the starship crews. And if we ever colonize a really hostile planet, we may be forced into hibernation like the human colonists in Sydney van Scyoc's science fiction Barohna trilogy.

The more radical alternative to hibernation is freezing—hence, the term *cryogenics.* For the last few decades, optimists have been storing their bodies—or, to save on fees, just their heads—in nitrogen tanks. There, they await the technology that can resurrect them, just as the Seventh-Day Adventists await the Rapture.

So what is standing in the way of us going cheerfully into suspension cocoons, like those docile folk in "Emanations" (VOY)? What's the problem with freezing?

If you read any biology textbook, sooner or later (usually sooner) you come upon the amazing fact that our bodies are 70 percent water. It's everywhere—in our blood, our lymph nodes, the casing around our brain, our cochleas (inner ears), our eyeballs, the interior of our cells, the interior of our nuclei. To a first approximation, we are really a multitude of enclosed ponds.

But to a first approximation only. In reality, cells are not those boring-looking circles you see in textbooks. They actually resemble miniature space stations, bristling with sensor arrays, docking bays, and armaments.

The cells and their nuclei are not just water bags with free-floating components. If they were, it would take too long for interacting molecules to locate one another by chance encounter or passive diffusion. The cellular and nuclear interior is highly organized by extensive and sophisticated struts—the cytoskeleton.

There are three cytoskeletal components—the actin, intermediate, and microtubule filaments. These three strut systems contain different proteins, create beams and cables of different diameters and strengths, and execute overlapping functions. Briefly, however, they play three vital roles. They are the train tracks that transport molecules and organelles (intracellular structures of defined structure and function) within the cell. They are the skeins that direct chromosomal movement during cell division. They also act as arbiters of cell shape—molecular corsets, if you like.

The cell enclosures are equally crucial. All our functions depend on these membranous fences, which, as Robert Frost said in a different context, make good neighbors. They act as windows and doors to the outside world. Receptors, synapses, molecules that facilitate cell recognition and movement—they are all embedded in the semiliquid membrane, platforms and derricks floating on a lipid sea.

Yet we still remain watery creatures; water makes us, and water undoes us. Previously, I extolled the virtues of water as a solvent. We even like it when it freezes because it floats, allowing life to go on beneath it. But when ice forms in our tissues, it behaves like Genghis Khan's Golden Horde. With a multitude of crystal daggers, it punches the membranes, saws through the cytoskeletal scaffolding, shreds the DNA. There go the carefully nurtured ponds with all their meticulously separated ecosystems.

Ice also concentrates solutes, effectively dehydrating cells and collapsing both the cytoskeletal scaffolding and the membrane components. When mammals freeze, they die—and if they are thawed without benefit of a fixative, they resemble either mush or leather.

Fixatives, of course, are even worse because they literally pickle the tissues (this permanent unfolding of cell constituents is known as denaturation). The Egyptian pharaohs didn't have the remotest chance of resurrection once their bodies got perfused, regardless of the cost of the myrrh.

Hold on a moment, I hear you say. What about all those frozen gametes used for in vitro fertilization, or the frozen embryos fought over by divorcing couples? Don't forget that these are single or at most double cells. We can freeze them if we add an antifreeze substance to the water—glycerol, glycol, or dimethylsulfoxide. We weren't the first to perform that trick—fish in cold seas have glycol in their blood, and for the same reason.

I freeze mammalian cells routinely in the lab. Some survive better than others, but that's the end of the road. At this point, we cannot freeze/thaw anything larger or more complex than a collection of cells—not organs, not a body. Most importantly, not the brain and the mind that it contains.

There are optimists (Eric Drexler and Ralph Merkle among them) who believe that this feat can be accomplished by nanotechnology.

Nanotechnology literally means microscopic machines. Drexler and Merkle suggest that, once the contents of the body and the brain can be cataloged atom by atom, they can be stored as computer programs. When the moment comes for the thaw, assemblers (machines the size of molecules) will go into the brain and repair the damage. Sort of a replay of *Fantastic Journey* or *Innerspace,* except that we won't have to worry about the assemblers deminiaturizing.

Star Trek wholeheartedly embraces this version of events. Nanotechnology is a given both among humanoids and in the Borg collective. Suspended animation apparently began as early as twentieth-century Earth: the dictator Khan and his followers, found frozen on the *Botany Bay* in "Space Seed" (TOS), hail from that time. The Klingons and Cardassians are into liquid-nitrogen tanks as well—whole platoons are put into cold storage as emergency backups during extended wars (the Klingon starship *T'Ong* and its crew in "The Emissary," TNG; a Cardassian space station and its military personnel in "Empok Nor," DS9).

Can we really tuck ourselves into Dewar's flasks and hope to be awakened with the glad news that death has been conquered? People who have paid handsome sums to Alcor and Trans Time Corporations obviously believe so, having faith in the eventual advent of nanotechnology. I am less sanguine.

The problems that our bodies present are tractable, at least theoretically. I agree with the optimistic lot who believe that preserving the rest of the body is a matter of time, once we can regenerate organs and stem cells. At this point, we rely on organ transplants. This is a brute-force way to go, since we have to wrestle with graft rejection. Yet we are just beginning to investigate alternatives that may eventually make present tools of medicine look as primitive as leeches and barbers' blades look to us.

All cells of an organism contain exactly the same genetic information. However, they display radically different shapes and fulfill diverse functions by expressing only a subset of that information. Think of the vast difference between a neuron and a skin cell: this is called differentiation. It is generally extremely difficult to "retro-engineer" a differentiated cell—

that is, reverse its state and render it capable of assuming another form and function. Differentiation is irreversible because the genes that have been turned off collapse permanently into dense clumps (called heterochromatin) and cannot be coaxed back out of their retirement.

Nevertheless, our body is actively into organ replacement without any help from the medical profession. We are completely made over every few years, some parts of us even more often. For example, our intestinal walls are completely renewed about twice a week. This miraculous rejuvenation stems from stem cells, progenitor cells that are undifferentiated—i.e., uncommitted—and can give rise to more than one kind of cell (multipotent).

Once we have completely defined the gene set that gets expressed in each cell type, we can program an undifferentiated cell line to give us the right descendants, and eventually a whole organ upon specification. We can do that already in tissue culture, up to a point.

Some molecular programmers are venturing even further. Recently, Jonathan Slack of Bath University generated a frog torso by suppressing the genetic program that specified the rest of the embryo. This opens up the possibility of "organ farming"—cloning sections of ourselves and generating organs that won't be rejected.

Such repair capacity would make cryogenics as superfluous as swordsmithing. However, not all of us can be repaired. There is a lone holdout. The central nervous system—brain and spinal cord—is a beast of a different stripe (interestingly enough, these are the only two organic components of the Borg queen in *First Contact,* ST8).

Jeffrey Macklis of Harvard University recently introduced neuron progenitors into rat brains and got successful reenervation (i.e., connection of the newcomers to the target host neurons). This is a step in the right direction, but the most important question is still unanswered: Dr. Macklis hasn't yet determined whether these rats remember how to run the mazes they were familiar with prior to the surgery.

No one knows if we can truly regenerate our central nervous system. It is also far from certain that we can re-create it. And where the central nervous system goes, our identities go—as inseparable as the bonded Miradorn twins in "Vortex" (DS9).

LOCK PHASERS ON TARGET

This tight intertwining of brain and mind brings me squarely against a question that I've been circling cautiously since chapter 3, like a starship trying to avoid a gravity well. I can't avoid it any longer, though, because it is going to follow us like an imprinted duckling for much of the book. It is *the* central unsolved question in biology (as well as in psychology, philosophy, and religion). And it is, *How does the brain create a mind?*

Many technologies and processes in *Star Trek* require transfers of consciousness: suspended animation, uploading, the transporter, the holodeck, Odo's shape shifts, Dax's symbiosis with Jadzia. All these beg the question of where, if anywhere, consciousness resides. Is it localized or diffuse? Something in us is continuous and feels coherent, even though our cells turn over.

If consciousness—more specifically, personality—resides in the synapses of our brain, any cryogenic preservation, prosthetic substitution, or brain transfer that does not retain the detailed synaptic network will kill us as effectively as more conventional methods (and far more expensively).

I will put my cards on the table right away and declare that I'm neither a Platonic dualist nor a quantum neurobiologist. That is, I do not believe that there is something unique about our brain that is beyond science or contradicts universal laws—a ghost in the machine. However, neither do I think that the workings of the mind can be solved by evoking quantum theory, as Roger Penrose of Oxford University has done in his books *The Emperor's New Mind* and *Shadows of the Mind.*

So how *does* our brain work? Let us climb this Everest of a question in easy stages, like wise mountaineers.

Does the brain operate like a computer? In my opinion, the answer is a resounding *Yes, repeat no*—the honored traditional answer of British Intelligence when asked if one of its field operatives had been captured.

I can list several points of physical similarity between brains and computers. The nature of the connections is similar: both essentially look like an extended switchboard. Brains and computers use the same method of signal propagation—namely, electrical impulses. Finally, signal reception in both is directed, not an all-points bulletin.

A vital difference is that our brains rely on parallel processing, whereas most computers still execute their tasks linearly. Parallel (multiple simultaneous) processing is relatively slow, but in the end both the speed by which it converges on a solution and the complexity it can handle are immense.

The AI people have duly noticed this. Artificial neural networks and supercomputers are now built on parallel processing principles, giving the first glimpse of hope that one day we may construct androids like Data.

Of course, the computer is not the only (semi-)valid analogy for the brain. The brain has also been likened to a hologram, and for a good reason: the quality of a hologram depends on the correct interaction of all its light sources. Start degrading or reducing the sources of a hologram and it loses resolution.

The mammalian brain does the same. Karl Lashley's experiments with rats and the existence of near-normal children who required extensive brain surgery at birth indicate that the critical factor is total amount of missing brain matter, rather than specific area. What counts is the number of the connections and the multiple feedback loops. Our brain is the ultimate Internet World Wide Web: everything is connected to everything else.

The locations of many brain functions have been roughly determined. The hindbrain regulates automatic mechanisms, the midbrain mostly processes sensory information, and the forebrain analyzes, synthesizes, and decides. However, all the "high" functions—attention, memory, language, problem solving, novel ideas, thought, the sense of self—are diffuse. Some (language, which we'll visit in chapter 8) have discrete processing centers, but are still generated globally. Others (memory) have been lumped under one name, when in fact they represent several phenomena.

Everyone is familiar with short-term memory, which is chemical and located in the hippocampus, and long-term memory, which is reflected in the configuration of the synapses and resides in the cortex. Another division of memory is shown in "Conundrum" (TNG), in which the short- and long-term memories of the crew have vanished (they don't know who they are), but their procedural memory (basic skills) has not. Such a loss is unlikely, but it tells me that *Star Trek* writers have been guiltily stashing *Scientific American* inside the covers of their scripts.

Of course, the most crucial question concerning our minds is, *Who is the Narrator that tells our story?* What in that jumble of neurons and glia perceives itself as a singular identity and pronounces the word *I*? Who integrates all the incoming stimuli into a coherent picture?

This question is known in neurobiology and the behavioral sciences as the Binding Problem. Some neurobiologists (Michael Gazzaniga of UC Davis among them) believe that the brain operates in modules, and one of the modules is the Interpreter—the integrator.

Others believe that the brain is like a highly talented orchestra who can play without a conductor. In that case, the "I" would be the music that the brain orchestra produces. There is nothing metaphysical about this: music, unlike a disembodied emanation, is a physical phenomenon that can be recorded. So is the mind. Alternatively, the "I" may be a spotlight sweep that checks all activity in discrete bursts that happen too frequently to be detected as discontinuous (just like our eyes integrate pixels or rapidly flashed successions of images into continuous input).

This may sound far-fetched. However, Rodolfo Llinás of New York University, using magneto-encephalography, has recently recorded coherent 40 Hz oscillations that travel from the thalamus (the processing center for sensory input) to the cortex and then back again. These waves are reset by a sensory event if we're either awake or dreaming, but not during deep sleep, when we're totally unresponsive to any but the strongest stimuli.

The thalamus and cortex behave like oscillators, which are coupled during the aware state (think of two tuning forks vibrating in unison). The former provides content, the latter context. Perhaps the coupled oscillations are a glimpse of the integrating sweep that makes us whole. Interestingly enough, the 40 Hz waves are random or absent from people suffering from Alzheimer's disease, strengthening Llinás's hypothesis.

Stuart Hameroff of Arizona University has come up with a very different proposition. He (and Roger Penrose) has assigned the task of brain coherence to microtubules.

If you recall, earlier in the chapter I mentioned that microtubules are one of the three cytoskeletal systems that keep cells in shape inside and out. Penrose and Hameroff suggest that microtubules are ideal for the integration of brain activity, because they are poised between the macro- and microcosmic. In this theory, they are hailed as panaceas to all mind/brain problems.

The quantum microtubule theory purports to answer the various questions of consciousness by pairing each of them to a fundamental property of elementary particles. Thus, binding is supposedly achieved through the property of nonlocality, which arises from the dual energy/matter nature of elementary particles—as dual entities, they can be anywhere. Intuition is explained as a superposition of several possible "states" of microtubules, again in an analogy to particles. Problem-solving by the brain is expected to come about by collapse of the microtubule wave-function, which means that one solution has been chosen among many candidates. The theory even covers free will, which presumably comes of the fundamental indeterminacy arising from the Heisenberg uncertainty principle (which states that the position and velocity of an elementary particle cannot be determined simultaneously).

I should have loved this theory. Not only does it solve everything in one fell swoop, but it actually elevates the humble microtubules to center stage. It just so happens that the gene that I work with in my research produces a microtubule-associated protein called tau (an appropriately named target for a Greek and a science fiction lover). What could be more welcome than Hameroff's theory for someone in my position?

Alas, however, though microtubules are important, there is nothing mystical about them. For one thing, they occur in all cells, not just neurons. For another, they are not unique in either their scale or their functions. Penrose and Hameroff might as well have chosen filaments or collagen or the myelin sheath.

No one molecule can hold up our brain, like Atlas holding up the world. There is no corner office in our mind, inhabited by a CEO or a general. In the end, I think that our brain is the most primitive kind of democracy evolved to its highest stage—the town hall meeting grown to encompass a whole world.

MEAT CAGES

If our brains define us, it stands to reason that we are obsessed with both their workings and their preservation. This is reflected in the scientific fashion of the times. Like physics, molecular and developmental biology have been concentrating on the two ends of the spectrum—beginnings (how the genetic program patterns a body) and endings (how to prolong life); the very small (genes) and the very large (the brain). The body in the middle tends to get neglected and taken for granted, unless it rebels.

Star Trek follows this trend. They are fascinated by the life of the mind. The bodies of our heroes are content to carry their genes and their brains. They know, poor things, that they are like unskilled migrant labor: if they clamor for attention, they can be deported and replaced by prostheses, by another body, or even by a computer frame.

Noncarbon life-forms particularly dislike the frailties of carbon-based bodies, human or nonhuman: Nomad in "The Changeling" (TOS) stands ready to vaporize them as imperfect. The conscious hologram in "Revulsion" (VOY) has resorted to bludgeoning them, instead. I find it interesting that all perfectionists exist as some version or other of a cleaning program, classifying all bodies as inherently messy and fit only for the garbage heap.

However, we see the other side of the coin, too—reveling in life's inherent messiness. In *Star Trek,* whenever aliens take over human bodies, they get drunk with the sensations. The Kelvans in "By Any Other Name" (TOS) go on a spree that would put frat parties to shame, and in "Return to Tomorrow" (TOS) Sargon and Co., highly evolved as they are, still lament having to give up the human bodies that acted as their hosts.

Yes, our bodies can be both a blessing and a burden. However, they are not to be ignored. I disagree with Hans Moravec of Carnegie Mellon, who believes that they are just passive vehicles for our minds. In fact, the old joke about the intestines rebelling and holding the rest of the body hostage (the lofty brain included) by blocking the anal exit highlights the complete interdependency of our various parts.

It is true that a brain starts gaining entropy rapidly and irreversibly if it remains uninhabited by a mind for any but the briefest interval. Brain cells start degrading almost instantly upon cessation of brain activity. *Star Trek* is aware of this, as shown in "Code of Honor" (TNG), in which Tasha Yar can only resolve a conflict by killing, then immediately resurrecting, an adversary. On the other hand, I doubt that a *human* mind can exist without a brain, contrary to what is shown in "Lonely Among Us" (TNG), in which Picard beams his "neural pattern" into space—and has his pattern survive long enough to realize what an error he has committed. Our brain and mind evolved together, intertwined.

Our mind, like all complex systems, is poised between order and chaos. Constantly seesawing between stability and flexibility, it needs external reality to act as an arbiter of input. We get seasick if we cannot see the horizon because our ears and eyes are giving us conflicting information. Under prolonged sensory deprivation, we hallucinate, then go mad. So we need heads and hands at least, if not the rest of our body.

Even if it were possible for our minds to be disembodied, I suspect that they would be helpless invalids—and I'm using both words quite literally. The parts of our brain that became superfluous, which coordinate automatic functions such as the heartbeat, digestion, and motion, or which regulate hormonal output, would flail around looking for their proper connections—just as people now can experience sensations from lost limbs (phantom-limb pain). It is quite possible that the result of uploading may be not expansion of horizons but psychosis, truly creating a ghost in the machine.

Star Trek partly agrees with this assessment. In "Schizoid Man" (TNG), Ira Graves, brilliant though he is, can't keep himself together when he usurps Data's body. When Graves does the final transfer, into the *Enterprise* computer, his knowledge stays intact, but his consciousness is lost. I don't think he would have lasted even that long. I think that his consciousness would actually have dissipated the moment he entered Data.

On the other hand, these restrictions do not extend beyond the human mind. The particular requirements of our physiology do not preclude a stable intelligence within a computer, which arose within the frame and recognizes that place as home, just as our mind is born of our brain.

But eventual stability aside, are our minds uploadable at all? On this, I'll hedge my bets. I personally think that the information that needs to be transferred is of such quantity and quality that it would take too long a time to do so—certainly much longer than the few moments it takes Ira Graves to co-opt Data in "Schizoid Man." Our brain has several billion neurons, which create trillions of connections. To upload all that information without making errors seems to me as acute a problem as transporter transfer, which will occupy the next chapter.

To avoid the final dissolution, the denizens of *Star Trek* have gone far down the slippery slope of believable science. If one part of their body fails, they replace it with a prosthesis, which is possible. If they have a generalized disease like cancer—or political enemies with clout—they resort to cryopreservation, which is unlikely. If their bodies are too far gone to save, they try to upload their minds into android bodies or computers. This is probably impossible. And if all else fails, they have . . . the holodeck.

The holodeck is the place of last resort. So let us enter the holosuite. Computer, activate program *Roy Bean, Hanging Judge.*

HEROIC MEASURES

You are on a beautiful beach of white sand. Two gentle suns beam down radiance. Waves lap at your toes, and the sweet smell of wine and bread wafts from somewhere next to you. You turn around to speak to your companion and it's . . .

Me, speaking to you about the biological wisdom of the ages. That's how you'd experience this book in one of *Star Trek*'s holodecks.

The holodeck, the transporter, and the universal translator give enormous trouble to us biologists (we'll cast a jaundiced eye on the latter two in chapters 5 and 8, respectively.) All three technologies, even if we extrapolate with abandon, are still too close to magic to be viewed with any feeling of comfort—and this holds whether we're physicists, biologists, or engineers.

The starship holodecks (holographic environment simulators), a combination of holographic, replicator, and transporter technology, are apparently as dear to Starfleet personnel as television is to contemporary humans. They certainly seem to be the favored method of starship entertainment. In the latest *Star Trek* series, the starship *Voyager* is almost one hundred thousand light-years away from home. It's surrounded by enemies and has limited choices for replenishing its energy (or its constantly vanishing shuttles). Yet it has never occurred to Captain Janeway to discontinue the holodeck, which must draw an inordinate amount of energy. Perhaps she keeps it for crew morale. If you can't give them bread, at least give them circuses.

But before I go on to grumble about the contribution of the holodeck to decadence, spiritual poverty, and juvenile delinquency, let's first see how the holodeck is supposed to be able to extend life. Apparently, it can give temporary holographic bodies or body parts to those deprived of their appendages.

In VOY, our heroes run afoul of the Vidiians, aliens who are suffering an interstellar version of leprosy and have resorted to organ scavenging. To that end, they have perfected equipment that can extract the required organ and insert it in themselves. In "Phage," they remove the lungs of Neelix, the *Voyager* morale officer. He must then content himself with holographic lungs till real ones can be replicated. In "Lifesigns," the reverse happens: a holographic body is created for a Viidian woman whose brain is being attacked by the disease.

In "Our Man Bashir" (DS9), holographic bodies are also required, although this time the transporter is the culprit: in one of the all-too-common transporter screwups, the "patterns" of four members of the control center get lost in the shuffle. Then a truly Cartesian division occurs: the minds of the four hover in transporter limbo; their bodies, however, rematerialize on the holodeck and get animated by programmed personalities.

The Viidian organ-snatching is bad as metaphor and even worse as science. Have these beings heard of graft rejection? The fact that they can successfully use organs from different species tells me that they may well have circumvented the problem. In that case, they're medically advanced enough to create a vaccine or antibiotic against their disease and thus no longer need to snatch others' organs.

What about the holodeck organs and bodies themselves, though?

The Star Trek Encyclopedia informs me that the holodeck operates by generating a special form of matter that can only exist in the holodeck, under magnetic confinement. In particular, matter from either the replicator or the holodeck is "reconstituted only to the molecular, not the quantum level" (which is supposed to explain why replicator food tastes bland). I bet that once they thought of this, the creators of the series lay back and heaved a sigh of relief, assuming that they had assuaged the physicists and engineers. They were obviously not expecting to face indignant biologists.

In the real world, exotic and "ordinary" matter interact according to consistent rules. The encounter can end with a bang or a whimper. Whole universes can theoretically be born or destroyed when matter and antimatter interact. Conversely, another type of matter, "dark matter," one of the candidates for the missing mass of the universe, is almost impossible to substantiate because it is not expected to interact with everyday, garden-variety particles (hence its alternative name, *shadow matter*).

Holographic matter doesn't fit either category. According to *The Star Trek Encyclopedia*, holographic matter is unstable beyond its protected niche. Yet our heroes can touch it, eat it, inhabit it, without any precautions.

Star Trek cannot have it both ways. If holographic body parts are made of "special" matter, I cannot fathom how they mesh so seamlessly with conventional matter, as they did with Neelix's body. On the other hand, while Neelix breathes with his holographic lungs, he's forced into complete immobility. This restriction would make the holographic method of organ replacement equivalent to an iron lung, and as inviting as today's dialysis machines.

I have similar reservations for holographic bodies. How exactly do they reunite with the "neural pattern" stored in the transporter buffer if they degrade or evaporate once they are removed from the magnetic confinement of the holodeck? For "Our Man Bashir" (DS9), the series writers can argue that what gets restored is not the holographic matter itself, but the information of the bodies, placed back into "real" matter. However, that argument cannot be used for the transfer that we see in "Lifesigns" (VOY). Furthermore, that particular transfer is equivalent to uploading, and the same cautionary points apply: holographic bodies may not be up to the task of stably housing a mind.

The holodeck extends life with a vengeance, indeed. And it goes even further. It doesn't merely provide our heroes with spare parts; it also gives them live dolls to play with.

DANCING GIRLS AND TOY BOYS

Starship denizens spend an inordinate amount of time in the holodeck. Occasional lip service is paid to "balance" (as when Geordi lectures hapless Reggie Barclay on holo-addiction in "Hollow Pursuits," TNG). However, it is only within the walls of the holodeck that our heroes can drop their inhibitions and indulge in the two pastimes that have become overly cerebral in their real lives: love and war (actually, sex and violence). Judging from the addictive appeal of immersive interactive computer games, this behavior is not far from the truth.

Living in our heads can be as satisfying as the real thing, and far less risky. Ever since the first crude virtual reality helmets came on-line, cybergurus and cyberpunk SF writers have been hailing the advent of the parallel life. Already, the Internet has given us freedom to indulge our fantasies by assuming different personae. Virtual reality is an extension of daydreaming, just like the interactive role-playing computer games. (Is *Riven* great, or what?!)

Dreaming and daydreaming are subjective time. In that sense, the holodeck also extends life, because subjective time does not flow at the same rate as real time. When do products of our imagination acquire life of their own? Will we be confronted by cyberpeople demanding their own rights to life, liberty, and the pursuit of happiness?

That is precisely what happens in *Star Trek:* cyberpeople. The holodeck has generated at least two overbearing life-forms—Professor Moriarty ("Elementary, Dear Data" and "Ship in a Bottle," TNG) and the Holodoc (VOY). Both of them object vociferously when it's closing time. The female holodeck creations are more suitably demure and submissive—Minuet ("11001001," TNG) and Moriarty's paramour, the countess, acquiesce to their own disappearance.

Holodeck-generated life-forms must run through two overwhelming gauntlets. First, they are required to be "fully interactive." That is, they must (and do) respond to the program participant as if they were real people. Second, to all intents and purposes they must appear real—when Will Riker kisses Minuet, or Jadzia Dax engages with a Klingon warrior, they must sense warmth, a pulse, a scent, etc. How can the holodeck produce and direct such creations?

If the holodeck is to respond to the wishes of the participants, some type of physical connection may be necessary. In today's virtual reality, the participants have to put up with unwieldy helmets and gloves. There are no such constraints on the starship holodecks. Holodeck sensors may read the participant's pulse rate, temperature, voice tone, movements, etc., and gauge a rough estimate of mood, just as we do in our daily encounters with other people. However, paranormal abilities aside, the holodeck cannot read the thoughts of our heroes and anticipate their wishes. Alternatively, if the holodeck does read minds, it is as guilty of gross invasion of privacy as the universal translator (which we'll examine in chapter 8).

What about the other face of the coin—namely, the holodeck life-forms themselves? The odd nature of holodeck matter again returns to bedevil both them and us. In fairness, the holodeck has to recruit matter if it is to generate anything that approaches corporeality. Holodeck programs that depended entirely on hologram technology would be empty calories: a feast for the eyes, but not to be touched. They would also be incapable of manipulating real objects.

For example, a purely holographic simulation of Dr. Lewis Zimmerman (VOY) would be unable to jab everyone with syringes or scalpels. Also, none of the adversaries in the fighting programs could raise weapons of any weight. Fighting with shadows is not the best way to train, you must agree. Yet by sidestepping this problem, the makers of the series have introduced several others.

If the holodeck recruits matter, there will be a huge explosion whenever the holodeck entities disappear, magnetic confinement or not. Alternatively, let's for the moment take the *Encyclopedia*'s word that the holodeck-generated matter is unique and evanescent. After all, cosmologists posit exotic particles to fill out their proposed symmetry groups or remove infinities from their equations. Then holodeck-created entities should be unable to leave the holodeck.

The adherence to this is spotty. Two holodeck villains indeed evaporate when they leave their proper domain ("The Big Goodbye," TNG), and Professor Moriarty, despite a show of independence in "Ship in a Bottle" (TNG), is finally shown up as an illusionist rather than a sorcerer.

On the other hand, the Holodoc (VOY) roams the ship ("Future's End"), leaves on away missions ("Revulsion"), and can even sustain injuries ("Projections"). The confinement beams have conveniently become portable. Equally odd is that, although hololife can fulfill all other possible functions, including sex, it cannot cause injury to the real participants. This is an unexpected restriction, especially since I haven't heard Asimov's Robotic Laws mentioned once with connection to the holodeck.

Even if we swallow the "unique matter" designation, the amount of information required to produce a moving, breathing, living Minuet ("11001001," TNG) is staggering. Even worse is the case in "Shadowplay" (DS9), where a village full of people turns out to be a simulation. The simulator is so sophisticated and powerful that it even allows the birth of holographic children!

This approaches hubris to such an extent that the *Star Trek* creators should be wary of lightning bolts. What stored patterns form the genetic, physiological, and behavioral program of these life-forms? If the holodeck "borrows" patterns of real people, it's soul-snatching—or copyright violation, which is just as bad. If it generates novel patterns for its life-forms, we are dealing with something that has the attributes of a god.

In "Our Man Bashir" (DS9) we see that the combined technology of the holodeck and the transporter can shift "neural patterns" (a.k.a. minds) back and forth between bodies, real or holographic. This strongly suggests that by combining the holodeck and the transporter, our heroes could become immortal without fear of decrepitude or dementia, in which case I could have spared you the doom and gloom of this chapter.

Finally, we must field the question of the creators' responsibilities toward their creations. A holodeck life-form that behaves like the real item is close enough to it to merit rights, just like a sentient computer. Using self-aware holodeck-created people as toys is as reprehensible as slavery. Turning their program off would be tantamount to murder—or, in a kinder interpretation, equivalent to putting the holodeck character in suspended animation.

Given all these ramifications, it's not surprising that Riker is more haunted by Minuet (his holodeck soulmate in "11001001," whose memory persists in "Future Imperfect," TNG) than by Deanna Troi—empathy, décolletage, and all. Captain Picard does not feel any twinges about deceiving Moriarty in "Ship in a Bottle" (TNG), but Captain Janeway recognizes the moral obligation by giving the Holodoc control over his program in "Eye of the Needle" (VOY). While *Star Trek* clearly reflects the middle-American values of the audience that it woos, the holopeople are a dark chapter in its morality book.

THE END OF THE ROAD?

If prostheses enhance and extend the senses, cryogenics, uploading, and virtual reality extend the concept of life itself. With prostheses, we baby-step into the knowable. With the others, we launch into the truly unknown. The logical extrapolation of these technologies, if they are successful, will change human lives as radically as Borg-level nanotechnology.

By investigating such possibilities, *Star Trek* proves scientifically adventurous and places itself firmly on the side of the optimists, who see the future as an endless garden of benign exotic fruits. Yet musing on the evidence, in whichever direction I lean on how far life can be extended, I'm still uncertain whether the brain can be disembodied or uploaded without, well, losing its mind.

However, my opinion of the holodeck is firm. As envisioned by *Star Trek*, it is a Faustian piece of equipment, inviting abuse of ourselves and eventually of others. Fortunately, I think that the holodeck is not even science fiction, but pure fantasy. I'm relieved to assure you that the best and only reliable holodeck is the traditional one, within our dreaming brain.

ACT II.
INTERSPECIES CROSS-TALK

The Musical Score Develops

SCENE 5:
FALLOUT FROM TRANSPORTER FISSIONS

Unchained Doppelgängers and Monsters from the Id

You step into the booth. A ruddy Irish face bobs above the controls.

"Coordinates set, sorr." "Energize, Mr. O'Brien!"

Instantly you find yourself in a richly furnished Victorian office. A well-dressed man with a beard and glasses sits in a high-backed chair, holding a notebook. He gestures to a couch.

"*Ja!* Another visitor from the U.S.S. *Enterprise!* Make yourself comfortable, *bitte,* and tell me about your mother."

When you step on the transporter platform in *Star Trek,* you're not merely entering an area of questionable science. You may well end up on a psychiatrist's couch, split into two people for that professional's profit and delectation.

Freud and his followers, of course, divided the human psyche into three watertight components. The visible one was the ego, which corresponds to everything accessible to our consciousness. On top of that rode the superego, which stores "higher" values, moral inhibitions—and most importantly, can administer doses of guilt like castor oil. Last but not least, submerged below our consciousness lurked the id, which contains everything that has been repressed, fermenting like a compost heap.

While contemporary psychologists question the validity of Freudian theory, the concept of the suppressed shadow twin, Mr. Hyde to Dr.

Jekyll, id to ego, has been a recurrent motif in human folklore and literature. I wonder if it springs from the time when humans were forced to sacrifice one from a set of twins, rather than risk starvation of the mother and both infants.

Fiction and science fiction writers have always made liberal use of psychological splits and compartment breakdowns in stories and films. One of the most famous uses of the id concept is in the 1956 film *Forbidden Planet.*

I first saw *Forbidden Planet* during my sophomore year at Harvard. Until recently, folks in Greece were not much into science fiction; I had to come to the States to indulge my vice. I can remember my hair standing on end when the rungs of the metal ladder bent under the weight of the invisible destroyer who had been picking off the crew of the starship visiting Walter Pidgeon's planet. The Id Monster has the dubious honor of eliciting one of my rare moments of the fight-or-flight reaction.

The Id Monster, of course, was an expression of the suppressed part of Walter Pidgeon, a frightening entity derived from the subconscious of a decent man. Older and more cynical now, I wonder if he'd entered a defective *Star Trek* booth.

With distressing regularity in *Star Trek,* transporter accidents have split persons' essences along an axis. Such plotlines make for the easy character-oriented melodrama that *Star Trek* likes so much. They also give me the opportunity to discuss the actual biological feasibility of the splits shown in the series, transporter-caused or not.

SING THE TRANSPORTER BLUES

Enterprise ensign Reggie Barclay has a distinct phobia about transporting ("Realm of Fear," TNG), and I don't blame him. The transporter causes so many problems in *Star Trek* that I don't understand why they insist on using it, plot convenience aside.

How does the transporter function? Again, *The Star Trek Encyclopedia* conscientiously explains this technological enigma. In the transporter, the complete specification of a person or object is transmuted into a "pattern" of information. The pattern is stored in the transporter buffer as "phased matter," then beamed to the desired point of rematerialization.

This sounds just like the way I cut and paste buffers and clipboards in my word-processing and drawing programs. While in the transporter buffer, a person's pattern is in limbo, just like the buffer while I decide where to place it next. Very convenient—it removes the necessity for entering and exiting planetary atmospheres with ungainly star vessels. Unfortunately, the device is really bad news: whenever you enter it, you play an interstellar version of Russian roulette.

Now, I'm not an advocate of careful living. Before my shoulder tendons gave out, I used to fly single-engine planes, which are essentially compacted sawdust, held together with glue and staples. If there's a Mars mission with people aboard, I'll try to bribe or coax a spot on it, radiation and thin carbon dioxide atmosphere be damned. However, if I were in the *Star Trek* universe, I'd be more easily persuaded to enter a black hole event horizon than use the transporter.

To begin with, it's unclear to me whether transport as shown in *Star Trek* is at all possible. Remember my careful arguments concerning the correlation of body and mind? There are two ways that we can envision transport happening: either body and mind travel together, or only the mind goes.

Let's check out the two scenarios. Both of them would cause trouble at dematerialization—we should see spectacular explosions whenever people are converted into their information patterns. The enormous energy released from an atomic bomb essentially results from a few grams of matter converting into energy. Think $E = mc^2$ where E is energy, m is mass, and c the speed of light, and you see that even a tiny mass multiplied by the speed of light squared gives you tremendous amounts of energy. An average human weighs sixty to ninety kilograms—transporting one would release roughly ten to fifty thousand times the energy of an atomic explosion.

Star Trek could employ the transporter as a destroyer of entire solar systems—why bother with fancy weaponry when a few grains of sand in the transporter will suffice? Then again, perhaps this is where the celebrated annular confinement beams of the transporter prove their worth. In the *Star Trek* universe, these play a role similar to the magnetic coils of the real world, which can confine artificially produced antimatter, thereby prolonging its life span.

If the transporter buffer stream shifts both the physical substance and the information bits of its target (genetic template and synaptic connections as we defined them in previous chapters), the information may well exceed the available atoms in the universe.

This sounds bizarre—how can a single human contain more information than the entire universe? The reason is that, unlike holomatter, the reconstructed person must be the real item, not a pale imitation thereof. Therefore, the transporting computer must catalog the exact location (three coordinates) and state (several quantum numbers) of each elementary particle making up the person to be transported. A much larger data set than the original transportee, you must agree. Transporting would then take a good deal longer than the almost immediate shift we see in *Star Trek*—several lifetimes of the universe, by my estimate.

I also have trouble with "phased" matter, which sounds as dubious as the holodeck matter that I lambasted in the previous chapter. Call me an old fogy, but I dislike states of matter or life-forms that beg for special dispensation, like lawyers seeking flimsy reasons to annul contracts. On the other hand, unlike holodeck matter, at least "phased" matter is not expected to interact with normal matter.

We can satisfy some of the physics requirements by postulating that the transporter separates body from mind, but then we bump into numerous steep obstacles of the biological kind.

First, separation of body and mind by the transporter is equivalent to uploading (explicitly so in "Lonely Among Us," TNG), over which I obsessed extensively in the previous chapter. *Star Trek* does not ease matters by waffling about whether people are conscious while they are in active transport. I would think that to remain conscious while your body and brain are being deconstructed is foolhardy, to say the least. Nevertheless, in "Realm of Fear" (TNG), Reggie Barclay is obviously conscious enough to locate crewmates wandering in buffer limbo. Probably too full of adrenaline to let go, poor guy.

On the other hand, in "Relics" (TNG), Scotty has been spinning in the transporter for seventy-five years, like an unpaired sock forgotten in the dryer. If transporting includes the body, he should have starved long ago. Alternatively, if he was conscious and disembodied all that time, the least we can do is study him intensively, to discover what gave rise to such incredible stability and endurance—regular doses of single-malt whiskey, maybe?

It's also difficult to sidestep an unpleasant fact. Removal of the "neural energy" from the body will leave behind a corpse—or a clone, depending on how the pattern is stored in the buffer. The two outcomes would correspond to "cut" versus "copy" in my word-processing program. Either way, it follows that the old physical body must be destroyed the moment the new one materializes. This is the position taken squarely in J. P. Kelly's harrowing story "Think Like a Dinosaur."

Back in the more dubious scientific world of *Star Trek,* the duplication of Riker into Will and Tom in "Second Chances" (TNG) toys with this unpalatable idea, then coyly turns aside by making the accidentally duplicated Rikers shake hands and part friends. I'm willing to go along with this one, though, because Tom Riker is what Will Riker should have been—a firebrand, a Maquis, rather than a Starfleet darling. His existence resulted in one of the best *Star Trek* episodes ("The Defiant," DS9).

"Symbiogenesis" (VOY) tackles head-on the moral dilemma of a composite being created by a transporter accident, resolving it with a variant of the "last hired, first fired" tactic: Captain Janeway "kills" the newly minted person, restoring the original crew members. If only the science of this episode were as incisive as its decisive stance.

What our heroes studiously avoid discussing is the fact that the transporter routinely works, regardless of which mode it may employ (both body and mind or mind only). This means that it *exactly* re-creates the target that it transports, which in turn leads to the inescapable conclusion that whatever is "there" is all physically tangible.

This leaves as much room for the soul as special relativity left for the ether. I personally have no trouble accepting that humans are the sum of their parts, as long as we recognize that they are complex systems that exhibit emergence. In fact, I spent most of the previous chapter arguing that minds and brains are inseparable.

But what happens when the transporter starts wavering? For the sake of saving about half of the *Star Trek* episodes, let's momentarily accept that the transporter works as stated. We still have to deal with its malfunctions.

PROCRUSTEAN FITS

Whenever the transporter hiccups, I can safely bet that it will split our heroes into odd halves. By now, we've seen just about every possible permutation: separations into good and evil ("The Enemy Within," TOS, which actually corresponds to a division between the "low"/midbrain versus "high"/cortical emotions), Klingon and Human ("Faces," VOY), body and mind ("Lonely Among Us," TNG), even a fusion ("Symbiogenesis," VOY).

All these violate not only mass conservation but also biological principles. What kind of information is the transporter transmitting? My specific objections will differ depending on what constitutes the pattern in the buffer.

Let's tackle the bottom-up transport mode first. This theorizes that the transporter sends a complete genetic blueprint of the person in transit.

Such a method of transport is implied in "Unnatural Selection" (TNG). In that episode, Dr. Pulaski's abnormal aging is reversed by passing her through the transporter and sending along a "clean copy" of her genome at the same time. We also see it in "Rascals" (TNG), in which accidental rejuvenation of three crew members is reversed by another transporter pass plus insertion of "adult genomic sequences."

Yet although our genes determine whether we fly by growing wings or building airplanes, they don't decide the details within our brain that make us who we are. In particular, if the information that is sent is genetic, it would be impossible to get the "good/evil" split of "The Enemy Within" (TOS)—unless we also want to argue that morality is genetically determined, thereby totally abandoning the concept of free will. Complete specification of personality by genes is a position too extreme for even dyed-in-the-wool social Darwinists.

Furthermore, if the transporter can restore Dr. Pulaski to youth and health, it is incredible that it hasn't been used to make people immortal—or thin or beautiful or . . . take your pick. And if our heroes have again become children in "Rascals" (TNG), how is it that their memories and adult skills remain unaffected?

To drive one more stake into the genetic-blueprint transmission theory, there are no "adult genomic sequences" in humans. It is true that different genes are active at different times. Also, sometimes genes that fulfill the same function at different ages are strung in tandem arrays on chromosomes, in order of their activation. A good example is the globin family, whose members code for the protein part of hemoglobin, our oxygen carrier.

However, the triggers for the developmental switches, themselves the products of other genes, are not hierarchically coordinated either spatially or temporally. Instead, they are combinatorial—that is, they form overlapping networks, like the constantly shifting alliances of feudal princes. Given this organization, I cannot see accidental aging or rejuvenation caused by a single glitch in the transporter's biofilter.

I have reached similar conclusions about the possibility of dividing the humanoid hybrids into their parental contributions. Take B'Elanna Torres's division into Human/Klingon halves in "Faces" (VOY). Can the transporter (or any other machine) distinguish between Human and Klingon genes on chromosomes? Most of the time, we can't even distinguish between human and chimpanzee genes, given the 99.5 percent identity between the two. Even if we could, the genetic encoding of a human being cannot be neatly teased apart.

You may recall that our chromosomes crave variety as much as we do: when they're paired, they exchange homologous portions (recombination). Our chromosomes continue shuffling in the nuclei of all our cells throughout our life. A separation of genes according to parental provenance, as shown in "Faces" (VOY) would require reversal of all recombination events, precise excisions at gene boundaries in each cell, then painstaking reconstitution that would give *two* viable beings where one existed previously (the same applies in "Symbiogenesis," VOY). Think of trying to transform a baked cake back into raw eggs, flour, sugar, vanilla . . . and you get a simplified idea of the magnitude of this task.

Dividing the genes would still not give us a functioning genome. The complete human genome may well be known by the twenty-third century. Indeed, the Human Genome Project will probably give us the complete sequence of all human genes within the next few decades. However, getting a gene to act correctly is the work of several lifetimes. To make that happen, we would also need to throw in the sequences that control the expression of the gene in question. Control sequences (known by such descriptive names as promoters, enhancers, and silencers) are sometimes located far from their targets.

To activate genes at the appropriate place and time has for years been the grail of gene therapy. That progress in that field has been difficult and slow shows how tricky reconstitution of a single gene can be, let alone an entire genome and the being that it specifies.

Innocent bystanders get caught in serious crossfire when their genes get activated at the wrong place or time. This is demonstrated in chromosomal translocations, which accidentally move a piece of chromosome into another: such out-of-context gene expression shows up as spontaneous miscarriage, death in utero, hereditary disease, or proclivity to sporadic disease at an earlier age than the statistical average. Within the genome, context is almost as important as absolute content.

Finally, separating people chromosomally, the way B'Elanna is split in "Faces" (VOY), creates another serious problem—namely, the resulting fission twins are completely homozygous (all their genes are identical in both chromosomal copies). This is equivalent to being haploid—i.e., having a single set of chromosomes.

Remember that mutations are usually recessive: that is, a single good gene copy covers for its sibling. However, in completely homozygous cases, we should see the effect of any deleterious allele immediately. We see that in completely inbred mouse strains used in the lab. Some of these strains are so prone to diseases and early death that researchers have trouble maintaining them.

Nor are humans exempt from such woes. Each of us carries from a few dozens to a few hundreds of such alleles. This is bad news when we cannot yet cure them but have our health insurance voided because of them nonetheless. This is the infamous "preexisting condition" clause, which has already been invoked for women carrying certain alleles that predispose them to breast cancer. Complete homozygosity is also terminal bad news for the all-Human or all-Klingon B'Elanna, who will probably develop early cancer, heart disease, dementia . . . or all of the above. She would do better to stick to a shuttle hereafter.

I can summarize my objections to this possible method of transport as follows: unless the transporter is equipped with a real molecular biology lab, I cannot see it being able to handle complexities at the gene level. Whenever it malfunctions, it should generate either a mess or nothing. If the transporter cannot merely separate genes from almost identical species, but also cotransport their correct control sequences, the Federation might as well call itself Q and behave accordingly.

SOLOMONIC JUDGMENTS

Let's now tackle the top-down transport mode. This would have the transporter transmitting the exact number and position of synaptic connections within the transportee's brain.

First off, recall that our brain has synaptic connections in the trillions. Again, I think that this should cause the transporter to take a little longer than a few moments to read, write, and transmit. But let me be indulgent yet again and give *Star Trek* technology a very long rope. Could we then witness a personality separated the way Kirk divides in "The Enemy Within" (TOS)? That division doesn't correspond to a facile good versus evil. Instead, it's a split between "low" emotions, which reside in the midbrain, and "high" emotions, which generally arise in the cortex.

Our midbrain contains the hypothalamus, on top of which is perched the limbic system, also known as the R-complex. These two structures are involved in primary, "single-color" emotions: anger, fear, hunger, and sexual arousal. The neurobiologists call this quartet the Four Fs—fight, flight, feeding, and, ah . . . reproduction. These are essential to our survival and therefore sometimes need to bypass the normal decision-making-by-committee—one extra moment of hesitation, and we're bear lunch. Nuanced complex emotions arise from interactions in the cerebral cortex (forebrain).

Already, you can see the problem. If the division in TOS separates midbrain from forebrain, Kirk couldn't be alive in either incarnation.

The Kirk possessing only the midbrain would very definitely not be chasing Ensign Rand with lascivious ends in mind. What mind? He would be mute, devoid of what we'd call personality, and unable to function as a human at all. Fetuses missing a forebrain occasionally develop—the condition is known as anencephaly. The few that are not spontaneously miscarried die a few hours after birth.

Conversely, the Kirk owning solely the forebrain would not be agonizing over whether he was a good enough captain. He'd be lacking control over his endocrine and automatic functions and would be busy dying in any number of graphic and unpleasant ways—asphyxiation, internal bleeding, extreme dehydration, or diabetic shock, to name only a few.

Even if the transporter substitutes some kind of filler for the missing brain areas, the half-Kirks are still knee-deep in bat guano. As I discussed earlier, consciousness, although far from being understood, acts as a unified whole. Personality does not reside in a particular brain compartment. With few exceptions (for example, the language centers), if parts of the brain are destroyed, the picture doesn't spring gaps; it just loses resolution, gets fuzzier like a photo taken by an out-of-focus lens.

There is no command center to be found in our brain. The Narrator in us seems to be a composite sum of each moment—or the winner out of a group of choices. When shaping something novel—an idea, a sentence, a melody, a guess, a decision—our brain evaluates competing candidates like evolution weighs phenotypes. The losers in the draw are forgotten or cast into the subconscious, from which they only emerge during dreams.

The recent PET and MRI technologies, combined with results from electrode stimulation, have shown that there are different and overlapping "maps" for everything (in medical textbooks you see pictures of the "sensory" and "motor" homunculi, with their distorted body parts reflecting the proportional representation of various areas on the cortex). The variability among individuals is so high that neurosurgeons test every millimeter of the area they will go near during a brain operation with electrodes, to spare important functions as much as possible.

So as in the case of genomic splitting, unless the transporter can reintegrate partial brains into cohesive minds, the two half-Kirks will actually be zero Kirks.

There is, however, one interesting division in our brain. It is the lateralization of our left and right hemispheres, which control the opposite halves of our bodies. Surprisingly, this is a split that *Star Trek* has never explored. The amount of specialization between the two brain hemispheres varies in each individual (left-handers such as me routinely show less lateralization). There is only one consistent finding: the language processing centers invariably reside in the left hemisphere.

The two hemispheres can be isolated by lateral strokes or by severing the corpus callosum, a thick cable of nerve fibers that connects the halves. This operation is undertaken to alleviate severe epilepsy, by essentially reducing system overload and preventing the wave of seizures from propagating throughout the system. The results are fascinating, as Mr. Spock would state.

The left hemisphere can proffer verbal explanations or descriptions. The right is good at recognizing patterns and gestalts. Damage to the left half may produce aphasia (inability to speak), but problems of the right half have subtler manifestations. Such people essentially ignore their left half, even to the extent of only dressing the right. Their personalities also change in unpredictable ways. Severance of the corpus callosum brings to the surface two slightly different versions of the inhabitant, each rather dimly aware of the other's existence.

The left/right hemisphere split has been oversimplified and overinterpreted: there have been too many books crammed with advice about how to reach the "mute" right hemisphere with its "artistic," "intuitive" capabilities. There has also been a too easy identification of the mute right hemisphere with the id, Caliban indentured to Prospero and forced to do his bidding.

However, the location of the language decoding center in the left hemisphere does not mean that the right hemisphere inherently lacks language capacity: removal of parts of the brain in babies, because of vascular abnormalities that cause life-threatening seizures, results in rewiring of the brain—and if it must, language processing pitches its tents in the right hemisphere. Accommodation is better than death or disability.

Nevertheless, under normal circumstances the right half is silent—and the left half might not recognize any "voice" emerging from it as "self." This has been documented in split-brain patients. When their right hemisphere sees a picture, they can draw it with their left hand. Asked to describe what they saw, they deny having seen the picture.

This led Julian Jaynes of Princeton University to formulate a fascinating hypothesis in his book *The Origin of Consciousness in the Breakdown of the Bicameral Mind.* He theorizes that "speech" from the area in the right side of the brain that mirrors the language center on the left actually registers as external voices. He then suggests that such utterances were interpreted as the injunctions of gods, before the corpus callosum strengthened and unified the two halves.

Jaynes places this event in historical times, making the Israelites of the Old Testament and the Greeks of the *Iliad,* both particularly prone to oracular visitations, preconscious people. Perhaps the corpus callosum, and not the serpent, caused us to leave the Garden of Eden—separated from God but united with ourselves, a force to be reckoned with. No wonder the Old Man tried to subdue the humans again later, with the Babel Tower business. Be that as it may, this particular rich vein has been left unmined by *Star Trek*.

An event that mixes both genes and brains occurs in "Symbiogenesis" (VOY), in which the transporter creates a composite being (Tuvix) from Lieutenant Tuvok and Neelix, morale officer and ship's cook (although the quality of his cooking apparently makes his two functions incompatible).

Recall that these are two different species, Vulcan and Talaxian respectively. Furthermore, here we're dealing with chromosomal pairing in each cell as well as synaptic coherence of two brains/minds within one skull. The solution that our heroes hit upon in this case is to tag one DNA set with isotopes and beam it out, reconstituting the original two—much to the distress of poor Tuvix, who combines the best points of both.

I didn't know whether to laugh or weep about this one. Like David Cronenberg's *The Fly*, this episode is so eager to make a point that it mixes (and messes up) its metaphors as badly as its science. I'll leave the critique to you as an exercise.

So if someone asks me whether the transporter can do any of these neat tricks, I must firmly answer in the negative. On the other hand, *Star Trek* remains obsessed with divisions between ids and superegos. These abound in the series in settings beyond the transporter.

MANICS AND DEPRESSIVES

We humans prefer to think in easy-to-clump units. We can't help it—our brain is optimized for "chunking." We easily fall into dualistic thinking and seem to be oddly attracted to trinities. All these preferences are reflected in everything that we do or say—from dyadic or triadic philosophies and religions to the reflexive classification of anyone different as "other" to the overemphasis of either/or distinctions in the sciences.

Star Trek has used whole species as mouthpieces for extreme positions. Two obvious cases are the Vulcans and the Klingons. These represent the extremes of logic and emotion—superego and id species and societies, if you like.

You'd intuitively agree with the assessment I just made. Yet that conclusion is at best facile, at worst utterly false. Logic and emotion are not the opposites of each other. Nor do they respectively predominate in men and women, let old Aristotle say what he likes. In our brains and our minds, the two are inextricably intertwined, like the Escher prints that show two hands drawing each other.

One point that I must clarify right away is the word *emotion* itself. Just like the word *memory,* it's used inexactly and encompasses more than one phenomenon. In the previous section, I noted that there are at least two kinds of emotions: the primary, one-note ones from the thalamus and limbic system and the kaleidoscopic ones from the cortex.

Despite this superficial compartmentalization, all brain parts are in constant communication with one another. Both kinds of emotions are firmly ensconced in the brain, and no technology can distinguish cortical emotions from thoughts. Although I regret having to contradict Vulcan science, I must reluctantly report that feeling and thinking cannot be chemically separated in the vertebrate nervous system without producing a dysfunction many orders of magnitude larger than what *Star Trek* allows (such as autism).

In the previous chapter I presented several "theories of mind." Now is the time and place to introduce one more. This one, originating from the work of Antonio Damasio of the University of Iowa, does not contradict the others; it complements them instead. As Damasio explains in *Descartes' Error,* our sense of self depends on integration of input from the external world. In this way, our sensory apparatus is critical to our identity (uploaders, beware!). But the intertwining goes one step further: the coordination of emotion and thought is equally instrumental in shaping a coherent personality.

All four lobes of the forebrain (frontal, parietal, temporal, and occipital) help coordinate our personality. But the loose cannon, the one who is venturing where no one has gone before, is the frontal lobe, the most recent arrival. We know it's a newcomer because it is the brain area that gives us both the most trouble and the most pleasure (in lofty terms, of course; the pleasure centers that salivate specifically after base things such as chocolate and handsome boys reside in the lower brain parts). The frontal lobe also gives us our forward-jutting foreheads, unique among primates—unless, like Mayan nobility, we tie boards to our heads while we're still babies. Maybe the frontal lobe flattening that would inevitably follow this fashion explains the sudden, inexplicable collapse of the Mayan empire.

The immense disjunction that arises when thought is divorced from emotion becomes obvious in people with extensively damaged frontal lobes, whether by genetic propensity (autism), accident, or lobotomy. Their cognitive functions often remain unaffected—in particular, their memory and speech are intact. Autistic people can astonish us with feats of calculation that only a computer can rival—or with expert specialized knowledge.

However, autistic or lobotomized people are emotionally unresponsive or explosively unstable. Their emotional problems go hand in hand with compulsive, repetitive behavior and inability to make rational or long-term decisions. It's as if they don't possess a picture of the world against which to measure their actions—or as though they can't comprehend that what goes on inside their heads is also happening inside other people's minds.

So it looks as if emotion doesn't hinder or cloud reason. In fact, it has quite the opposite effect. Emotion acts as a focusing or filtering device for thought. In humans, the development of cognitive faculties precedes emotional maturity. Look at most adult humans, and you'll concede this point.

People don't turn to sentimental mush, catatonic lumps, or violent lunatics when their cognitive faculties are suppressed, as is shown in "The Naked Time" (TOS) and "The Naked Now" (TNG). In a counterintuitive outcome, people are actually reduced to such dangerous configurations when their emotive capacities fail. During World War II, when the

German occupying army executed entire Greek villages and sprinkled salt on the smoking ruins to discourage the resistance movement, there was nothing wrong with their *reason.* The id has been unfairly maligned, and the superego overvalued. Vulcans could use some leavening, as much as Klingons could use some discipline.

In the discussion between Commander Data and Ambassador Spock ("Unification," TNG), Data points out that he has been trying all his life to achieve what the Vulcans wish to dispose of: emotions. We can add at least two major points to his argument. The Vulcans will first have to survive the ground-level problems I listed for the divided Kirk in "The Enemy Within" (TOS). Moreover, if they succeed in their quest, they will become a race of zombies, unable to plan beyond the next few minutes and imprisoned in a permanent "now."

So, emotion is here to stay. Still, I'd hate to think that touchy-feely people are the next stage of evolution.

HEREDITY VERSUS ENVIRONMENT

In *Star Trek,* as in much of literature, the first line of struggle is always within. Internal conflicts find their voice in the transporter splits, the various dilemmas of the humanoid hybrids. Eventually, however, mirrored conflict moves from within a person to larger physical or conceptual units.

Star Trek has always greatly favored balance, moderation, integration. As a result, the series doppelgängers almost invariably appear as suppressed desires—a very Victorian manifestation. We see that on several levels: in persons, whether carbon or silicon (Tom and Will; Lore and Data); in groups (the Maquis within the Federation); even in races (the Vulcans and the Romulans).

Most commonly, the doubles are shown to be a defective version of the canonical. Lore is a Data manqué, despite his emotion chip. He is vindictive and destructive, as shown by his betrayal in "Datalore" (TNG) and his manipulation of the Borg in "Descent" (TNG). Tom Riker, although absolutely identical to Will, is nevertheless shown to be weaker, clumsier, slower. Perhaps the lack of stimulation in Nervala IV has caused this (I'll enter the environmental controversy shortly).

Some Romulans wish to follow Vulcan ways in "Unification" (TNG) and abjure violence and imperialism. Like political conservatives, they yearn for a kinder, gentler fantasy world, where all societies and races know their place and keep to it without prodding.

In a more extended division metaphor, some very interesting episodes in *Star Trek* have shown mirror universes, where values or personalities are reversed (we'll revisit this from the social angle in chapter 11). The progenitor is "Mirror, Mirror" (TOS). DS9 found the concept intriguing enough to dedicate three episodes to it ("Crossover," "Through the Looking Glass," and "Shattered Mirror").

Such portrayals inevitably bring up the question of hardwiring, which I touched upon earlier. Namely, how much of our personality is already set in stone the moment we emerge from the womb? And even if most of our personality is shaped by environment, how much free will do we really have?

These questions have been the major concerns of religion and society from time immemorial. Official religions, which have the most to lose from change, have clung to the concepts of karma or kismet. In fairness, sometimes stoic acceptance can ease an unavoidably restricted life. It may be better to survive and leave descendants who will successfully rebel than be cut in half by a katana in a premature uprising.

Social institutions have been equally eager to enforce obedience and conformity. For example, biological arguments have been used ad nauseam to prove that women cannot be creative thinkers, original artists, or top-notch scientists (depending on the era of the expert opinion, they lack the necessary apparatus, hormone, brain circuits—you name it) or should not be overeducated (bad for the womb).

Similar arguments have been used against people whose color, religion, or class differs from that of the ruling group. Personally, whenever I hear the sentence "Biology is destiny," I reach for my phaser holster.

Where does *Star Trek* stand in all this? Well, given that it must satisfy a wide audience used to the veneer of democracy, obviously it must side with the angels. Except it doesn't, quite.

The transporter splits that we have just dissected seem to indicate that *Star Trek* is leaning toward nature. For example, in "Faces" (VOY) they explicitly consider Klingon violence a genetic trait. Also, *Star Trek* gets away with stereotyping that would land it in very hot water on Earth. Just substitute the word "Chinese" for "Ferengi" in, say, "A Ferengi would kill his own brother to get ahead," and you get the drift.

On the other hand, all the *Star Trek* series show a great desire for equality, being the children of relatively enlightened times. Already, they have shown their dedication to multiculturalism by having a crazy quilt of crews that get along, especially DS9.

Additionally, when *Star Trek* shows duplicates of our heroes behaving despicably in the mirror universe, it is obliquely implying that this abhorrent behavior is the result of nurture. A benign environment, and Major Kira is a paragon of virtue, tolerance, and loyalty . . . most of the time, anyway (she is rather xenophobic in "Sanctuary," DS9). In a malign environment, she becomes the Intendant, the ultimate dominatrix in black leather and whip, with a temper that matches the outfit.

Star Trek has played it safe, in the manner of people who cannot decide which god to appease. So which one is it? Nature or nurture? Do we become slavering beasts if given the wrong food, or is the monster already within, covered by a thin skin of civility?

A good deal of confusion arises from the fact that different factions use terms sloppily to suit their own agenda. Nevertheless, regardless of final definition, it should be obvious that we're defined by both interior and exterior agents—and that the two are braided together. After all, what is evolution but the influence of the environment on genes? Only recently have we humans created our own rapidly changing environment, in which influences other than chance and genetic selection apply.

Even there, though, the old rules still reign. A slave may never have the time or energy to create great art. However, a king's son won't create great art, either, if he doesn't have the talent. Inclination and opportunity must be present at the same time.

As a molecular biologist, I cannot doubt that genes are decisive in our makeup. Single errors in genes can cause well-defined hereditary diseases or propensities for them. Everyone will recognize the disease names I'm about to rattle out: Down's, Tourette's, hereditary early-onset Alzheimer's, Huntington's, Lesch-Nyhan, Tay-Sachs, cystic fibrosis, muscular dystrophy, thalassemia, sickle cell anemia . . . the list could go on forever.

In studies with transgenic and knockout mice (the terminology means that a single gene has been altered or deleted, respectively), some behavioral traits have been linked to one or several genes. Extensive studies at the University of Minnesota have shown that identical twins separated at birth and reared by different families still eerily mirror each other when adults. Their tastes coincide, they are in similar professions, they choose comparable lifestyles and partners. They are like paired quantum particles, whose behavior can be predicted by observing one member of the pair.

Lastly, there have been the controversial studies of Dean Hamer of the National Cancer Institute. These purport to show a connection between male homosexuality and a region in the X chromosome (the fault of the mother yet again—and Hamer didn't bother with either a large sample or a control group).

The connection of genes with specific diseases is no longer controversial. The trouble starts when genes are discussed in connection with behavior, especially "undesirable" behavior. No one objects if tests show that their child is a genius. Moral and social arguments erupt when tests are used to limit access to resources and power by arguing for inherent, permanent differences—with the corollary, of course, that "different" automatically means inferior.

Diseases that were once considered environmental have now gone into the genetic fold. Schizophrenia and autism are not due to inadequate mothering. Cretinism can be prevented by thyroxin and mental retardation due to PKU (phenylketonuria) by avoiding phenylalanine in the diet.

The last two examples, however, point to the environmental connection. Although PKU is caused by a faulty gene, it can be controlled by eating soybeans and lentils. As we move across the spectrum of complexity, other diseases or propensities require a specific environment to manifest themselves.

Obesity is a classic example. The Pima Indians are the most obese group in this country and, as a result, suffer disproportionately from diabetes, hypertension, and heart disease. The members of the nation that remained in Mexico and still rely mostly on subsistence farming are of normal weight.

This is my opinion, as both a woman and a scientist: our genes are critical to our disposition. However, genes do not operate in isolation. I earlier mentioned chromosomal context; environmental context is equally critical. Both dispose us toward certain outcomes. For complex traits, the number of outcomes is very large and cannot easily be foretold by simple linear addition.

Our mind is like a ball poised at the top of a hill overlooking the many valleys of potential personalities. Some valleys are inherently inaccessible, but the ball can still roll into many others. Which valley the ball will end up in depends on the height and composition of the hill—but also on when and how the ball is pushed.

Yet we're more hardwired than we like to think, in this era that hails complete self-determination. As someone who at eighteen entered a totally different society from my natal one, I can tell you that when I left the homogeneous Greek environment, I thought I'd acquired X-ray vision. Since I've been in the States, I can categorize most people by nationality a mile away. The hardwiring can come from either genes or environment. Nonetheless, unless completely constrained by circumstances, we can still exert a fair amount of influence over both.

The concept of free will, so important in philosophy of religion and theory of governance, is not yet, if ever, demonstrable by experiment. That's the one thing that I'm willing to admit taking on faith. Whether it's true or not, it makes my life worth living, in lieu of conventional religious belief.

Morality and dignity require choice. Our struggles would become comic at best, pathetic at worst, if we're just puppets, jerking at the end of genetic or environmental strings. Not a very scientific argument, I know. Mr. Spock would not be happy with me on this point.

A HOUSE DIVIDED CANNOT STAND

Star Trek is too enamored of transporter technology ever to have its booths permanently decommissioned. On my part, I greatly regret having to pronounce the possibility of the transporter DOA. If transporter technology were at all feasible, I could just pop into the gadget in the afternoon, which is the time I get snoozy. I'd rematerialize in Greece, where my mom would be waiting with fresh spinach pie, and my dad, the other bookworm in the family, would discuss books with me. Alas, it's not to be, now or ever. Even if transporter services start advertising, given the dangers of the transporter, I'll still take my chances with Olympic Airways.

As for divisions of the self, ids and superegos are doomed to cohabitation, though they may once have been segregated in different rooms, long ago. What makes us human is not just our reason, but also our emotions. The *Star Trek* shadow twins and all representatives of extremes arise in the series precisely for the purpose of illustrating the desirability of the middle path, the golden mean of the pre-Socratic philosophers that we all seek.

In the end, *Star Trek* agrees with both current scientific knowledge and moral opinion by arguing that we do have leeway to decide and are therefore responsible for our actions, despite the raw materials that made us. Sometimes this is an overoptimistic conclusion, but it is the only one that will prevent us from backsliding into the cruelty of the mirror universes or the tyrannical obsessions of the doubles. These melodramatic devices reflect the real extremes of intolerance in human character. Despite my reservations on the biological distortions of *Star Trek,* I certainly think (feel?) that its heart is in the right place.

SCENE 6.
COLD FUSIONS

Symbionts and Parasites Search for Hosts

The very first aired episode of *Star Trek* was "The Man Trap," which showed a salt-needy, shape-shifting beastie out for Dr. McCoy's electrolytes. Written by George Clayton Johnson, whose work had appeared in *The Twilight Zone,* it was the first of many *Star Trek* plots that showed the biological interdependence of organisms, both as partners and as prey.

We humans are social animals, a biological phenomenon that gives us baseball and music concerts and allows us to attend them without (usually) erupting into riots, glad to be temporarily part of a crowd. We inherited this sociability from our ancestors, who developed it in order to survive. Clearly, a footloose Cro-Magnon face-to-face with a truly skilled hunter—say, a saber-toothed tiger—would be filet mignon. A dozen Cro-Magnons banding together had greater chances of survival against predators. The safety in numbers was a lesson learned through the ages and, finally, biologically programmed to the profit of warlords everywhere.

For all our snuggliness toward one another, though, we also have this deep-seated aversion to visitors who breach our boundaries—who get under our skin, so to speak. This instinctive dread is almost as powerful as our sociability. This extreme ambivalence may partly explain the almost universal pregnancy taboos, which forbid touching the new mother and/or child. Our instinctive revulsion may also explain the popularity of films in this vein, such as the *Alien* tetralogy and most Cronenberg productions: humans have a horrified fascination with symbiosis and parasitism, both as literal fact and as metaphor.

This is ironic, considering the biological reality. Practically every single life-form on earth is actually a colony, a true microcosmic society of actors benefiting from each other's presence, a symphony of symbionts.

Even single-celled organisms are in fact complex units. The cytoplasm of their cells contains smaller entities, the organelles (small organs). The most vital organelles are the mitochondria, which are the energy factories of the cell, and the chloroplasts, which in green plants convert light into oxygen and energy. Both were once freelancers—organisms that traded independence for an easier life as obligate symbionts. Larger organisms can rival Elizabethan royal households for complexity—and like them, they boast both productive members and hangers-on.

What separates symbiosis from parasitism? By definition, symbiosis benefits both partners involved, while parasitism is beneficial to one but harmful to the other. Short-term tactics favor parasitism; long-term strategy opts for symbiosis.

Star Trek tends to push our instinctual buttons of aversion against these kinds of relationships rather than investigate their biological reality. A disproportional number of episodes center around entities that "rob" series regulars of something vital, be it their bodies, their minds, or their gametes. Yet although *Star Trek* has again voted with the majority against parasitic "intrusions," it has put itself in interesting dilemmas by positing the race of joined Trills.

Whereas in reality parasitism and symbiosis can occur at any biological level, *Star Trek* invariably presents both phenomena at the level of the organism and often as metaphors for cooperation or coercion. Parasitism in *Star Trek,* for fiction that speculates on the future, has a distinctly medieval flair. As far as I can observe, *Star Trek* usually portrays parasitism in two modes that any devotee of thirteenth-century history could appreciate: demonic possession (or body snatching, if you will) and vampirism.

POD PEOPLE

The most commonly encountered parasites in *Star Trek* are body thieves. They may need a character's body because they've lost or are about to lose their own. They may also want to manipulate events in the upper echelons of Starfleet or the Klingon High Council, and only a specific person will do. Selected examples are the aforementioned "The Man Trap," "The Lights of Zetar," and "Turnabout Intruder" (TOS); "Conspiracy," "Aquiel," "Power Play," and "The Child" (TNG); and "The Passenger" and "The Assignment" (DS9).

Sometimes, the body snatchers in *Star Trek* are so desperate that they will appropriate an android body—to the perpetual discomfort of poor Commander Data. I wonder if it feels like being taken over by a computer virus, bent on overwhelming your hard drive. Data's body is commandeered in "The Schizoid Man" by Dr. Ira Graves and in "Masks" (TNG) by the intelligent but temperamental archives of a mysterious civilization, who are fighting among themselves and choose Data as the conduit.

Parasites take over bodies in *Star Trek* almost too frequently. Although the takeover mode is similar in most episodes, the fate of the host personality differs: the attacker may exchange bodies ("Turnabout Intruder"), suppress the host personality ("The Assignment"), or destroy the true owner, permanently appropriating the body ("Aquiel").

In our Terran environment, parasitism of the body-snatching variety happens at several levels. Cells are prey to viruses, which we'll discuss more extensively in a moment. Wasps and spiders lay their eggs in caterpillars, and the larvae consume the caterpillar when they hatch. Cuckoo birds place their eggs in the nests of other birds; the cuckoo hatchlings often peck their nestmates to death or push them out of the nest, forcing the hoodwinked parents to raise an impostor. Many insects will imitate prospective mates of other species, only to use the naive suitors as food.

And in species ranging from insects to mammals, males will try to cheat rivals (by either seducing females or pretending to be females), with the express purpose of enhancing their own chances of reproduction.

The case of parasites literally eating their host from inside out is encountered in several terrestrial species, including the wasps and spiders mentioned earlier. Yet the idea of a total takeover, in which the parasite effectively becomes the host, is not biologically tenable—though *Star Trek* and science fiction in general are fond of this variation. In nature, the parasite and host have completely different genetic programs and one cannot morph into the other. This sort of impossible shift occurs in "Aquiel" (TNG); when the "coalescent organism" *becomes* Lieutenant Rocha, it is no longer the original life-form.

Of course, the invader may have squirreled away its original genetic program like a dormant virus, to be taken out of retirement and brushed up when the parasite tires of the current host. However, if the result looks and thinks like Rocha "down to the molecular level" (according to *The Star Trek Encyclopedia*), this suggests that no hidden program can be detected by the formidable array of technology available to the Federation. In that case, we must ask who has actually died here and how we would know the difference.

Even if we assume that such a feat of genetic transformation is possible within each cell nucleus of the host body, we still have to deal with the brain. As we discussed in chapter 3, our personalities, our identities, are effectively contained in our brain—our memories and experiences are etched in the synaptic connections. So it is useless for Dr. Janice Lester to take over James Kirk's body in "Turnabout Intruder" (TOS), since his body also comes with his brain—and his brain contains his mind. The same is true of Tieran's takeover of Kes in "The Warlord" (VOY).

If the brain is to reflect the personality of the invader, it will have to be completely dewired and rewired. During that time, the host will behave like a newborn baby—actually, since the body is usually adult, like a catatonic idiot, with no sensory or motor control, let alone the more sophisticated thinking and decision functions. Such behavior will not let the interloper fool the rest of the crew for very long ("Data, why is Geordi drooling on the plasma coils?" "Looks like another takeover attempt, sir"). Furthermore, it is doubtful that such extensive rewiring is possible for an adult human brain, which has already created its association maps and has lost the plasticity it emerged with at birth.

Temporary suppression of the host personality is only slightly less remote as a possibility. People with personality disorders are often found to suffer from abnormal brain compartmentalization, to the point where they appear to be inhabited by more than one person. Schizophrenia, split personalities, or hearing voices do not correspond to multiple minds—just to a single one with poor interlinks. Of course, sometimes it may seem that a single brain does contain at least two minds, if the owner of the mind in question is indecisive enough.

However, in the case of body snatching, the brain of the original owner is not partly empty, like an underused attic. Although popular journals are fond of saying that we only use a small percent of our brain, the reality is that we do use most of our equipment—we just use it intermittently and sometimes inefficiently, but for a very good reason. If our brains become totally efficient, they may lose their capacity for accommodating new skills. One example of such a skill is reading, which made its entrance only three thousand years ago and which was clearly not on the survival list of apes swinging from trees.

For a mind invader to assert ownership, the brain circuits still have to be altered. Once they are altered, it is unlikely that the original personality can be retrieved even if the genetic pattern of the legitimate owner has been banked. Whatever is written in the genes is not reflected all the way up to the brain. Brain connections happen after most of the hardwired gene programs have been expressed, and after all the neurons have been born.

Star Trek is correct in showing the consciousness of Dr. Graves disappearing when his mind is finally coaxed out of Data and uploaded into the computer ("The Schizoid Man," TNG). A similar problem would arise with Spock's *katra* (spirit, soul), which migrates into Dr. McCoy and is later retrieved and put back into Spock's reclaimed body (in ST2 and ST3, *The Wrath of Khan* and *Search for Spock*).

If the intruder is vanquished, the most likely remnant will truly be a clean slate, a tabula rasa. Worse yet, given that adult brains have lost a good deal of plasticity, the owner of such a brain may never again learn to speak or function like a fully adult human. We know that this is not an unrealistically bleak conclusion because, unfortunately, such people exist. Their brains were despoiled not by an invader, but by a careless nick of the surgeon's scalpel, or from stroke: a few seconds of oxygen deprivation are enough to starve the neurons. The loss of function associated with stroke would seem mild compared to the devastation wrought by the brain snatching envisioned in *Star Trek*.

I have read my demon exorcism chants. Looking into my little black bag, I see that I've also brought along a few sharpened wooden stakes.

I NEVER DRINK—VINE . . .

The second most common parasitic attack in *Star Trek* is a variant of vampirism, in which the attacking entity steals "psychic" or "neural" energy from its victim ("Time's Arrow" and "The Loss," TNG; "The Muse," DS9; "Cathexis," VOY).

Vampirism of the physical variety occurs in nature. Mosquitoes, ticks, and vampire bats drain blood from mammals and often compound their trespass by injecting additional parasites—malaria, Lyme fever, and rabies. The specific type of vampire first unleashed upon Victorian England by Bram Stoker in the unperson of Count Dracula (and more recently upon America by Anne Rice with Lestat) is a conflation of old Central European folk beliefs and of a real historical personality. This, of course, was Prince Vlad Tepes of Walachia, also known as the Impaler for his preferred method of punishment.

The ancillary characteristics of vampirism (pallor, bad breath, aversion to light) may have originated from the fact that the exact moment of death was somewhat harder to define prior to electroencephalograms. People occasionally go into a coma and recover. Just watching for breath to cloud a mirror is obviously inadequate and in the past may have led to inadvertent burial.

Vampirism of the psychological and social variety also happens among humans. You don't need a degree in psychology to notice how people have preyed on each other throughout history. Some types of social vampirism have been so common that they have made their way into myth and fairy tales (murderous stepparents; unsympathetic in-laws; abusive spouses; changeling children). Nor has this particularly improved. Whether it's Count Dracula, CEO, who siphons off his workers' ideas and presents them as his, or Vampire Lestat, coach potato, beating his wife and living on her welfare check, vampires are with us still.

A biological vampire—a parasite—may destroy a host's nervous system, killing the host. The Vegan choriomeningitis in "The Mark of Gideon" (TOS) can be lethal—just as its real counterpart, meningitis, can turn humans into the equivalent of cabbages by infecting the membranes of the central nervous system. However, no parasite can draw off a host's "neural energy," even if such a thing existed.

In *Star Trek*, "neural energy" is yet another code word for soul, just as the Force seems to be the equivalent catchword in the *Star Wars* universe. It is quite true that, like all life-forms, humans emit across the energy spectrum. Obviously, they register in visible light. Because they are warm, their outline shows up in infrared. Human beings also produce a small electric field—not surprising, since they contain conducting electrolytes. These fields may have led to the New Age concepts of auras and Kirlian fields.

In PET scans, brain activity shows up upon ingestion of radioactively labeled glucose molecules. PET and MRI methods have been vital in uncovering the workings of the brain. Neurons in certain brain areas can be "seen" firing when a word is read, in other areas when a word is spoken; when someone is unlocking a door, forming a novel idea, or suffering an epileptic seizure.

However, this neural energy is inextricably connected with the physical brain. It cannot be extracted, transferred, used, outside the brain. The efforts of Chakotay's disembodied spirit to save the *Voyager* in "Cathexis" (VOY) and regain his purloined body are academic—minds cannot move anything but the brain they find themselves in. In that sense, it is true that we are prisoners of our bodies, even though our minds are capable of encompassing the universe.

In the end, Stoker got it right: blood is a likelier food source for vampires than neural energy. However, very real vampires lurk not just among our *Star Trek* heroes, but among us today.

THERE AIN'T ENOUGH ROOM IN THIS TOWN FOR THE BOTH OF US

Parasitized hosts may not be able to wish their tormentors away, but neither do they give up without a fight. Most life on Earth is involved in an arms race against parasites—a race that consumes more resources than did the Cold War buildup. Plants evolve toxins to prevent insects or fungi from eating their leaves, animals grow immune to the toxins of bacteria and plants; bacteria retaliate by acquiring resistance to antibiotics, and viruses produce new variants so rapidly that the designated targets can barely keep up. The rapid changes that can result from sexual reproduction are a potent weapon against parasitism and a major reason for the adoption of sex as a reproductive strategy, despite the shortcomings we discussed in chapter 2.

Star Trek contains surprisingly few examples of "conventional" symbiosis or parasitism that are nonviral, and they all occur in the original series. The episodes that I can recall are "This Side of Paradise" (TOS), in which symbiotic spores keep the colonists of Omicron Ceti III alive despite their sun's lethal emissions, clouding their minds in exchange; "The Man Trap" (TOS), previously discussed; "Obsession" (TOS), in which a gaseous life-form siphons off human hemoglobin; and "Operation: Annihilate!" (TOS) in which pancake-size cells attach to our heroes' nervous system.

On the other hand, *Star Trek* is absolutely mesmerized by viruses, perhaps reflecting the disagreeable fact that, while we have conquered or accommodated just about everything else, viruses are antagonists still very much to be reckoned with.

Viruses have evolved expressly as genetic parasites. They consist essentially of a genetic program and a system for delivering it to its target host. Viruses combine both the evils we just described—vampirism and body snatching. They have no choice but to draw resources from their hosts, because they are not self-sufficient enough to propagate without help. Their arsenal has been calibrated for invading a host and deceiving it into turning its machinery over to the interloper.

The rest—replication of the viral genetic information and packaging it into new viruses—is done using the host's genetic program as blueprints, the host's own enzymes as engineers and builders, and the host's substance as building blocks. After the viruses have used up one host cell, they burst out of its husk and launch themselves toward the next target (the strategy of the interlopers in *Invasion of the Body Snatchers* and the *Alien* tetralogy). To add insult to injury, viral particles are eerily beautiful; some bear an uncanny resemblance to planetary landers, others are polyhedrons like Fuller domes or complicated snowflakes such as the Crystalline Entity in "Silicon Avatar" (TNG).

Yet viruses cannot afford to be too greedy. If they are too good at hijacking the host's resources, they will drive it to extinction and fall with it into the abyss. Truly successful viruses are finely attuned to their host, so that they merely weaken it. If the host is hovering at the brink, they will sometimes go into hibernation while it recovers. For example, most humans carry a dormant brain guest, cytomegalovirus. We still don't know if it's harmful or not—but there it sits, perhaps a quietly ticking bomb.

Nevertheless, viruses are extremely efficient killers, their killing capacity augmented by their rapid mutation rate. The genetic fluidity of viruses overwhelms the defense system of the host, which cannot easily keep up—even the versatile immune systems of vertebrates, with their modular flexibility, are no match for a virus on the move. Like all other life-forms, viruses turn vicious when backed to the wall. Relatively benign parasites become virulent when they are forced to choose a host different from their optimal one.

This is why smallpox is benign in cows, its optimal hosts, but lethal to humans; ditto with monkeys and HIV, or influenza and pigs: the original viral strain had not been designed for humans. The viruses that parachuted most recently from animals to humans are the most virulent. "The Quickening" (DS9) shows the havoc that a recent host switch can wreak—people are keeling over like mayflies in that episode. The sweeps of bubonic plague and AIDS look like balmy breezes when compared to the behavior of the Ebola virus, which seems to have discovered humans in sub-Saharan Africa sometime in the last decade.

When the optimal animal host came into proximity with humans during early animal domestication, viruses that boarded humans found them unsatisfactory and hence had no reason to spare them. Those humans that survived acquired an immunity of sorts. This event in turn changed the cultural face of the Earth, when immunized cultures such as Europeans, Asians, or Bantu Africans came in contact with cultures that had neither immunity nor domesticated animals of their own to return the favor, as was the case with American Indians, native Australians, and Khoisan Africans.

Star Trek seems oddly nonchalant about such problems, especially when one considers the moral restrictions of the Prime Directive (of which more in chapter 10). Some planets have viruses that are activated only upon departure ("Resolutions," VOY). This seems an odd strategy, unless we believe in the panspermic distribution of life that I discussed in chapter 1.

In *Star Trek* there are viruses that attack only adults ("Miri," TOS) and viruses that discriminate so little that they can be used as population control (Vegan choriomeningitis in "The Mark of Gideon," TOS). There is also the bizarre disease in "Phage" (VOY), which attacks a humanoid race of the Delta Quadrant, eating away at their bodies until they are forced to scavenge the organs of others as substitutes—a case of parasites begetting more parasitism.

Particularly prevalent in *Star Trek* is viral invasion of the brain, often at the expense of verisimilitude. In at least seven episodes, viruses attack either the neural nets of starship computers ("Learning Curve" and "Macrocosm," VOY) or the neural systems of humanoids. When viruses cause degeneration or death ("The Vengeance Factor," TNG; "Babel" and "The Quickening," DS9), the plots do reflect scientific fact. When they cause the lamented "instant evolution," about which I grumbled at length in chapter 2, they are clearly not biologically possible (the worst offenders are "Genesis" and "Identity Crisis," TNG).

Furthermore, when viruses attack specific brain centers, recovery of lost functions is shown to be completely reversible. For example, the aphasia virus in "Babel" first disables the language centers; upon being given the antidote, station personnel automatically regain speech capacity (as does Uhura when her brain is cleaned out by Nomad in "The Changeling," TOS). Such plasticity is decidedly absent from adult humans, though it is present in children whose age falls within the "permissive window." The brain will redirect its neurons and their connections only if the catastrophe happens early enough.

So far, I've listed dangers from without. Let's now move indoors and see what threats lurk in our own attics and cellars.

INCUBI AND SUCCUBI

Somewhere in the slippery slope between parasitism and symbiosis is the uneasy mixture of things that may be good in the short term but eventually harmful ("All good things in life are illegal, immoral, or fattening").

The brain is a marvelous instrument, the right mix of precision and breadth. However, if overloaded or misled, it can give a wrong map of the world. Humans who are under great stress or sensory deprivation will hallucinate. Excessive hunger, excessive thirst, deep grief, prolonged depression, sleep deprivation, or just interruption of dreaming—they all lead to people suddenly hearing voices, seeing what is not there.

In "Night Terrors" (TNG), the entire *Enterprise* crew is going insane because they can't dream anymore. It turns out that a crew of an alien ship is inadvertently jamming their REM waves. And, of course, such deprivations are standard instruments of torture and coercion—used, for example, during Captain Picard's interrogation in "Chain of Command" (TNG).

Sometimes hallucinations are sought on purpose by members of cultures who embark on vision quests (including the Vulcans). Traditional shamans are convinced that they can exit their bodies with the help of cannabis or peyote; voodoo worshipers are sure that they can be "ridden" by the orisha (spirits); and prophets are equally certain that they hear the voices of their gods, usually to the grief of everyone within range. In "In the Hands of the Prophets" (DS9), the insufferable Vedek—later Kai—Winn is so convinced of this that she will eliminate dissenters. Sound familiar?

Such phenomena have been brought under the flashlight of science because hallucinations can also be induced chemically—by psychoactive drugs contained in plants—coca leaves, cacao beans (yes, Virginia, chocolate *is* a mild euphoriant), poppy pods . . . We have added to this rogues' gallery ourselves, with sedatives, tranquilizers, antidepressants. How do they do it? Neurons communicate by neurotransmitter molecules, which launch their canoes from a synapse to the awaiting receptors on neighboring neurons. Drugs affect transmission of the neuronal impulse by either enhancing or blocking the action of neurotransmitters.

All of our guilty pleasures have molecular partners. Here are some dancing pairs: nicotine/acetylcholine; angel dust/dopamine (which is why users often end up frozen with instant Parkinson's disease); LSD/serotonin; tranquilizers/GABA (gamma-aminobutyric acid); and ethanol, which is not picky and will cheerfully pickle everything in sight.

More recently, we have met the enemy and discovered that he is us: the reason that we are susceptible to opiates and their relatives is because we have such molecules in our brain, the enkephalins or endorphins ("endogenous morphins," first characterized by Candace Pert and Solomon Snyder at Johns Hopkins). Endorphins target specific receptors on neuron surfaces in the limbic system. This part of the brain coordinates and processes the sensations of pleasure. Substances that block pleasure (methadone, prostaglandins) work by either degrading these active molecules or preventing them from binding to their receptors.

Pleasure is a powerful motivator. When rats have a choice between food and stimulation of their pleasure centers, they go for the latter and die paper-thin but happy all the way (Elim Garak narrowly escapes a similar fate in "The Wire," DS9). Humans are more complicated, but addiction is a well-documented woe in societies from antiquity to the urban present.

Demons in *Star Trek* generally work on the same principles as addictive drugs. In "Sub Rosa" (TNG), Quint, an "anaphasic life-form" (read incubus) has been nurtured by the female ancestors of Dr. Beverly Crusher. Yet the poor demon has given his best in return: he may have induced hallucinations in these women and perhaps slightly shortened their lives. However, watching the expression on Crusher's face, he has also given them many glorious little deaths (grin) prior to the big one.

Conversely, too many entities in *Star Trek* seem to get their jollies from feeding on the brain emanations of humans. An energy entity has been prolonging a planetary conflict in "Day of the Dove" (TOS) because it lives on hatred. In "Time's Arrow" (TNG), shape-shifting Devidians feast on human fear. In "Shades of Gray" (TNG), the life of Will Riker is threatened by microbes that (of course!) attack his neurons and thrive on endorphins. Dr. Pulaski's solution is to stimulate his R-complex, the part of the brain directly above the spinal cord, which we share with reptiles—hence the name. Riker's R-complex comes to the rescue by literally pushing the microbes out, an appropriate response for a brain region that apparently houses the instincts for both territoriality and aggression.

What happens in "Shades of Gray" is *just* possible. We know now that our thoughts and emotions can influence our physiological state through regulation of the hormonal and immune systems. The thalamus, hypothalamus, and pituitary, all housed in the brain, are major coordinators of our chemical well-being. Some of their action is involuntary and tied to the biorhythms that we discussed in chapter 2. Doctors have discovered that chemotherapy and insulin delivery are more effective at certain times of day and month. And all our systems tend to droop around three in the afternoon. The civilized solution to this is a nap, although barbarous cultures opt for a caffeine injection instead.

Of course, this is a far cry from the brain dictating physically impossible feats to the body. We may be able to partly fool our bodies with placebos. In some cultures we can be killed or turned to zombies by sorcerers or houngans. But no matter how hard we think, we cannot grow wings, nor can we wish a tumor away.

Enough, though, of the bad guys. Let's look at the bright side as well.

THE FIRST INDUSTRIAL REVOLUTION

You, I, and the crews of the *Star Trek* starships are all symbiotic units, though we may be repulsed by the idea of inhabitants within us. Without our cellular partners, we'd never have advanced beyond the stage of lowly anaerobic bacteria. Life on Earth today would be unrecognizable without cellular symbionts.

As we discussed in chapter 1, when oxygen first became prevalent in the terrestrial atmosphere, it literally caused a holocaust. Some survivors fled to the safety of deep ocean vents or sulfur springs. Others, pluckier and more adventurous, evolved to the point where they could use the new, lethal tenant as an energy source.

At some point, such organisms were engulfed by larger ones. If the oxygen-utilizing organisms were not immediately digested, some of the engulfing organisms must have discovered that their captives conferred certain advantages. Those who decided to grant eternal hospitality to their accidental guests left so many more descendants that they have become the dominant terrestrial life-form.

Today, all advanced cells contain these symbionts. They are called mitochondria and contain the long assembly line of enzymes that gingerly convert oxygen to useful energy. The giveaway to their independent past is that they still have their very own genetic material, which codes for several of their unique components. As further proof of their separate provenance, their genetic material is slightly different from that of their hosts. This genetic uniqueness, coupled with the fact that mitochondria (like all cytoplasmic organelles) are inherited exclusively from the mother, has allowed molecular biologists to track our lineage backward to a few related females, separating us all by less than the six degrees of the eponymous theater play.

Some advanced cells were even more hospitable—and benefited

even more. They engulfed a second type of bacterium, which had evolved the capacity to harness the energy of light itself. These organelles, found in green plants and called chloroplasts, use light to convert carbon dioxide to oxygen. This process, known as photosynthesis, established the feedback loop that eventually turned the Earth's atmosphere to almost 30 percent oxygen. The presence of adequate oxygen in its turn created the ozone layer, which filtered out ultraviolet light, making multicellular organisms a feasible proposition. Microscopic life, yes, but it turned a ball of roiling rock into our lush biosphere.

In addition to creating our atmosphere and our predecessors, ancestral chloroplast-containing organisms gave us yet another gift, this one double-edged. Most of the fossil fuels that we depend on so heavily are decomposition products of ancient photosynthetic organisms. Their remnants have made most of our recent technology possible; they have also made us capable of destroying ourselves and are irreversibly changing this planet's surface, weather, and atmosphere. The possibility of a runaway greenhouse effect, which has turned Venus literally into hell, now looms large in our future as well.

So the first round on Earth has gone (with reservations) to the symbionts. Contrary to the selfish-gene hypothesis so beloved of social Darwinists, those who cooperated have now inherited this planet, while the isolationists are cowering in tiny niches.

GOOD COP, BAD COP

On Earth, we encounter symbiosis frequently even beyond the cellular level. Lichens survive in the hostile tundra because they are a union of an alga and a moss, combining the hardiest qualities of both. Plants give bees and butterflies food in the form of pollen or nectar in exchange for fertilization. Certain types of fish can live freely with predators (pilot fish with sharks, angelfish with sea anemones), acting as guides or warning systems in exchange for food morsels from the communal table. Several bird species camp out on top of large mammals (rhinos, hippos, water buffalo) or near the jaws of crocodiles, exchanging cleaning duties for protection from other predators. Mammals gather in bands, bartering sexual favors or food caches for protection. And, of course, there are the complicated social arrangements of humans, which cover the entire spectrum between parasitism and symbiosis.

As an example of a mixed ecosystem, an average human body has a complement of life-forms quite possibly in the millions, both partners and moochers. It harbors intestinal bacteria (their destruction is the reason that massive doses of antibiotics cause stomach cramps), gum bacteria, which thrive on sugar, skin and hair mites, and several benign or mild viruses.

If the human in question is unlucky enough, s/he might also host more virulent parasites in the form of runaway cells (tumors), viruses (hepatitis, HIV), bacteria (cholera, bubonic plague), nematodes (trichinosis, guinea worms, and tapeworms), or insects (chiggers). Lastly, insofar as pregnancy in advanced organisms robs the mother of resources and can result in protracted illness, permanent disability, or death, it, too, can be considered a special form of parasitism.

In true liberal Federation tradition, *Star Trek* approves of symbiosis so strongly that it has extended it to its starships. Like all sailors and pilots, the crews of the *Enterprise*, the *Voyager*, and the *Defiant* are attached to their vessels, which become more than the sum of their circuitry. Since these ships are not merely warbirds, but exploration vessels, they are actually home—they contain families and their quarters, schools, gardens, promenades. When Kirk has to sacrifice the *Enterprise* in *The Search for Spock* (ST3), he does not make his decision lightly or cheerfully, gung ho as he usually is. The entire crew wistfully watches the falling star that was the *Enterprise*, as it burns upon entry into the atmosphere.

Given that Starfleet ships are equipped with bioneural circuits, they do straddle the sentience fence. Their computers certainly have distinct personalities—for example, the station computer in DS9 is much grumpier and more opinionated than that of the *Enterprise*, although they all have Majel Barrett's voice. Ships have been known to take tentative steps toward asserting mental independence ("Emergence," TNG), and they can even act as surrogate mothers to orphaned space forms ("Galaxy's Child," TNG). Just as ships are prey to barnacles and rust, so are starships vulnerable to parasites that attach to the ship and may drain energy from vital functions ("Elogium," "Macrocosm," and "Learning Curve," VOY) or threaten hull integrity ("A Matter of Honor," TNG).

Taking this one step further, a sentient ship and its crew seems to be an acceptable symbiotic unit in the *Star Trek* universe. In "Tin Man" (TNG), Tam Elbrun, a Betazoid gifted and cursed with excessive empathic skills, finally finds a home literally in the bosom of a sentient ship, Gomtuu. The ship has lost its crew and is moping suicidally, suffering from a terminal case of the empty-nest syndrome. On his side, Tam feels battered by the constant onslaught of others' thoughts and welcomes the calmness of Gomtuu's interior. The ship takes care of all his needs and buffers all his interactions with the universe outside.

Is such an arrangement possible? At first glance, we're tempted to say it sounds too cushy a deal for Tam to be true. But such a configuration most certainly exists, and it happens often enough. Once we strip away the technobabble about Gomtuu, what we're left with is obviously a womb, our first and best refuge before we have to emerge and unwillingly face the world out there.

With a few exceptions, pregnancy and birth in all animals except higher vertebrates is a casual affair, usually consisting of releasing clouds of eggs and sperm. Several animals are more careful parents—insects will often ensure that their eggs are laid on or near food sources (often other insects); some insects will actually carry their young around while they mature (wolf spiders immediately come to mind); sea horses shepherd their young around in a tight ball; some fish aerate their eggs by fanning them with their tails; crocodiles carry their young carefully inside the safe cage of their teeth.

Going up the evolutionary ladder, birds invariably take care of their eggs, making sure that they are properly aerated and incubated. The parents then spend all their time and energy feeding the hatchlings and later teaching them the skills appropriate to their specific kind. Birds are born with the equipment to fly and/or swim, but they have to be taught the craft.

Mammals, the most recent arrivals, have gone to extremes as far as care of progeny goes. They evolved a new piece of equipment called the placenta, which allows the young to develop within the body of the mother. Nutrition, immune protection, a safe and warm place to grow in—the mammalian womb offers all these (that the fetus is entirely dependent on maternal antibodies makes mincemeat of Dr. Bashir's "discovery" in "The Quickening," DS9, that fetuses have unique lifesaving antibodies. Really, guys!). The young born in this fashion can be quite large, and brain size is especially favored. Yet once again, this advance is fraught with danger—and this is particularly true for humans.

The large brain allows humans to be born with their neurons less "frozen in place" than those of less advanced vertebrates. This means that they are more in control of their brain workings and less hardwired for instinctual actions. The accompanying disadvantage is that they are born helpless and need a long training period to become competent. With society becoming more complex, the point of competence has moved up; the needle now rests roughly at twenty-one years. The long and ever lengthening period of dependence seriously impairs the mobility of the mother and may have contributed to gender inequalities in primate and human groups.

Human pregnancy has additional, more tangible associated dangers. The position of the pelvis necessary for upright posture interferes with labor. Human women are rare among animals in routinely having birthing difficulties. The sociobiologists opine that "men are designed for a short, nasty life; women for a long, brutal one"—but they must have based this conclusion upon recent statistics. Until the twentieth century, premenopausal women died considerably younger than men and in slightly larger numbers. The main cause of death was childbirth complications.

Even in normal pregnancy, the child draws nutrients from the mother, causing all sorts of health dangers—anemia, gestational diabetes, eclampsia. This is reflected in an old saying: "For every child, a tooth." Yet in most societies (and despite the dangers of overpopulation), the status of women is still so closely connected to procreation that they will go to any lengths to conceive, ignoring the dangers of hormonal infertility treatments. The more affluent can now escape pregnancy, however, with the advent of surrogacy.

The Federation, equipped with transporters, warp drives, and cloning devices, still frowns on any other method of procreation than the original one (we'll revisit this in chapter 9). Back in the real world, too, while medicine has taken great strides in conception—hormones, in vitro fertilization, in vivo implantation—an artificial womb is still not in sight.

Until it arrives, humans will be born in the traditional manner. However, I have heard few women extol the joys of pregnancy—after all, who enjoys fallen arches, a squeezed bladder, dangerously high blood pressure, and labor pains?—although they naturally love and cherish the children that result. Now imagine, if you can, a case of voluntary lifelong pregnancy—and you get a Trill.

MERGE, HONOR, AND OBEY

In *Star Trek,* a joined Trill consists of a sluglike symbiont joined to a humanoid, with shared "personalities" and experiences. The symbiont seems to be lined along the spinal cord of the humanoid host, and it lacks all conventional senses. Successive hosts can be either male or female. Symbionts share memories of their previous hosts with the current one.

Our first glimpse of such an entity is Ambassador Odan in "The Host" (TNG). The race proved intriguing enough to merit a regular representative, Jadzia Dax—the science officer in station DS9 and current partner of Lieutenant Worf. The Dax symbiont has already had six official hosts (plus an unofficial one, forcibly revealed in "Equilibrium," DS9). Jadzia is intelligent, confident, and matter-of-fact, though in my opinion still an imperfect replacement for lost K'Ehleyr, who was a hybrid in a class all by herself ("The Emissary," "Reunion," TNG).

Our knowledge of the Trills is tantalizingly limited. We know that only a small percentage of Trill humanoids are joined (one in a thousand is the ratio that comes to my mind). Although joining is grueling, sometimes dangerous, and irreversible after ninety-three hours, it is considered an honor. Nonjoined Trills compete for the few available symbionts and go (willingly!) through a selection process that sounds like a combination of U.S. Marine boot camp, the Harvard entrance exam, and the mind games of the Cardassian Obsidian Order.

The Trills have ushered in a host of uncomfortable questions in the normally calm *Star Trek* home front. On my undoubtedly partial list I can count homosexuality ("The Host," TNG, was the first time that *Star Trek* grappled with the issue, although, as usual, it chose soft-core lesbianism as less threatening); memory transmission and survival of personality; social stratification (in "Invasive Procedures," DS9, it becomes obvious that nonjoined Trills form a dispossessed underclass); and host versus symbiont rights (variant of: if during a birth you can save only the mother or the child, which one will you choose?). It is emblematic of the unease surrounding these issues that the episodes focusing specifically on Trills can be counted on the fingers of one hand, whereas Klingon or Changeling episodes are too numerous to list, and Borg-centered episodes have been the nucleus of recurring plotlines.

Biologically speaking, it is unclear if a joined Trill can be considered a case of symbiosis or parasitism. The benefits to the symbiont are obvious—sustenance, sensory input, available bodies to inhabit. The advantages to the host are vague at best. The most I can come up with is that, like Tiresias of Greek myth, the host of a Trill symbiont accumulates the wisdom of several lifetimes, retains fuzzy memories of predecessors, vicariously knows the joys of both genders. Also, as long as the symbiont remembers, all its hosts gain an odd sort of immortality.

The case for parasitism is bolstered by clear indications that the symbiont is the dominant partner. Social conventions often reveal the balance of power. Women have traditionally been absorbed in their husband's family by adopting his last name. In an equivalent convention, the last name of a joined Trill is that of the symbiont; the host must give up her/his family name upon joining (Curzon Dax . . . Jadzia Dax).

Equally suggestive is the expression of whims or desires. The humanoid hosts are clearly expected to subordinate their emotions to their symbiont; this extends to feelings of sexual attraction, even though the symbiont sees the world through the senses of the host. The only restriction on symbionts is the famous taboo against "reassociation," shown in "Rejoined" (DS9), which forbids the renewal of a relationship between two symbionts once they have changed hosts. The taboo is enforced by banishment, which deprives the symbiont of future hosts. If the two hosts happen to be attracted to each other, too bad. What matters is new experiences for the symbiont.

The clincher is relative value and weight under the law. The symbiont, not the host, is responsible for the actions of the joined entity, and a current host can be prosecuted for crimes committed during the tenure of a previous host ("Dax," DS9). On the other hand, promises made by the host are not binding and can be broken without consequences ("Blood Oath," DS9). This reduces the host to property or, at best, to the status of a minor.

Finally, there is no doubt whatsoever that if the life of a joined Trill is in danger, the symbiont gets preferential treatment; this is unambiguously shown in "The Host" (TNG) and "Equilibrium" (DS9). Just the fact that joining becomes irreversible *for the host* after ninety-three hours shows that the host is expendable. In "Equilibrium" (DS9), we confirm our suspicions that if host and symbiont cannot mesh well, the host is simply discarded (although the symbiont retains traumatic memories of the event as well).

On the other hand, the irreversibility of joining is thrown in doubt in two episodes: in "The Host" (TNG), Riker separates from the Odan symbiont yet survives. Let's accept that this happens because Riker is not a Trill. A more serious case comes up in "Invasive Procedures" (DS9), in which Verad, a desperate nonjoined Trill, temporarily steals the Dax symbiont. Since Jadzia survives this experience, I for one wondered if joining is in fact used on the Trill planet as a method of social control. My suspicions were confirmed in "Equilibrium" (DS9), in which we discover that the Symbiosis Commission allows many fewer joinings than are possible "for the sake of stability"—and also, it goes without saying, in order to keep their power and their jobs.

Between class distinctions and casual treatment of the host's life, this union has ominous undertones indeed. A similar treatment, but without the idealization of *Star Trek,* is given in Octavia Butler's outstanding and disturbing story "Bloodchild," in which humans new to a planet inhabited by sentient aliens face a situation similar to that of the Trill hosts. Their dilemma is compounded by the fact that, in a reverse ratio to that of the Trills, there are not enough of them to go around.

Putting the moral dilemmas aside for the moment, can we evaluate the possibility of such a life-form? The presence of an entity within a humanoid body is quite feasible, whether we classify the symbiont as a parasite, a partner, or progeny. Beyond their mitochondria and their children, humans often "host" tapeworms that are yards long and still survive—though the ordeal leaves them anemic and prone to other infections. The reproduction of the Trill symbiont is shrouded in mystery, but can be sidestepped by positing reproduction prior to joining. However, other aspects of the Trills once again present us biologists with serious problems.

Compatibility issues are apparently formidable. Symbionts are only compatible with Trills, not with any other humanoids. In an emergency, they can be grafted onto a non-Trill (Will Riker in "The Host," TNG), but the immune system of a non-Trill host will reject them. This means that Trill hosts and symbionts are finely tuned, which in turn implies coevolution.

But like a Hydra's nine heads, coevolution sprouts a huge array of problems: if the two coevolved, Trills could not have common ancestry with other humanoids. But I already mentioned that in "Children of Time" (DS9), we meet Yedrin Dax, Jadzia's son by a non-Trill. Moreover, if the two coevolved, joining should be easy and must have occurred routinely prior to the development of technology. If this is true, why is surgery involved and why is a Symbiosis Commission (seen in "Equilibrium," DS9) necessary for overseeing, midwifelike, the joinings? And if the symbionts cannot exist "unhosted" (an automatic definition of parasitism), where do they come from?

Star Trek can't have it both ways: either the host and symbiont came into existence together (and hence neither surgery nor Yedrin) or the symbionts cannot exist independently and picked humanoid colonists as hosts relatively recently—in which case they are not symbionts but parasites.

Furthermore, the question of the continuity of memory from host to host is hard to answer. If host and symbiont share memory, they must share neural connections—and the alignment of the symbiont along the host's spinal column is suggestive. If they share neural connections, the death of a previous host should dramatically alter or even erase the memories and personality of the symbiont.

In "Facets" (DS9), Jadzia goes through the Trill ceremony of "closure," during which she meets her former hosts. To do that, the personalities of the former hosts take over another person (shades of demonic possession and body snatching), so that Jadzia can see them as separate entities.

Where are these memories kept? It is true that humans do not have full access to their mind. Several functions are "automated" and largely beyond our conscious control—otherwise it would take forever to digest or take a step. Our memories, too, are not always automatically at our beck and call: sometimes we have to shuffle through several folders and stacks before we retrieve the right file.

It is possible, of course, that the memories are kept in the brain (or its equivalent) of the symbiont. But if that is the case, it contradicts the fact that current hosts remember what past hosts have said or done. Who or what decides what is accessible and what is not? In "Equilibrium" (DS9) we find out that the Dax symbiont underwent one joining that failed, but Jadzia remembers nothing of this. Once again, we are forced to believe that the host may be a mere marionette, its mind strings pulled by the symbiont.

Another big problem is that, as I mentioned in chapter 2, Trill symbionts seem to have a large soft spot for humanoids: in "The Host" (TNG) Odan falls for Dr. Crusher; in DS9, Dax is smitten with Worf; and in "Facets" (DS9), we discover that Dax-in-Curzon yearned for Jadzia before she was joined. Yet given its form and the de facto impossibility of reproduction between it and a humanoid, a Trill symbiont could not possibly be attracted to humans.

And to venture a little beyond biological matters: although *Star Trek* humanoids seem to think nothing of mating with each other regardless of race, they seem considerably less enlightened with respect to same-sex partners. When Odan's next host proves to be a woman in "The Host" (TNG), Dr. Crusher backpedals frantically, although she was quite receptive (to put it demurely) to the symbiont when it inhabited Will Riker. To give the series credit, though, in "Rejoined" (DS9) there is no fuss over the fact that the two symbionts that contemplate breaking the reassociation taboo are both within female hosts—though an episode with two *male* hosts is apparently still below the event horizon.

THE GREATEST GOOD FOR THE GREATEST NUMBER

Overall, *Star Trek* has been responsive to the all-too-human fear of being taken over. I'm happy to report that most kinds of parasitism that show up in the series are, thankfully, unlikely in biological terms. On the other hand, *Star Trek*'s concern with viruses is not misplaced. Viruses are as real and as frightening in the here and now as they are in a fantasy future. In fact, I'd go even further and say that in the case of viruses, reality is stranger than fiction—even stranger than science fiction.

Although symbiosis is as common as parasitism in nature, it has received short shrift in the *Star Trek* universe. The series enjoys using it as a Three Musketeers metaphor ("all for one and one for all"), but it has let countless fascinating possibilities lie fallow.

Certainly, we have the Trills, who are feasible enough as far as symbiotic living goes. However, I'm highly dubious about the shared-memory part—and even more so about poor Yedrin Dax. Just from our everyday wanderings, we Earth bioscientists can spin out remarkable symbiotic yarns for potential *Star Trek* stories, based not just on informed speculation, but actual fact.

SCENE 7.
REMOTE CONTROL

Projections and Invasions by Empaths, Telepaths, and Espers

A subject of perennial fascination among humans has been the possibility that the human mind might harbor hidden powers. In earlier ages, such manifestations were classified as occult or sorcerous, and those who possessed such putative talents were either worshiped or burned. However, in the Industrial Age, with its strong urge to plumb the unknown, psychic phenomena came under the critical eye of science—and into the much more permissive domain of fantastic literature. By showing extrasensory powers as de facto occurrences, *Star Trek* is merely following a long fantasy tradition. However, *Star Trek* by now has such a large following and is so integrated into world culture that I worry that its endorsement of ESP might be taken at face value by the public at large.

In the real world, extrasensory powers of perception and movement really have currency only amongst scriptwriters, New Age disciples, and the Department of Defense, crowds that either have relatively large budgets or can operate under an institutional suspension of disbelief. Running out of story ideas? Give Gilligan the power to read minds! Running out of stuff to spend money on in military research and development? Invent a psychic gap between the United States and the Soviet Union!

For the rest of us, however, all we have are these occasional unsettling occurrences that we are at a loss to explain: knowing what is going to come out of someone's mouth before it emerges; a palpitation before the phone rings with news of a death; a strong sense that we've experienced something before. Still, the fact that we have language for these kinds of events and abilities means they represent some kind of experience.

Who hasn't had one of these episodes and wondered if there are senses beyond the traditional five? Or are we just catching a glimpse of our minds mis-synchronizing or performing some linked cascade of pattern recognition at a level of consciousness that we can't command?

In many episodes and through the introduction of psionically gifted non-Terran characters, *Star Trek* speculates on the development of such powers in humanoid beings. Yet it also backs away from allowing Humans to evolve these kinds of powers as new senses. The psionic abilities are supernormal powers that *Star Trek*'s protagonists are not allowed to evolve without great peril, apples perhaps best left unpicked.

Is *Star Trek* hedging again or is Terran mind-reading avoided because we are entering dangerous waters—faith, the soul, the sanctity of the mind? Thought-reading in particular is touchy territory, in some ways eliciting the same revulsion we harbor toward parasites who invade our bodies. In this instance, though, the intrusion is upon the one thing that defines us as singular identities: our minds.

Paranormal psychic abilities are roughly classified into four groups. These are telepathy (reading thoughts), clairvoyance (knowledge without sensory input, also known as remote viewing), precognition (sensing future events), and psychokinesis (manipulating matter with the mind).

What the paranormal abilities all have in common is perception or exertion of force at a distance—defined by space and time—without recruitment of the known resources contained in our bodies, but by sole use of our thoughts.

Yes, it is a beguiling concept. Magic for the common man, wish-fulfilling tools for people who find themselves in a complex, frustrating, and imperfect world. Therein lies both their novelty and the biological weakness in any argument for their existence or potential potency. What fuels these powers? What confluence of neurological and physical phenomena could animate them—if they exist at all?

Imagine trying to purify and define the mythical alchemical element of quintessence. This is pretty much what we are faced with in finding and describing the biological basis for psionic powers. Science has looked at these phenomena repeatedly. Scientists would like to be able to perform psionic feats as much as anyone else. Furthermore, what distinguishes science from religion is that the former *never* rejects evidence, even if such evidence forces the abandonment of an elegant or encompassing theory. Nevertheless, despite repeated experiments, the accumulated evidence for psionic abilities that passes inspection has been—none. Not that that has ever stopped Roddenberry and his spiritual heirs, who have merrily spread these abilities all the way to the twenty-fourth century.

A CHOICE OF POISONS.

Of the many possible ESP abilities, *Star Trek* has picked a favorite. Its creators are head over heels in love with telepathy. I guess there's a lot more dramatic potential in having a protagonist zap a Klingon with a mind message saying he smells like a camel than in giving a protagonist the power to lift a Klingon with his mindforce alone. Telepathy also undoubtedly saves tons of money on special effects. But before I elaborate on *Star Trek* telepathy, let me quickly run through the depiction of other psionic abilities in the series.

I cannot recall anyone gifted with bona fide precognition in *Star Trek*. I suppose that the closest to it is the El-Aurian race, which numbers *Enterprise* bartender Guinan (TNG) and Soran (*Generations*, ST7) among its members. These people are described as "listeners." They have a spider sense that tingles if the timeline has shifted or has been altered. This convenient attribute allows Guinan to warn Picard with vague misgivings in "Yesterday's *Enterprise*" (TNG). Maybe the El-Aurian brain microtubules, unlike ours, do sense quantum fluctuations!

Psychokinetic powers, which include teleportation, telekinesis, fire-starting, and distant healing, spring up with alarming frequency in Stephen King's rural Maine (could it be something in the water?). On *Star Trek*, though, they're primarily limited to beings from more than four spacetime dimensions—most visibly the Talosians in "Menagerie" and the Organians in "Errand of Mercy" (TOS); Q and his Continuum in TNG; and the wormhole aliens—Prophets to the religious Bajorans—in DS9.

Psychokinesis also breaks out sporadically among humans in the series. When that happens, it almost invariably comes before a character's dramatic fall from grace. If those thus blessed are series regulars, they either renounce such powers (Riker in "Hide and Q," TNG) or lose them, like Charlie reverting to idiocy in the film based on Daniel Keyes's classic *Flowers for Algernon* (Reggie Barclay in "The Nth Degree," TNG).

If they're guest stars, their fate depends on their intrinsic goodness. If they're nice guys, they undergo "transformation to a higher form" (Kes in VOY; John Doe in "Transfigurations," TNG). More prosaically, if they turn nasty, they get killed (Gary Mitchell and Elizabeth Dehner in "Where No Man Has Gone Before," TOS).

Star Trek has compensated for its circumspection on psychokinesis by going all out for telepathy and clairvoyance (which includes empathy). Telepathy is so prevalent in the *Star Trek* universe that two humanoid races—the Ferengi and the Cardassians—are resistant to it, like people whose immune system has developed antibodies against a disease.

Those who are susceptible are rarely left alone with their thoughts. Someone, somewhere, has the ability—and often the desire—to read or write on their minds. There's so much telepathic traffic in the series that I often wonder that the mind waves don't get jammed like the Italian telephone network. To direct this frenetic activity, each of the series has at least one psion among the long-term characters, like a house doctor on call.

In TOS, Mr. Spock with his Vulcan mind-melding abilities owns a special form of telepathy. Spock can meld with anything in sight, whether animal, vegetable, or mineral: he does it with the Kelvans from the Andromeda Galaxy ("By Any Other Name," TOS), with the silicon-based

Horta ("Devil in the Dark," TOS), with Nomad's metal carapace ("The Changeling," TOS). He gives real meaning to the phrase *communing with nature.*

Spock's father, Sarek, is no slouch in the melding department either, as we see in "Journey to Babel" (TOS) and *The Search for Spock* (ST3). When Bendii Syndrome slackens Sarek's discipline, he emits mind waves powerful enough to disturb everyone within his effective radius ("Sarek," TNG).

In TNG, ship's counselor Deanna Troi has mind powers. She is of the empathic Betazoid race and is suitably cuddlesome, as wide-eyed as a Care Bear and actually half-Human. Her full-Betazoid mother, Lwaxana, more gifted and less scrupulous, also sweeps grandly in and out of both TNG and DS9.

DS9 stands out in having no obvious esper among its regular cast. We must discount Odo's occasional flare-ups of telepathy, caused by plasma storms ("Things Past"). They are an obvious plot afterthought and as irregular and as unpredictable as bouts of sneezing.

VOY, the most prone of the four *Star Trek* series to New Ageism, makes up for DS9's parsimony by having two psions; Lieutenant Tuvok, a Vulcan, and Kes, an Ocampan crew member.

It is interesting to note that in *Star Trek,* as in most science fiction, empathy (passive reception) and telepathy (active transmission) neatly fall into the traditional feminine/masculine split and are treated accordingly. Telepathy, because of its potential to invade and manipulate other minds, is both more valuable and more dangerous. Empathy, the softer, fuzzier, weaker sibling, faces no such constraints—but neither is it particularly prized.

Humans who attain excessive ESP powers in *Star Trek* end up destroying themselves after harming others ("Where No Man Has Gone Before," "Charlie X," TOS; "Man of the People," TNG). In other cases, espers are allowed their special powers, but must "pay" for the gift by foregoing one of the conventional senses, just as Odin had to sacrifice an eye for knowledge of the runes in Norse mythology. Dr. Miranda Jones in

"Is There in Truth No Beauty?" (TOS) is blind but a superb melder; Riva in "Loud as a Whisper" (TNG) is deaf, but a powerful directional thought-transmitter.

In this manner, *Star Trek* manages to keep ESP while voicing its reservations about mental powers. I have a few biological reservations to register myself on the subject.

MAKE A WISH

How likely are all these literally sensitive minds? And can our mind rule over time or matter? To put it bluntly and succinctly, within the laws of physics and biology, no.

If precognition were true, it would defy our cherished concept of free will. It would also contradict the direction of the arrow of time, the Heisenberg uncertainty principle, and the unpredictable behavior of live beings (especially humans) as complex emergent systems. If precognition worked, no casinos in their right mind would continue operating. Mind you, precognition is by definition exact and hence different from broad predictions, which someone can do well if they are dealing with a simple, well-defined system that they know intimately (for example, the game of blackjack).

As for psychokinesis, all action at a distance needs a field and a carrier particle in order to function. Terrestrial life-forms generally rely on action by contact. Practically all our systems, from our chromosomes to our entire bodies, operate as levers, locks, and keys, transmissions along cables, flywheels. There are three notable exceptions, which do rely on fields and carrier particles—vision, hearing, and speech. To see, our retinas register and process incoming photons (light). To hear, the exquisitely balanced ear bones transmit compression (sound) waves, which then displace tiny hairs in the inner ear. To speak, we produce sound waves by vibrating our vocal cords.

Of course, speech is ESP insofar as it can influence the actions of animate matter at a distance (we'll discuss the putative particles of language in the next chapter). Yet Kirlian auras notwithstanding, our mind does not emit thought "particles" that can operate in inanimate matter without involving our bones, tendons, and muscles.

It is true that in physics there are well-known fields whose associated particle has not yet been captured by experimentalists. The most obvious one is gravity, whose putative carrier—the shy graviton—is still eluding cosmologists and physicists.

However, gravity itself and gravitational waves are well documented. In the case of psychokinesis, there isn't even a shred of evidence to substantiate a single occurrence. An undocumented phenomenon, without a resulting field and with an unobservable particle, clearly falls under the faith category. Carl Sagan put it eloquently in his book *The Demon-Haunted World* when he compared such concepts to someone's insistence that there's a dragon in his garage—except that the dragon is completely undetectable even with the most sophisticated equipment.

Psychokinesis in *Star Trek* is generally an arbitrary event, literally a whim of the gods—or powerful aliens, which is the same thing. However, in one interesting episode ("Plato's Stepchildren," TOS), mental control over matter is neither inherited nor bestowed, but instead dependent on the environment. Kironide, a substance specific to one planet, allows expression of latent human psi powers by interacting with pituitary growth hormone. The sole person lacking such powers is an achondroplastic dwarf. Perhaps we should search for kironide in the soil of Maine.

At least *Star Trek* got the biological part of its science right in that particular episode. Dwarfism of all types results from lack of growth hormone. The episode also wore its opinion on its sleeve about heredity versus environment.

By making most telekinetic manifestations equivalent to miracles, *Star Trek* has evaluated them correctly. The series' creators wisely refrained from getting too involved in mental hold over matter. If only they had shown equal restraint about the thought-sending and thought-receiving capabilities.

THE SWORD AND THE CHALICE

In contrast to its caution on psychokinesis, *Star Trek* apparently considers telepathy and clairvoyance a domain potentially open to all. However, this ease of admission to the telepathic club brings along its own set of troubles.

Telepathy and empathy seem to have been apportioned arbitrarily within the humanoid races of *Star Trek,* once again showcasing the oddity of their interbreeding. Mixed humanoid hybrids always exhibit ESP if one parent has it. This inheritance pattern implies that such capacities are not merely genetic, but dominant.

That brings me up against the first biological bump. If ESP capabilities are inherited as simple Mendelian traits (that is, in yes-or-no "quantum" fashion), they must be the product of a single gene. No such gene, real or latent, has been found in any terrestrial life-form, and certainly not in humans.

Of course, we don't know the entire text of the human genome—although we will soon enough, when the Human Genome Project has been completed. Nevertheless, a single gene with such an obvious phenotype would not have remained hidden for long. We're not talking subtle shadings here; it would be equivalent to someone showing up with wings.

But let's assume that the telepathy or empathy gene is as elusive as the graviton (it certainly seems to require as high an energy input to manifest itself). If telepathy and empathy are biological traits that affect the workings of the brain, they must have a neurological underpinning.

However, the recent PET, MRI, and CAT technologies, which allow us to observe the brain as it works, have uncovered no hidden power sources or fairy circles within our brains. What is there is marvelous, certainly, but it doesn't include mind reading of the sort that Lwaxana Troi indulges in.

Telepathy, the active transmission of thoughts, additionally falls under a shadow similar to the one lengthening over psychokinesis. Namely, as action at a distance, it must have a carrier particle. And this requirement will cause us, willy-nilly, to make the acquaintance of psychons. I am *not* making this term up. Such a particle has been theorized. Next we'll be treated to free-radical thought-provokers that inspire musical improvisation: cadenzons and jazzons.

Sir John Eccles, otherwise a renowned neurobiologist and a Nobel Prize winner, thought up the psychons. His theory postulates that concepts are "frozen" in the brain like whorls in petrified wood. Various ideas, thoughts, memories, are stored as synaptic connections. Specifically, they are stored as configurations in the dendrites, the neuron extensions that receive input—hence the term *dendron.*

Well, you ask, isn't that what you described as long-term memory? I did indeed, and I have no trouble with that part of the theory. It's the next part that leaves my dendrons unmoved, to put it mildly. Sir John next suggested that whenever a mental event occurs—that is, whenever a given dendron shakes its branches—it emits an elementary particle: a psychon. Thus, the psychon is the postulated thought unit. Consciousness supposedly arises from psychon interactions.

What we have here once again is dualism camouflaged under a fancy name. My kingdom for another paradigm! What poverty have the monotheistic religions wreaked upon our imaginations? Instead of brain and mind or body and soul, we now have dendrons and psychons.

Dualism springs eternal in human thinking and science. Recently, a younger sibling of the psychon, the meme, has been making the rounds as the latest attempt to separate the brain from the mind (we'll meet it in the next chapter). I must admit, though, that it's a pity that there's zero evidence for psychons: they are obviously tailor-made to allow telepathy.

What about empathy, the passive reception of thought? The more extended flights of fancy, in which Counselor Troi "feels" someone's aura at a distance (or when Obi Wan Kenobi doubles over in pain when the Death Star obliterates a planet), are impossible, unless the event that the empath feels has been perceived by conventional senses.

Yet empathy is actually possible at "one remove"—when it happens within an individual brain. In that sense, empathy is extrapolation of knowledge of a person or a situation, the classical "putting yourself in someone else's shoes." In fact, empathy in its broader definition of uncanny understanding—such as the astonishing environmental knowledge of pretechnological societies or the uncanny solicitousness of geishas—is often gained by painstaking apprenticeship and constitutes a powerful survival tactic. As such, it is the preferred tool of people who are not masters but either partners or subordinates.

That is why empathy is traditionally a feminine attribute and why, in that respect, Deanna Troi is a rather pernicious stereotype. *Star Trek* unwittingly reinforces this view in "The Perfect Mate" (TNG), which showcases an "empathic metamorph." This is a life-form programmed to register the fantasies of her chosen mate and mold herself mentally to his desires. We're told that male versions of this exist, but we never see them. To make matters worse, she is being traded as a peace offering, much like the slave Chryseis in the *Iliad*.

Perhaps I should order one of these "empathic metamorphs" by mail catalog. But then again, I dedicated a considerable chunk of chapter 3 to explaining that shape-shifting is impossible, let alone continuous rearrangement of brain circuits to keep up with someone else's desires. Hoisted with my own petard.

Beyond molecular concubinage, another physically impossible thing happens routinely to *Star Trek* empaths—and less frequently, to its telepaths. It is what I call "acquisition of stigmata"; that is, physical effects of thought reception.

Naturally, thoughts alter our brain circuits and can affect our actions. However, thoughts, no matter how hostile or powerful, cannot cause wounds by themselves (as seen in "The Empath," TOS, "Dark Page," TNG, and "Cold Fire," VOY). If that were the case, humanity would solve its overpopulation problem overnight; I wouldn't have any enemies or competitors left; and we'd be back into the days of the Old West, with mindslingers strutting their stuff and taunting those slower on the mental draw.

For good or ill, this will never come to pass. The healing touch will remain metaphorical. Negative emotions may affect our hormones, may even suppress our immune system—and thus weaken our capillary vessels and break our bones indirectly by making them brittle. But that's the extent of their control over matter, and you will note that once again it's not action at a distance.

I realize that in dealing with psionic abilities I enter into questions of faith. Faith cannot be challenged or changed by experimental proof. What I can say is that, if we measure by biological metrics, it looks dim for most ESP manifestations. Does any unconventional mental *Star Trek* activity pass biological inspection?

I FEEL YOUR PAIN!

In *Star Trek*, the most famous special case of ESP is, of course, the Vulcan mind-meld. What is particularly intriguing about it is that it shares characteristics of both empathy and telepathy, making it the other side of the coin to the Vulcans' suppression of emotion.

Of all the psionic manifestations, the Vulcan mind-meld is actually the likeliest for the simplest of reasons: like faith healing, it requires the laying on of hands. We're back to action by contact. Thus, if the initiator of the contact is capable of sensing the neuronal transmission flux or hormonal status of the person s/he is touching and can translate that into her/his thoughts, mind-meld has been achieved.

Could fingertips be attuned to molecular fluxes? That sounds outlandish, but we find many peculiar sensors within the terrestrial animal kingdom. For example, some bacteria can sense magnetic fields by virtue of iron-containing particles in their cytoplasm. Nevertheless, the requirements of a meld are a tall order. Such sensitivity of the fingertips would interfere with daily activities.

Imagine your genitals are at the tips of your fingers. Now visualize picking up a hot cup of coffee with them. Now imagine that sensitivity cubed. Okay, you can stop screaming! The traditional musicians' worry over their hands would be trivial compared to those of the melder.

Also, how can the melder control what thoughts to send or receive? And how many of these thoughts are firmly ensconced in the mind being read, rather than evanescent impressions, not yet cataloged or evaluated? People who edit the diaries of famous people invariably comment on how chaotic they are. Diaries would actually look like models of orderliness next to the attics of our minds with their thoughts at various stages of sorting.

If the melder wants to register hormone levels at the source, that's a tough assignment. The parts of the brain that regulate hormonal flux (thalamus, hypothalamus, pituitary, amygdala) are deeply buried under the cortex. The cortical layer itself, where thoughts usually course, is more accessible. It's close to the skull, a thin veneer over the brain mass. However, as I must have said one time too many, thoughts are not localized in one particular brain area. The melder is more likely to receive a cacophony of signals, like the sound of a gull rookery.

This, incidentally, is also true of reading thoughts at a distance. *Star Trek* has actually shown this, although only extraordinarily gifted or poorly trained espers suffer from sensory overload. In "Tin Man" (TNG), the Betazoid Tam Elbrun regularly wilts under the barrage of thoughts from the people around him, until he finds the equivalent of a soundproof room in Gomtuu.

There are two ways to filter the white noise of our thoughts, and our brain uses them both. We weigh our thoughts—usually—before we open our mouths. Language, a directed, collimated beam rather than a general emitter, is an effective filter for focusing the mind. *Star Trek* has caught on to this, and at least one episode has shown telepathic species trying to learn conventional language ("Dark Page," TNG). I can easily see why. By its sheer diffuseness and lack of selectivity, telepathy can cause a headache both literally and metaphorically.

The brain also discriminates between thoughts by choosing which ones to select for long-term memory. Since memory acts as another filter, perhaps a melder can get a satisfactory picture by strictly accessing memory.

As I mentioned in chapter 4, memory is one of the few functions of the brain for which a computer analogy is valid. We can do a one-to-one mapping: instant information is buffer, short-term memory is RAM (random access), long-term memory is the hard disk. Short-term memory is in the hippocampus and is probably in chemical form. Long-term memory is in the cortex, most likely in the form of specific configurations of synaptic connections.

So if we go by accessibility, it seems that long-term memory is literally closest at hand. That bodes well for the melders, since this is memory that has been inspected and approved for long-term storage. But even after such approval, human memory is not completely reliable.

The brain is not an infallible machine. For one thing, it has inherent limitations. That is a natural outcome of its evolutionary path. For example, we don't grasp statistical arguments very well (hence we keep driving cars, while being afraid of airplanes). Nor do we easily absorb concepts that run counter to our senses.

The particular wiring of our brain is in fact pertinent to our acceptance of paranormal "phenomena." We'll undoubtedly remember the time that someone called when we were thinking about them. We conveniently tend to forget the countless times that the phone *didn't* ring when we thought it might.

Human memory is a good but imperfect tool. Just interview three eyewitnesses to the same event. Our mind is very good at filling the gaps, whether they occur in a pixelated picture or a sequence of events, and it doesn't much care whether the filler is true or false. It's also good at seeing patterns even when none are there—shapes in the clouds, a meaningful pressure on the hand by an autistic child. The latter led to the heartbreaking facilitator fallacy, in which people directed the hands of autistic children toward the desired words on keyboards. When the testers ensured that the facilitators couldn't see what the autistic children were seeing, the responses of the children became random. The mind of the facilitators provided the crucial missing link between the picture shown and the pressure of the child's hand.

In times of stress, the brain filter gets even more porous. In the previous chapter, I described the outcome of stress and sensory deprivation—hallucinations, out-of-body experiences. Memory can throw a monkey wrench, too, in the form of false recollections: déjà vu and so-called recovered memories. Electrode probes in people about to undergo brain surgery can strongly evoke both of the latter phenomena.

Also, people susceptible to seizures (including several canonized saints) have invariably reported significantly larger numbers of visions and out-of-body experiences. The connection between epilepsy and visions was well recognized in the ancient world. Epileptics, "God-touched," were often used as oracles. This indicates that many instances of paranormal phenomena do in fact happen, but only within a person's brain—as misfiring of neurons. Finally, both age and its associated diseases erode memory in inverse order of acquisition—short-term first, then long-term.

So a melder will get as good a picture as the brain under her/his hands can project. Therefore, melding is a bad tool for acquiring knowledge, although an acceptable way of getting general impressions.

There is one other interesting analogy between mind-melding, memory, and the computer. *The Star Trek Encyclopedia* informs me that mind-melding works by "synaptic displacement," which involves the re-creation of a virtual representation of the person being probed in the melder's mind.

This sounds exactly like the various software programs that allow communication across hardware platforms (SoftPC, for example). Anyone who has tried those knows how fragile and cumbersome they are, giving us a good idea of the quality of service we can expect from the mind-meld. The need to re-create a whole other mind also explains why telepaths can sometimes be drained practically to death, something that happens in "Second Sight" (DS9).

So the mind-meld is a mixed blessing even among very like minds. Moreover, the mind-meld labors under one more major limitation. There must be substantial similarity between the neuronal wiring of the two communicating individuals, so that the initiator can "map" the input onto known thought patterns.

Hence I consider it highly unlikely that Spock can achieve a productive mind-meld with the Horta in "Devil in the Dark" (TOS). A human or humanoid would be as able to read the thoughts of a non-carbon-based life-form as the universal translator would be to understand its language. The failure of Picard to achieve meld with the energy cloud in "Lonely Among Us" (TNG) and the troubles that Troi has with the telepathic aliens in "Night Terrors" (TNG) confirm this estimate—at least in the *Star Trek* universe.

Still, science fiction likes to pose the question, *What if telepathy were possible?* Well, even if it were, it would still trail huge streamers of problems.

THERE OUGHT TO BE A LAW

The various physical and biological problems with sending and receiving thoughts are obvious and thorny enough. However, such troubles pale before the ethical dilemmas that ESP capabilities would create. The most obvious problems are mind control and the use of such abilities as weapons of destruction.

Since telepaths send thoughts, they can literally invade a mind. By either projecting their own memories or suppressing memories that they find, they can alter the memories—and thus the personality—of the mind they're accessing. This happens in *Star Trek*. In "Remember" (VOY), B'Elanna Torres is implanted with someone else's memories—a convenient receptacle for safekeeping memories that the original bearer did not want extinguished.

In a variant of this, the mediator Riva in "Loud as a Whisper" (TNG) employs a chorus. Each member receives and then transmits one aspect of his personality. I consider such transmission unlikely, since the scientific evidence shows that the high-brain functions cannot be disentangled in this manner. Nevertheless, I wonder if the chorus members like being used literally as mouthpieces, mental equivalents to the Trill host.

At least in these two cases the long-range motives are defensible. Something much more frightening and repulsive happens in "Man of the People" (TNG). In that episode, we discover that Alkar, a highly gifted diplomat, has achieved his professional distinction by channeling his negative emotions into others. Those privileged to receive these emotions become violently unpleasant, age rapidly, and die. This is highly reminiscent of Oscar Wilde's *Picture of Dorian Gray*, except that Alkar uses live people as receptacles—actually, to use the correct word, as toilets.

Which brings us to a related but specific problem with telepathy. If used improperly, it can result in the psychic equivalent of rape. *Star Trek* is too savvy not to have made this connection. In "Violations" (TNG) it shows a literal interpretation of this possibility, by having a telepath rape people in their dreams.

The point is sharpened in the encounter between Ensign Suder and Lieutenant Tuvok in "Meld" (VOY). This time, the violation is amplified by multiple mirrors. There is, of course, the vast difference in rank. Also, Suder is Betazoid, an empath, so he is playing the "passive" part to Tuvok's "active" one.

Finally, whereas Tuvok is a Starfleet officer, Suder is a member of the Maquis, the downtrodden rebel group suffering neglect and harassment at the Cardassian border. Therefore, the encounter unintentionally shows the power layers within the nominally classless Federation (of which more in chapter 11). Rape has always been the prerogative of conquerors or of the ruling class, from the medieval droit du seigneur to the calculated rapes that establish prison hierarchies or that invading armies inflict on the women of the vanquished.

In *The Undiscovered Country* (ST6) we run across the most jarring abuse of ESP powers, jarring because it is performed by a highly respected figure. Spock forces a meld on Valeris, his protégée, when he concludes that she has betrayed the Federation.

With such a protector, who needs enemies? Captain Janeway shows more consideration to the Holodoc, a mere program, than Spock shows to a fellow Vulcan. Worse yet, he is not deemed lesser by that action. Perhaps the lessons he has to teach the Romulans in "Unification" (TNG) are not all sweetness and light, after all. Telepathic powers combined with the Vulcan emotional detachment create a potential for lethal abuse.

Being scrupulous about privacy, *Star Trek* has placed limits on how much someone's mind can be read without permission. Races whose telepathy makes them dangerous have been declared off-limits (the Talosians in "Menagerie," TOS).

In this, the series has fallen in line with prevailing tradition. In *Babylon 5, Star Trek*'s main rival, the Telepath Guild is under harsh strictures not to exceed its very specific mandate. Similar restrictions apply to psionic guilds wherever they are encountered in science fiction literature.

Moral strictures also prevail in *Star Wars*, where Jedi knights are exhorted to harness their telepathic and telekinetic powers to benign uses. As Q would say, how boring. If all Jedi had adhered to the code, we'd have been deprived of Darth Vader, the most interesting character in the trilogy. Actually, come to think of it, we'd have been deprived of the trilogy itself. No Dark Side, no conflict, no Lucas franchise.

The dastardly behavior of Darth Vader brings us to the second major problem of ESP misuse—psionic powers as weapons.

It seems that lack of empirical evidence for ESP capabilities is not a barrier for the Department of Defense, the most active and well-funded speculator into events paranormal. If you can call it research, there is a history of Pentagon-funded inquiry into the psionic powers in institutes as orthodox and prestigious as Princeton, Stanford, and Los Alamos.

Starting after World War II, the Department of Defense put a good deal of money into the paranormal branches. Apparently, the United States had to bridge a psychic gap, in addition to the nuclear one. "Sensitives" have tried to locate Soviet submarines by clairvoyance or to mess up their electronics with telepathy.

John B. Alexander, the ex-director of the Los Alamos division of Non-Lethal (or Less-than-Lethal) Weapons, is a believer in the paranormal and has been an enthusiastic participant in spoon-bending parties. He also believes that at some point we will send out a psionic warrior to face our enemies, a combination of John Rambo and Luke Skywalker—

another incarnation of the golem or Majin, the Japanese equivalent. Before you start chuckling, you might want to know that this soldier of the future has already been assigned an official name: Jedi knight.

The convergence of Less-than-Lethal Weapons and ESP makes a twisted amount of sense, since several of the former are action at a distance. Through our sensory system we are vulnerable to invasions not only by putative telepaths but by energy emissions as well—infrasound, microwave, laser. All developed countries have tested and deployed such lovely additions to their arsenal as sonic bullets, ultra-low-frequency and high-intensity sound emitters, or tasers (long-range pulse-shock emitters).

Such emissions mostly fly under the radar of our conventional senses, but do affect the pattern of neuron firing, cellular structure, and chromosomal integrity—and in fact may be the basis for Romulan disruptors and both the stun and kill settings of *Star Trek* phasers. Many of the electromagnetic weapons I listed earlier have actually been used for riot control against the civilians of the country that developed the weapons.

You can sense some effects of subsonics (ultra-low-frequency sound) in rock concerts, in which the thrumming can result in nausea and dizziness. I use sonic disruptors routinely in my experiments to homogenize tissue, i.e., break down all super- and infrastructure into a "soup." Noise in general, by virtue of being distracting, can actually prevent formation of short-term memories (ask anyone with a teenager or a new baby).

Lasers can burn neat holes in retinas—or in muscle, if left focused on one area long enough. And microwaves cook tissue as effectively, and much faster, than conventional infrared. I guess the classification of "Less-than-Lethal" must be considered linguistic license, similar to calling the neutron bomb "clean." And I assume that the ESP weapons, if they ever descend upon us, will be used not just to foul up tanks and submarines, but also to produce torture-proof operatives or for populace "pacification."

However, I'm not unduly worried about this particular eventuality, for the simple reason that I've already stated: evidence for ESP is zero. Given that fact, perhaps use of money to play with harmless theories and toys is better than creating real weapons. I doubt that the military will ever be able to use "amplified" telepathic powers as "focused" weapons—an outcome predicted by John Alexander and shown in "Gambit" and "The Battle" (TNG).

So although you see Spock communing via mind-meld and Troi reading emotions at long range on *Star Trek*, you won't see any of this in our future.

PSIONICS: SCIENCE FICTION OR SITUATION COMEDY?

Let's face it. Looking for the basis of psionics in the hard sciences is like trying to explain a leprechaun sighting with a microscope. Given the billions that General Alexander of the Non-Lethal Weapons Division had to throw into psionics, if there were anything to it, Qaddafi and Hussein would be gone. They'd be dispatched by unkind thoughts directed at them by psi-warriors fighting for freedom in their BarcaLoungers at an ultrasecret psi fortress.

If there is a basis for psionic events, it can best be examined by the softer social sciences. John Mack of Harvard University has been roundly vilified for recording the reports of people who claimed to have been kidnapped by UFO occupants. I don't endorse his research. However, his findings on the fantasies of suggestible people are a bellwether of our times, a social barometer if you will.

We humans react strongly to the idea of sharing our bodies and our brains. The possibility of having our minds remotely scrutinized is a source of even greater anxiety and has given rise to countless conspiracy theories—witness the perennial popularity of films such as *The Manchurian Candidate.* Given the power and ubiquity of information technologies, what's on our mind is the last province of privacy, although modeling systems will soon be able to predict our desires, a sort of derivative mind reading. Our only defense then will be to lie to market researchers or live in a tree house.

On the other hand, we would not object if our mind enabled us to accomplish physical deeds, unaided by either brute strength or the crutch of technology. We have little control left in our lives. We're as tightly stuck to hectic schedules and encroaching hardware as insects in a web.

Belief in the paranormal tends to surge whenever we humans feel uneasy with our technology. It is not coincidental that séance salons bloomed at the same time that the Victorian mills belched smoke and child labor was prevalent. We see a similar increase of so-called New Age maxims in our times, when people are preoccupied with the increasingly frenetic pace of life and have grown disillusioned about the powers—or the benevolence—of technology. However, people who believe in these phenomena are on as safe a physical footing as Wile E. Coyote when he walks on air. Like all victims of deception, he ends up splattered on a canyon floor.

I don't remember seeing all these palmists and psychics when I came to the States in the 1970s. In the past four or five years, they've sprouted everywhere, even in relatively sophisticated locales with skeptical, inquiring populations such as Cambridge. I can walk to two "psychic advisers" from my own house. I blame the coming turn of the millennium, of course, the latest of many artificially manufactured hysterias.

Star Trek, by its blanket credulousness toward ESP, has not aided the cause of science. There are so many real wonders in the universe that the series does not need to recycle old *Bewitched* scripts. In this, *Star Trek* is definitely treading where many have gone before—and with a much flimsier excuse.

SCENE 8.
ROSETTA STONES AND BLACK MONOLITHS

Can a Universal Translator Function?

"Ich bin ein Berliner," John F. Kennedy triumphantly announced to West Berlin in 1963. No doubt, Kennedy's handlers, hearing the roars from the assembled throng, thought the young president had charmed the Germans. But neither he nor they had any sense of the context of the language he was abusing on that historic occasion. Had they listened closely, they might have heard some well-bred guffaws escaping the crowd. After all, they had just heard the leader of the free world proclaiming that he was a jelly doughnut.

This episode illustrates the challenges that technology, no matter how advanced, confronts when facing the task of translating languages. Language is both a medium and a process. More importantly, language is an artifact of culture and experience that gives mere words—discrete sounds or symbols—the delicious fullness of their meanings.

Thus, the universal translator, which mediates dialogue between our *Star Trek* heroes and their various allies and enemies, has abilities that border on omniscience. Its capacity to read minds is not just scientifically debatable but also constitutes a serious breach of ethics—it invades privacy.

To support this observation, I would like to introduce you to one of the most contentious questions in the biological and behavioral sciences: *From where does language arise?* Given the serendipity of events that conspired to give us uppity bipeds the ability to communicate with shared syntax, grammar, and words, we can only stand in awe—or in sneering skepticism—before the universal translator. This, after all, is a machine that not only reads the electrical activity in our brains, but also knows where to look for it in brains it has never before encountered. It then goes even further by instantly turning those impulses into stilted dialogue.

So let's delve a bit more deeply into the origins of this extraordinary capacity of ours, which has made us so different from all other animals.

HOMO LOCUTUS?

Spoken language is one of the few characteristics that distinguishes us humans from other advanced mammals, including our ape cousins. Chimpanzees have a repertoire of about thirty-six sounds, which make up not merely their entire vocal cache but also their entire vocabulary. Human phonemes are not infinite either, but a well-educated human can have a vocabulary of one hundred thousand words.

When did this differentiation occur? Something changed during the ice ages, at the same time when our cerebral cortex was expanding and our frontal lobe pushing forward. We don't know yet what happened, or how. We're fairly certain, however, that spoken language only sprang up among the Cro-Magnons, a.k.a. *Homo sapiens.* The Neanderthals had culture by any other standards: they used tools, they adorned and buried their dead, they probably played music. But reconstructions of Neanderthal faces by Philip Lieberman of Brown University show that their larynx and vocal cords were not up to the task of clear articulation.

The question of whether language promoted consciousness or vice versa is still a hotly debated topic. Sharing and transmission of experience does not require language, but having a language makes it easier to form such a collective knowledge pool. Language helps to group information in chunks. This "chunking" results in two positive feedback loops: it increases information storage capacity as well as speed of information transmission.

In recent years, language has been used as a substitute for other qualities once considered uniquely human, such as use of tools, manufacture of tools, cooperative relationships, female orgasm, face-to-face sex, self-awareness, etc. Like any self-respecting explicator of consciousness, language must account for the "neural energy" (soul) posited by the dualists, who insist that the mind is separate from the brain. The soul substitute that has been ascribed to language is called the meme.

The meme theory has been primarily advanced by Richard Dawkins of Oxford University, who also invented the concept of the selfish gene, and has been further elaborated by Daniel Dennett of Tufts University. A meme can be a cliché, a joke, a commercial ditty, a proverb, a mental image (think sound bites). The meme is supposed to be to consciousness what the gene is to evolution.

Memes are thought to be colonizing informational "viruses" (or symbionts), which have taken up their abode in the human mind, granting us language. In return they roam our minds, competing against each other for propagation during both wakefulness and sleep. The concept of the meme as a mind virus was widely popularized in Neal Stephenson's seminal novel *Snow Crash*. *Star Trek* has obviously been keeping up on its fad science reading, since it uses the concept of a virus that mimics memory engrams in "Flashback" (VOY).

How does Dawkins visualize the correspondence between memes and genes? In his book *The Selfish Gene* he postulates that bodies are mere vessels for their genetic programs. The genes are defined as inexorable entities that wish to propagate and outcompete rivals and have chosen DNA as their replicator. In the extension of this theory to consciousness, memes are "mental entities," minds (or neural connections of varying strengths) are the vehicles—and language is the replicator. So in equivalence to our gene pool, the accumulated nongenetic knowledge of humanity represents our "meme pool."

Heady stuff, but like bubbles in champagne, it subsides quickly. The idea of the meme is about as subject to dis/proof as the anthropic principle that I briefly tackled in the prologue, and for similar reasons. The concept is yet another continuation of the dualistic thinking that has both helped and blinkered Western thinking for the last four millennia.

Dualism is as old as the Zoroastrian religion, with the opposing moral poles of benign Ahura Masda and evil Ahriman, but just like any other reductionist approach, it has its limits. In previous centuries we had the head versus the heart, woman/nature versus man/culture, brain versus body, then brain versus mind. Now that the brain seems to create the mind, rather than passively contain it, along comes the meme to fill the "neural energy" gap.

Analogies are fruitful ways to visualize difficult concepts, but sometimes they go too far. There is no question that ideas (and languages, or even words within a language) evolve and compete, in what can be considered Darwinian fashion. It's also true that ideas and mental concepts require the correct environment in which to flourish. However, language is not a viral parasite.

Viruses exist in computer networks just as they exist in organic hosts, true, but wherever we find them, they are still physical entities. And if memes are indeed viruses or viroids (virus precursors), they must follow the rules of evolution. That is, they must have a precursor—and one still with us, since the human jump to language happened rather recently.

Where is that precursor in apes? I am even willing to accept a precursor that is executing a different function, just at the verge of switching (this "switching" phenomenon is now commonly accepted in evolution and explains how specialized organs evolved, such as the mammalian eye). Yet the meme viroid precursor has been more elusive than the Scarlet Pimpernel.

Lastly, the entity/replicator split is as valid and as productive as the medieval hairsplitting over whether the Holy Ghost emanated only from the Father, as the Orthodox believe, or from both the Father and the Son, as the Catholics believe. Our genes do not "use" DNA as a replicator, unless we consider genes an abstract idea. DNA *is* the genes, just as our brain *is* our mind. Dividing mind from brain is like separating an elementary particle into discrete matter and energy "halves."

Language is not an interloper that has invaded us; it has evolved in us and is an inextricable part of our brain circuitry.

THE HAUNTS OF THE BEASTIE

I've have been talking of localized and diffuse brain activities throughout the last four chapters. Language is one of the few high functions of the brain that has a dedicated decoding location. Actually, there are two way stations, both in the left hemisphere. Wernicke's area initially unscrambles the received code in Scotty's brain when Kirk asks for more power. Broca's area is what Scotty uses to respond, "Cap'n! The engines canna take any more!"

Both these areas are roughly above our left ear, close to the top of the skull. Between the two, a brand-new dedicated area has winked into existence in the last few millennia: the reading center, which decodes written language.

People who have sustained damage in Broca's area understand speech but in return can only produce "telegraphese"—short, disconnected bursts of words. In contrast, those with damage to Wernicke's area bring forth mellifluous, articulate nonsense. When the personnel of Deep Space 9 succumb to the aphasia virus in "Babel," the symptoms are characteristic of an affront to Wernicke's area.

There are no equivalent areas in the right brain hemisphere, which is in charge (broadly) of visual and spatial relationships—gestalts, patterns. Unexpectedly, brain scientists discovered that deaf people fluent in sign language process it in their left hemisphere, though that language involves spatial and visual recognition. Also, whereas amateur musicians delegate music analysis to their right hemispheres, professional musicians do it with their left, mostly in the language centers. The implication is strong that language per se is in a category of its own regardless of its medium.

Language decoding is localized, but language encoding is diffuse. Stimulate Broca's or Wernicke's area, and you don't get a torrent of words.

Language generation is somewhere else—or everywhere, as seems to be true with most high-brain functions. And to make it all even harder to unravel, native language paths are different from those carved by any language learned later in life.

How does all this relate to the words that *Star Trek* writers process onto their scripts?

SCALPEL OR HAMMER?

Mother language, learned language—it doesn't matter in *Star Trek*. Impatient with the niceties and plot longueurs that would result from real language decryption, the series has once again opted for an easy solution, postulating a device that takes care of translation needs across all species.

Of course, there are a few stubborn species—such as the insectoid Jaradans in "The Big Goodbye" (TNG)—who hold out for the real thing: they demand greetings in their own language and exact perfect delivery, too. Everyone else has bowed to homogenization. The ploy of the universal translator gets the plot going, all right, only to create troubles of its own, like an iatrogenic (doctor-caused) disease.

In "Metamorphosis" (TOS), Kirk uses a handheld translating machine to talk to the Companion, which is realistic enough. In subsequent series, the machine (or implant or body modification) is taken for granted. It is never shown or discussed, except in the case of Quark, the Ferengi bartender and black marketeer who wears it in his ear (DS9). The canonical explanation for the gizmo is that it registers brain waves, compares them with its menu of known brain signals, and then chooses comparable concepts as a basis for translation.

Where does the translator live? In most episodes it is apparently incorporated into the starship computers, a practical move. Yet when alien species meet our heroes on a planetary surface, outside the protective shell of a starship, they still understand each other perfectly (selected examples are "A Private Little War," TOS; "Darmok," TNG; "Rocks and Shoals," DS9).

There is one notable exception: in "Arena" (TOS), Kirk and his Gorn antagonist have to resort to clumsy handheld machines, which makes their plight concrete and immediate. So in face-to-face encounters we must be dealing with some kind of implant. This opens the floodgates of both the dubious and the objectionable.

Language translation issues would be more plausible if *Star Trek* showed initial lags upon encounters with new species, then less hesitation and fewer errors over time as the translator sorted out the patterns of the new language. That never happens. There is no time lag at all between the alien utterance and its translation, even on first contact (examples are "Pen Pals," TNG, in which Data communicates with an alien girl *by radio;* and all the Human/non-Human interactions in VOY that are de facto first contacts, since Terrans have never been in the Delta Quadrant before).

Now, I'm totally bilingual in English and Greek, but even I sometimes stumble slightly during transition between the two languages—and transposing two completely familiar languages in your head is as close to instant transmission as you can get.

The closer we look, the odder things get. The starship computers recognize all voices instantly, just as they instantly recognize and analyze all life-forms. The sentences come out in fluent, idiomatic English. Moreover, the translator seems to have no trouble at all sifting out extraneous thoughts and only conveying the pertinent ones. This sounds like the mechanism of selective attention—in which case we are dealing with much more than language.

Even if we assume that the translator is incorporated into the starship computers, this is getting a bit too close to magic for comfort. For one thing, I mentioned in chapter 3 that, in fact, voice recognition is a serious and consistent problem with computers. For another, even with nanotechnology, there should still be a lag between the original words and their translation. A universal translator, regardless of its programming, could not go through all possible permutations fast enough to generate instantly comprehensible patterns, even if it went through decision forks (for example, classification of the alien language by phonemes) rather than linear exclusion of alternatives.

Worse yet, I cannot remember the universal translator *ever* making a mistake, large or small. For dramatic tension, *Star Trek* has milked malfunctions of either the transporter or the holodeck for all they are worth and then some, as we discovered in chapters 4 and 5. But it has completely ignored the mayhem that would ensue from malfunctions in the universal translator.

An accidental or deliberate mistranslation during important treaty negotiations—what plot twist could be juicier? I can just imagine the exchange between the Federation and a race fastidious about bodily functions. The Federation representative: "Live long and prosper." The universal translator (chuckling to itself): "Fart long and loudly." The result? Chaos, galaxy-wide war, and Nielsen ratings right through the stratosphere.

If the translator is embedded in the ships' computers, it should be affected as often and as much as the rest of the components, but it seems miraculously exempt. Furthermore, problems arising from failure of the universal translator would be quite realistic plot engines, because fatal misunderstandings have occurred routinely during first meetings of cultures here in our own Terran backyard.

However, these are nitpicks compared to the central issue: How does the translator really work? One way that will not stretch credibility is if it acts as a one-to-one word mapping—in other words, a dictionary. Yet we know it's more than that because not only is the translation perfectly idiomatic, but it also carries the speaker's mood and attitude.

I must therefore conclude that we're dealing with a thought-reading device. Reflect on this one second and you see that we have just opened a large and malodorous can of interstellar worms.

If I had to evaluate the Federation's politics, I'd cautiously classify them as libertarian liberal. The Federation values individuals almost to excess, often at the expense of the collective good (the *Enterprise* has endangered itself countless times to rescue a single missing crew member). Members of the Federation frown on cloning and coercion and are fervent believers in free will. They are queasy about integrity of consciousness and go to extreme lengths to safeguard it from any intrusion, whether physical (extensive prostheses) or mental (telepathic invasions).

Yet all members of the Federation tolerate—no, actually calmly and constantly use—a device that has such invasive potential that the Borg assimilation techniques would wilt before it. At least the Borg are upfront about what they are doing; the universal translator is mind-scanning cloaked in the clothing of brotherly understanding.

You might ask, what is the fuss about? Didn't you just say that language decoding is localized? The universal translator simply needs to access the Broca and Wernicke areas, or the equivalent areas of a nonhuman sophont (a wonderfully expressive word, coined by Poul Anderson, that carries the connotation of wisdom on its Greek root).

That would work if the translator were just a dictionary, but it's not. Since the translator conveys not merely the content but the context of the speech as well—tone, mood—it must be accessing the rest of the mind/brain, not merely the connections and thoughts associated specifically with language. In that case, it is committing a grave breach of ethics, regardless of the motives of its makers.

The near-infallible mind reading of the universal translator ushers in a few other difficulties. If it is so good at reading minds, we could forgo all courtroom dramatics in *Star Trek* and most equipment crises as well. Since the translator can filter thoughts effectively, it is the ideal focusing device for starship control panels, which routinely respond to voice commands. There go half the episodes.

The translator also obviates the need for empaths or telepaths such as *Enterprise* counselor Deanna Troi. She is totally superfluous if the universal translator does a precision job of reading minds, because she is limited to fuzzy impressions of gestalt (on the other hand, I do concede that the universal translator doesn't slink around in low-cut, skintight . . . er, uniforms). In this connection, the Cairn species, which have chosen to learn spoken language after communicating only by image-oriented telepathy in "Dark Page" (TNG), need not have bothered—the translator can unhesitatingly turn their images into words.

Let us leave ethics and delve a little deeper into universality. If the universal translator is in fact accessing the speakers' brains, maybe it is already systematically malfunctioning, since what comes out of it is almost distressingly uniform. In *Star Trek,* everyone seems to share all the important concepts—even non-carbon-based forms (an extreme example is "Galaxy's Child," TNG, which endows an energy cloud with mammal-like maternal feelings). The diversity of mind-sets is less than that found in a small village, and the universal translator is almost an overkill: like the United Nations interpreters, it is presiding over essentially petty local disputes.

It is characteristic of *Star Trek* to give with one hand and take with the other, so to speak. First it goes too far in postulating interfertility among all its humanoid species. Typically, it then compensates for this daring by making them all speak essentially the same language. Even taking the universal translator into consideration, most life-forms encountered in *Star Trek* speak "humanese"—and a humanese suspiciously close to the mind-set of the West Coast, at that.

Star Trek has grown increasingly anthropocentric and anthropomorphic in its successive incarnations. This tendency has reached its apogee in VOY, which has obviously taken literally the bogus tale of galaxy-seeding ancestors told in "The Chase" (TNG) and has trumped it with its own, even worse version in "Tattoo" (VOY). That episode competes with *Close Encounters of the Third Kind* for smarminess and condescension, by postulating benevolent aliens who decided to bless an Amerindian tribe with the gift of language.

Yet even if we concede universal humanoid-like thoughts, we still run into road bumps. Language conveys a mind-set. If the mind-set is different enough, the same words may denote different meanings. Within the humanoid family, similar mind-sets are plausible—but only barely. We need only to consider the dreamtime of the Australian aboriginals or the nonlinear time concepts of several Amerindian cultures to realize how radically different worldviews can be within humanity alone, or, for that matter, a religious fundamentalist and an agnostic within the same culture.

In fact, an unusual episode ("Darmok," TNG) highlights how rocky communication can become when words are shared, but not concepts. The Tamarians in "Darmok" are humanoid, and that they think exclusively in extended metaphors still does not defeat the translator: the sentences that come out are perfectly recognizable, but the context is missing—almost like talking to someone with damage in Wernicke's area.

Another episode takes a different approach, but once again the problem is clearly a plot convenience: in "Sanctuary" (DS9) the universal translator has inexplicable trouble decoding the language of the humanoid Skrreeans, although their thought processes are obviously familiar once they are decoded.

Maybe the difficulty stems from their matriarchal organization; according to Freud, it is hard to know what women want—though the translator works fine for the Vulcans, Cardassians, and Bajorans, all of whom seem to have several matriarchal elements in their governing structures.

BEYOND THE FIELDS WE KNOW

If the universal translator works as shown in *Star Trek,* it needs to solve a few other physical problems. We mentioned in chapter 2 that even humanoids in *Star Trek* have their brains differently organized. The Vulcans and Betazoids have paranormal abilities, the Ferengi sport four cortical lobes, and the Trills must have special neural connections for symbionts. There is no guarantee that their language centers will coincide. On the other hand, if the translator has access to the entire mind/brain, this should not be much of an obstacle, since then it has the power to sort out the structures.

When facing a radically different species, even more fundamental difficulties rear their ugly heads. Language reflects the map of reality. In chapter 4, I discussed how our brains are constantly poised between chaos and stability. They need periodic reality checks against the world outside the body. This implies a very particular organization. If the universal translator works by comparing "brain waves," the creature on the other side of the linguistic divide must have a brain recognized as such by the translator. If we cannot make up our minds whether apes are intelligent, it is unlikely that either we or the universal translator will register the body language of a living rock.

In particular, the translator seems optimally geared to language that has evolved on Earth-like planets. I wonder if it would work at all for a "language" that has evolved in response to different dominant sensory input—or one emanating from a silicon life-form. In fact, our heroes don't even consider using the universal translator on the Horta in "The Devil in the Dark" (TOS). They immediately take the mind-melding route instead.

Even in our parochial planet, animal senses extend across the electromagnetic spectrum. Some insects can see in the near ultraviolet: what to us is a petal of unbroken color looks to them like a landing strip, with corridors and even flags clearly demarcated. Vipers can sense their prey by its infrared (heat) emissions. Cetaceans and bats sense their surroundings and locate their food with sound waves (echolocation). Electric eels and fireflies harness electricity and send out Morse signals to their species or stun their prey. And everything, from insects to mammals, emits scents, to mark territory or signal sexual receptivity.

With such variety just on one small planet, it is certain that the sensory apparatus of extraterrestrial life will not correspond to ours. Science fiction writers have had a field day describing such variations.

For beings whose senses are centered in bandwidths of the spectrum very different from ours (infrared, ultraviolet), or which are not carbon-based, the Rosetta Stone necessary for one-to-one mapping is absent; they will be unable to decipher either the plaques placed on *Pioneers 10* and *11* or the CDs placed in *Voyagers 1* and 2—though they might grok Chuck Berry, making all other intelligence tests redundant.

And although the wormhole entities have sent vision-inducing Orbs to Bajor in DS9, creatures of pure energy cannot communicate with material beings, because time collapses onto a point in their frame.

Captain Sisko almost loses the wormhole because he cannot explain the concepts of past and present to its inhabitants in "Emissary" (DS9). Neither translators nor telepathic connections seem to aid him. Paranormal abilities and the translator will be equally helpless when dealing with beings that truly live in less (on cosmic strings in "The Loss," TNG) or more (the Q Continuum, TNG) than four dimensions.

So what happens when words fail us?

SWAGGER AND STRUT

Communication does not begin and end with vocally expressed language. Even plants, traditionally considered insensate, have evolved sophisticated, high-density media for communication. By studying rapid changes of chemistry in leaves, botanists have discovered that certain trees are capable of warning each other of predators. If attacked by insects, the trees manufacture defense toxins, as well as send out a chemical alarm. Neighboring trees receive the alarm and begin to create the toxin in anticipation of the invading hordes. Plants also communicate to animals by shape or scent, especially when they want to attract pollinating insects.

Animals also have widely varied communication methods. The most complicated displays are reserved for the all-important business of attracting a mate and discouraging poaching of either mate or territory by rivals. Insects can court by scent, by sound (cicadas and crickets produce their song by rubbing their back wings or legs), or by electricity (fireflies). Birds, like medieval Provençal minstrels, use their song both to serenade their chosen mates and to defend their castle, the nest. Many male fish, birds, and mammals go to extremes of plumage or body appendages (tusks, antlers, manes). Throughout the animal kingdom, both sexes also go through elaborate courting rituals.

However, there are cases of communication that are not merely aids to propagation. Bees show their hivemates where to find pollen by an elaborate dance, which shows the direction, distance, and amount of the food source. Members of canine bands express their mood and position in their hierarchy by body posture, tail position, ear angles. Cetaceans communicate with all kinds of clicks and whistles, which graduate in length and complexity to the intricate laments of the great whales. And all mammals are capable of producing various sounds that are used either in mother/infant interactions or for cooperative fight-or-flight situations.

Especially in primates, face expressions and body gestures affect the quality of band life. Field and laboratory work with primates (led by Jane Goodall's seminal work on the Gombe chimpanzees) has shown that our ape cousins are as complicated in that respect as we are. Competition such as rank disputes, cooperation in food sharing and grooming, the feasibility of pursuing and wooing a potential mate, the nurturing and socializing of juveniles—all activities within the primate band are minutely calibrated from body language.

One of the most controversial and fascinating questions is whether apes are capable of communication similar to that of humans. Although the vocal apparatus of apes does not lend itself to spoken language, they can and do use sign. At least two chimpanzees, Kanzi and Lucy, not only mastered modified language—lexigrams and Ameslan, respectively—but also invented new words. The implication is strong that innate capacity for language is not a quantum leap: at least some requirements were laid down before the primates speciated into separate branches.

Nonverbal communication is limited in *Star Trek.* One reason is the scarcity of nonhumanoid fauna—in chapter 1, I lamented the paucity of either predator or prey in all the planets that we see. Another reason is the existence of paranormal abilities and of the universal translator, both of which obviate the need for subtle signals. Body language seems a lost art in *Star Trek,* which favors the rigid, full-frontal delivery stance of pharaonic Egyptian statues. TNG is particularly guilty of this. Throughout its first season, I wondered repeatedly and aloud if the whole crew was sedated.

However, body language occasionally helps prevent misunderstandings in *Star Trek.* Examples are the mutual backpedaling of Human and Horta to prevent each from damaging the other in "The Devil in the

Dark" (TOS), and the antiphonal hums of the *Enterprise* computer and the Crystalline Entity when they're establishing communication in "Silicon Avatar" (TNG). And of course, all humanoids in the series (especially the Romulans, the Klingons, the Cardassians, and the Kazon) are as adept at—and as prone to—verbal swaggering and posturing as Homeric heroes or samurai in early Kurosawa films.

Still, the comparative lack of body language is not the only missing component in *Star Trek* communications.

DOES ANYONE SPEAKA THE ENGLISH AROUND HERE?

One of the oddest things in *Star Trek* is that each planetary society that the Federation encounters, with or without help from the universal translator, seems to speak a single language (we'll get back to this in chapter 11). Such linguistic uniformity on Earth is always strictly local spatially and temporally. The prevalence of Latin in Europe, English in India, and Quechua in western South America resulted from forcible conquest. The dominance of Greek around the Mediterranean basin and Dutch in the Indonesian archipelago as linguae francae arose from trade superiority.

English seems to be the lingua franca of the Federation, to the exclusion of all others. Even Human crew members with different native languages never seem to meet compatriots, to exchange a few words in their mother tongue. Surely, the isolated human settlements encountered in the series are most likely to speak something other than English and would in fact be cultural depositories of lost languages. The Ekosians in "Patterns of Force" (TOS) should speak German if they have modeled their society after the Third Reich. The 4/892 civilization in "Bread and Circuses" (TOS) should converse in Latin if they are Romans in all other cultural aspects. And the Bringloidi in "Up the Long Ladder" (TNG) are obvious candidates for speaking Gaelic.

This *Star Trek* stance may well reflect humanity's (or, most likely, Gene Roddenberry's) desire for order and ease of access. But there is one lone island in this homogeneous ocean of Terran English—Klingon.

It may be true, as Noam Chomsky of MIT has suggested, that we humans are innately wired for language—although experience with deaf and "wolf" children shows that we never learn it if we don't acquire it within a narrow critical window, during the first year of life. For this reason, Uhura can never realistically relearn to speak after she has been mind-wiped by Nomad in "The Changeling" (TOS).

However, those who speak more than one language know that they differ in construction—some are cathedrals, others are symphonies. About six thousand languages are spoken on Earth today, and the extinct ones must have been at least as many.

Speaking the same language never seems to prevent civil wars. Nevertheless, rationalists of the nineteenth and twentieth century hoped that strife might abate if everyone spoke the same language—the same approach, incidentally, taken by mediator Riva in "Loud as a Whisper" (TNG). Some, more optimistic than the rest, went ahead and created such languages. The best known is Esperanto. The creator of these artificial languages took pains to make them regular and easy to learn, handy communication tools like standardized wrenches. However, none of these constructs ever grew deep roots into people's minds.

I think there is a deep-seated reason for this, beyond human orneriness. Languages such as Esperanto are one layer deep; worse yet, they are a patchwork of vocabulary, which makes them look as inviting as a Borg with a full load of prostheses. Language, beyond its physical manifestation, evolves out of shared experience. It does not perform well in a cultural vacuum.

This may explain the unexpected success of artificial languages that are quite complex. Good examples are J. R. R. Tolkien's invented languages for the various races in *The Lord of the Rings* and its associated stories (Old Earth Numenorian, Elvish, Dwarvish) and Marc Okrand's tlhIngan-Hol, the language of the Klingons. Artificial they may be, but those who take the trouble to learn these languages enter cultures with their own history, politics, customs, and quirks.

The Klingon language, because of the inordinate allure of a warrior culture to the couch space explorers who make up most of the *Star Trek* audience, has taken off spectacularly. Currently it boasts at least one language institute and several translations of the classics. Shakespeare, from whom *Star Trek* has borrowed heavily in other ways (plots, script lines), figures prominently in the Klingon canon.

When spoken, especially by someone with the vocal apparatus of Michael Dorn, who plays Lieutenant Worf, Klingon sounds like a combination of Arabic and German—awash in gutturals and glottal stops. Exotic all right, but only to people who know nothing but English. Klingon falls into the group of the staccato, mostly monosyllabic languages such as English and Chinese that seem poised to inherit this planet during its next historical cycle.

I got a kick out of reading in *Wired* magazine that Klingon sentence construction (object-verb-subject) is unique and never encountered on Earth. I wrote to them that, actually, such word order is commonplace even among our familiar Indo-European group—Greek, Russian, German. Most Indo-European and Semitic languages are inflected, which leaves much freedom to syntax. I pointed out that, in fact, Klingon syntax and grammar are rather similar to that found in British Border ballads and in Elizabethan rhetoric, perhaps not a bad choice for swashbuckling barbarians. The *Wired* people are good sports—they published my letter.

Nevertheless, if you go through *The Klingon Dictionary,* you discover that Klingon is closer to a pidgin language. Such languages develop at trading posts, whose inhabitants tend to be polyglot, or in areas that don't have a shared language. Such a language has developed in Papua New Guinea, which, because of its isolating mountain ranges, is home to one-fifth of Earth's six thousand languages.

The Klingon language finally betrays its artificial origins by the fact that its vocabulary does not reflect the concerns of the people who speak it. People who live in the Arctic have many words for snow, though I think the reputed one hundred in Inuit is an exaggeration. Those who live in deserts have multiple words for sand and sandstorm—a select sample comes up in Michael Ondaatje's *The English Patient.* People culturally concerned with honor tend to have several nuanced words for it. Greek has three, Japanese half a dozen. Not so tlhIngan-Hol: every third or fourth word out of a Klingon's mouth is *honor* or *battle*—but *The Klingon Dictionary* shows a single word for each.

Klingon has gained enough status that American *Star Trek* watchers will put up with subtitles—a considerable sacrifice for the culture that invented dubbing and TV remote controls. That marks the far extent of the *Star Trek* fan's concession to multilingualism.

THE DEAD SPEAK

Star Trek is not the only forum where communication with alien civilizations has been the focus of serious and extensive efforts. For the last few decades, powerful radio telescopes have been scanning the heavens, searching for a regular signal that would unmask the presence of an extrasolar civilization. In sending artifacts or signals of their own, humans have endlessly debated what to show or say that would be detectable and decipherable by other sophonts. Similar questions apply to a signal that we receive. How will we know that it sprang from an alien intelligence, rather than a rotating supernova remnant?

One day we will receive a signal that cannot be attributed to anything but intelligence. After we have excluded all other possible artifacts, we have only just begun the journey: now we must decode the message. We can predict the troubles that we will have during this task, because we've met them already on our own planet.

The most likely scenario for civilizations light-years apart is that they will never meet face-to-face and decipher each other's language by the simple expedient of pointing at something and naming it. Undoubtedly, the transmission will be some kind of coded script.

This is known ground to archaeologists, who must often decipher a written language script with no living descendants. To do so, it is necessary to have some sort of mapping key, either a closely related language or literally a Rosetta Stone that contains side-by-side texts in multiple languages. Otherwise, a language can be perfectly readable but still incomprehensible—Etruscan is a prime example of that—or, more commonly, completely opaque to posterity—Minoan Linear A, the Mohenjo Daro scripts of the Hindus valley.

Wrong assumptions that lead to nonsensical conclusions have set archaeologists back for decades. There are two particularly famous cases—the Mayan hieroglyphs and the Linear A/Linear B syllabary. In both, grand old men with a personal stake in the matter (Eric Thompson and Arthur Evans, respectively) held the field captive to their beliefs and reinforced their opinions by withholding the rare script examples that were available. The same could easily happen with a message from an extraterrestrial civilization, so I hope that the various government agencies enamored of classifying documents are reading this and taking notes.

The latter of the two stories will suffice to illustrate my point. Crete had developed a unique civilization, the Minoan, a sea empire whose complex cities were unwalled and alive with Art Nouveau–like frescoes. This mercantile civilization, a crossroads between Egypt and the Fertile Crescent, flourished for almost a millennium before it was extinguished by the Thera volcano explosion. The catastrophe was of such magnitude that it is still remembered in myth as the destruction of Atlantis. The power vacuum of that collapse left the door open for the Mycenaeans, the first Indo-Europeans to come down the Greek peninsula.

The invaders spoke their own language, but were strangers to writing. Not so the Minoans, who had developed a script. So when the archaeologists were sifting through the palaces, they found only one script, though it was possible to tell that there were two versions: Linear A, in which Minoans wrote, and Linear B, the descendant that they bequeathed to the Mycenaean usurpers.

Archaeologists tried for years to decipher the languages, with zero success. During that time, Heinrich Schliemann found both Troy and the golden hoard at Mycenae. His discoveries validated the Homeric epics as history. The Bronze Age people described in the *Iliad* and the *Odyssey* apparently spoke an old form of Greek. Occam's razor is the logic maxim that postulates that the simplest of competing theories is almost always the right one. Therefore, if Linear B was the script that the Mycenaeans used, it should be Greek as well. But Evans would not even consider this possibility and frowned at dissenters, with dire consequences for their careers.

Finally, young Michael Ventris, a British codebreaker during World War II, took a shot at the scripts. Not a professional archaeologist, he did not quail before Evans's wrath and went on the assumption that Linear B was, in fact, Greek. Bingo. Entire fragments suddenly made sense.

There are two more wrinkles to the story, both pertinent to signals from the beyond. As is the case with most early remnants of writing, the Linear B tablets contained mostly mundane lists—sheep, slaves, wheat bins, olive oil barrels . . . Also, Ventris could decipher Linear B because it had evolved into a still-living language. The inconsiderate Minoans spoke a language that was neither Indo-European nor Semitic. To this day, Linear A remains unsolved.

So the first moral of this story is that the extraterrestrial signal will be business-like. They will not send poetry, unless we receive their random radio transmissions rather than a directed narrow-band signal.

The second take-home message is that deciphering an unknown language without some kind of key is impossible. The regular patterns that the inorganic life-forms create on sand in "Home Soil" (TNG) would definitely alert us to their intelligence, but mutual comprehension is another matter. If a resident of Manhattan sees an Australian or Navajo sand painting, how much will s/he register beyond aesthetic pleasure?

Perhaps our galactic correspondents will send a key along with the message, as is shown in the film *Contact.* But also as is shown in *Contact,* there is only one universal signal that can reliably be decoded—mathematics. Any extraterrestrial civilization that is sending a signal must have developed technology, which implies science, which in its turn requires mathematics.

When the phone rings at the Arecibo radio telescope array or in the

SETI headquarters, it won't be ET calling home—it will most likely be a numerical string. A recognizable arithmetic progression will be conclusive proof that the signal is artificially generated—for example, prime or Fibonacci numbers. Transmitting primes to show sentience is precisely what Picard does in "Allegiance" (TNG). If the transmission is at the 1.42 gigahertz hydrogen-emission "universal frequency," so much the better. It means that not only are they scientifically adept, but that they think like us as well.

THE PASSWORD TO THE GALACTIC CLUB

Thanks to the universal translator, I've been able to take you on a whirlwind tour from the brain to Linear B to radio telescopes. It's a pity that as a scientist I have to pronounce the translator impossible, because such a tool would be useful. On the other hand, its immense abilities cause a huge pile of problems that *Star Trek* has been hard put to sweep under the rug. The dangers of such a piece of equipment are so dire that it's best left on the drawing board of the mind as an image only—a new meme?!

But if science appears merciless, it can also offer consolation. Science has reason to believe that even exotically different organisms will recognize the fundamental principles of mathematics, although their particular brand of mathematics may be radically different from ours. The mathematical commonality will unequivocally establish the presence of intelligence and compatible science. After such a contact, we can exchange information knowing that we understand each other. Eventually, we will progress to arguments over poetry and politics—and debates over which of the four *Star Trek* series was the best of the bunch (my vote is for DS9).

ACT III.
FAMILY MATTERS

The Libretto Unfolds

SCENE 9.
ALL IS FAIR IN LOVE, WAR, AND STARFLEET ENTRANCE EXAMS

From Mendel's Sweet Peas to Tailored Life-Forms

You live on twenty-fourth-century Earth, in the era of the Federation, when humans roam from star to star, following their dreams. You have a dream yourself. You have a child.

Your child—your only child—has just started at the best school you can afford. You're anxious for him to do well, so that he can later go to college, which in turn will help him get a good career in an increasingly complicated and demanding workplace. Yet soon your heart sinks as you're forced to notice that something's amiss.

The child is not thriving at school. Inexorably, he's slipping behind his classmates. He can't write coherently; he can't grasp simple math. Kindly but firmly, the teachers make it clear that the paths you've envisioned—doctor, engineer, scientist, lawyer, Starfleet officer—are closed to your child.

It's the twenty-fourth century, though. There is one last recourse. It's expensive, it's illegal. But it's the least you can do for your child, the only way that he'll not end up as a "sanitation engineer" in the medical school where you'd envisioned him becoming a doctor. So you convert your savings, you forge papers, you squeeze a pocket of time away from your small business, and you take your child to an unmarked, inconspicuous building.

You hand the enormous fee to the people inside. "Please make my child smart," you whisper.

This is how it might happen in the twenty-fourth century, and who would blame you for wanting the best for your kid? Once it was enough to find a compatible mate and produce normal children. Now, both companion and progeny must be the distillation of physical, emotional, and intellectual perfection. Once it was acceptable to live a life relatively free of disease and oppression. Now high quality of life and eternal appearance of youth have become the imperative. Humans are relentlessly, remorselessly dissatisfied. As the hierarchy of needs changes, desires and dislikes escalate accordingly. We make our choices—and then we look for more.

As is shown in *Star Trek*, many of these demands can potentially be addressed by genetic engineering. This gives rise to two major questions: Is it ethical to change people genetically? And if it is allowed, will it once again be the exclusive privilege of the powerful and rich?

When nonscientists hear the words *cloning* and *genetic engineering*, they often recoil. Conditioned by the media and popular culture, they immediately visualize an army of like-minded automatons or a concentration camp where brutal eugenics experiments are conducted without consent of the participants.

Yet people have routinely used low-tech genetic engineering for millennia. Selective breeding and ruthless culling have generated improved or desired plant and animal hybrids—even human ones. Think of incestuous royal marriages. Consider, too, the suspiciously high percentage of sons in many developing countries, where lineage is paternally defined.

At the same time, widely divergent visions of the future beckon from the battlements of contemporary biotechnology. On the beneficent side, we may look forward to improved crops that help combat hunger, vaccines for cancer and AIDS, eradication of birth defects. On the malign side, we may end up with genetically custom-made slaves and biological weapons.

In the debate on genetic manipulation, *Star Trek* has once again chosen the safe, politically correct side. Cloning by biological means is illegal in the Federation. In all four series, tailored life-forms are generally villains or employed by the villains. The most prominent representatives, respectively, are Khan Singh, member of a genetically altered group—beautifully tanned and muscled monsters who instigated the Eugenics Wars ("Space Seed," TOS; *The Wrath of Khan,* ST2)—and the Jem'Hadar, the feared foot soldiers of the Dominion (DS9).

Frowned upon yet accepted are men engineered to be "ideal warriors" ("Captive Pursuit," DS9) and women engineered to be "ideal companions" ("Mudd's Women," TOS; "The Perfect Mate," TNG)—polite terms for slavery, slaughter, and prostitution. Such species are usually covered by Federation cultural noninterference laws similar to those that prohibit the Western nations from preventing female genital mutilation in Africa and the Near East.

Let's take a look at the real science from which all these speculative *Star Trek* characters spring.

THE REVOLUTION THAT WASN'T

Star Trek may be timid, but it has an excellent sense of timing. One episode of DS9 ("Doctor Bashir, I Presume?") revealed that Julian Bashir had undergone genetic enhancement. Like the child that I envisioned earlier, his anxious, loving parents wanted to ensure that he could enter the Starfleet Academy. This episode aired the very week that newspaper headlines were screaming about the cloning of the sheep Dolly from adult cells. Actually, unlike Dolly, Bashir had had his DNA "resequenced," which translates to somatic retroengineering. So he's not a clone but a eugenics product—a genetic cousin of Khan Singh.

The progenitor of genetic engineering as we know it today and as it appears in *Star Trek* is gene splicing (also known as recombinant DNA). This field uses various techniques of molecular biology to create new combinations of genes, with the express purpose of discovering their function and regulation. The term *gene splicing* is confusing because it is used to name both an artificial and a natural process.

When artificial gene splicing first arrived on the scene, people were petrified by scenarios that prophesied the imminent emergence of monster bacteria that would swallow cities and spit out goo and matchsticks. Al Vellucci, ex-mayor of Cambridge, prohibited recombinant DNA research in the city, causing a major exodus of Harvard and MIT scientific faculty. Fortunately, reasonable guidelines eventually prevailed—instituted and enforced, I should add, by the scientists themselves the moment they started doing the experiments.

Just when the dust was settling, two teams at MIT and Cold Spring Harbor discovered endogenous (natural) gene splicing, which I described in chapter 3. It turns out that splicing and recombination are happening constantly within the cells of all organisms—and much more rapidly and intricately than we can do them in the lab.

The genetic material within our cells is never static. It constantly shifts to respond to environmental challenges. Whole chunks of DNA get reorganized whenever the immune system meets another antagonist. Genes use alternative splicing to vary their output according to external stimuli. Gametes mix and match their chromosomes when they meet, so that you end with your mother's eyes but your father's dimples.

Even disparate organisms trade genetic information by exchanging small DNA circles (plasmids) that can replicate autonomously. That's how bacteria acquire antibiotic resistance and plants sometimes grow resistant to plant viruses. In their turn, viruses occasionally ferry genetic bits of their hosts around, a property used in gene therapy.

These processes are so vital to the correct functioning of our cells that, if genes had obeyed Mayor Vellucci's *fatwa,* there would be no life left in Cambridge except *E. coli* and its cousins.

Gene splicing was originally performed on bacterial strains. Since then, recombinant DNA work has expanded into other organisms, gaining the more general sobriquet of genetic engineering—that is, changing the content of the genome for a specific purpose.

At this time, genetic engineering is principally being used for basic research, to dissect the wheels within unknown genetic clocks. Everything that we have discovered about us and our genes in the last two decades comes directly or indirectly from the use of recombinant DNA technology.

Along the way, we've found ways to apply this knowledge to create fruit that won't rot easily; crops that are resistant to plant or animal parasites; organisms that produce antibiotics or important human gene products (for example, blood-clotting factors or growth hormone). Most recently, this technology has given us the capability of growing organs to solve the shortage in transplants.

In *Star Trek,* the Federation has reportedly eliminated disease and hunger. Its medical practices look very much like an evolved version of ours. Federation doctors obviously graft organs such as Picard's artificial heart in "Samaritan Snare" (TNG) and Geordi's new eyes in *First Contact* (ST8) without any fears of rejection. Federation scientists make no secret of the fact that they are using recombinant DNA techniques the way we now use aspirin.

That's not surprising. The Federation sprang from Earth, and we humans love the fruits of technology and medicine. However, *Star Trek* also shares the eternal ambivalence of humans toward science.

Whenever scientists annex provinces that were traditionally considered the domain of religion, people start worrying about hubris. Some folk are afraid that, like Pandora, scientists will unleash something that they can't control. In *Star Trek,* even the benign warp drive proves to inadvertently damage the fabric of space in "Force of Nature" (TNG).

Given that the first applications of new technologies are almost invariably military, I'd say that some of this fear is justified. It's almost irrelevant to argue that such decisions are always taken by politicians or members of the military, rather than scientists. What complicates matters is that, although science and ethics routinely intersect, they are really like apples and oranges. Science is the pursuit of knowledge about the physical universe. Ethics, in contrast, deals with the principles that distinguish right from wrong. And whereas scientific discoveries are morally neutral, science can be used by heroes and villains alike.

Scientists themselves add to their troubles. With their odd habits, their detached viewpoint, and their reams of jargon, they make convenient scapegoats. Conversely, when they insist on looking at consequences, they become unpopular with the ruling groups who have always had a stranglehold on science funding.

This is strongly reflected in popular culture. Can you recall the latest film or book that unabashedly endorsed a scientist as a hero or heroine? I can't. Starting with Mary Shelley's *Frankenstein,* scientists have usually been portrayed as pride-puffed egomaniacs masquerading as gods, greedy and ambitious schemers or, at best, naive innocents whose goofy idealism makes them dangerous.

Star Trek is gung ho about biotech and medical gizmology until it reaches the usual boundary: genetic intervention in humans. Then it gets the willies and runs for cover under conventional, ill-informed wisdom.

YOU CAN STRETCH MY FACE, BUT DON'T TOUCH MY GENES!

In people's minds, it seems, the critical division of acceptable versus questionable is between germ-line and somatic cells. The germ line resides in our eggs and sperm, which fuse to give the next generation. Any alteration in the germ line is inheritable and will show up in all the cells of the descendants.

Somatic ("body") cells are the lumpen proletariat that make up all the rest of us—skin, internal organs, muscle, bone, brain. Alterations in those are not inherited. This vital distinction lets Julian Bashir's parents off the sharper hook—unless they had Julian's germ cells redone as well, trying to also ensure improved grandchildren.

Genetic engineering in multicellular organisms can take three general forms. In successive degrees of difficulty, and causing decreasing moral outcry, it can alter germ cells prior to zygote formation; it can alter somatic or germ cells during early embryogenesis; or it can genetically manipulate a fully formed living body. At this point, the first two can be done with varying degrees of success, depending on the organism targeted. The third, which is in the center of "Doctor Bashir, I Presume?" (DS9), is not yet possible, but I suspect that it will become feasible in the future.

At this point, we routinely use germ-line alterations to generate custom-mutated organisms (transgenics) from yeast to mice. Now we can investigate the importance of a gene product by deleting (knockout) or by overproducing its gene. We can activate them in specific cell types or at specific times during development. Engineered mice, in particular, have been vital for deciphering the functions and complex interactions of mammalian genes.

In humans, the major application of genetic engineering is gene therapy, which attempts to correct inborn errors of physiology or metabolism. Gene therapy is still taking steps as tiny as those of its patients. The major problem, which we discussed in chapter 5, is getting the desired gene to express at the correct place and time.

A more specific problem arises if the missing or defective gene product discharges its function in the brain. Due to the blood-brain barrier, most gene delivery vectors get detained at the gates to the brain, like immigrants trying to enter a country with stringent visa requirements. This has been partially alleviated by recent advances that allow delivery of drugs to the brain—but the downside of this is that the most promising vehicles are viruses.

Some people are worried that viruses are inherently dangerous vehicles, because of their rapid mutation rate. *Star Trek* has foreseen such a development. In "Miri" (TOS) a therapeutic virus gone awry now kills everyone at the onset of puberty. On the other hand, weakened viruses have been routinely and safely used in the past as vaccines (most notably the polio vaccines and vaccinia, which was instrumental in eradicating smallpox).

The Federation clearly has the technology available for doing genetic engineering at all three levels. This is not just implied by Bashir's alterations. We also learn that Geordi's decision to retain his VISOR was voluntary—and the VISOR has disappeared in *First Contact,* ST8. Furthermore, we don't see anyone else with genetic defects beyond

Geordi La Forge. Such defects should be rife in a society that is subject to radiation from both space-faring and from the broad use of nuclear fusion and fission technology. Those confined to wheelchairs are there because of a disease or an accident and would exchange their crutches for reengineered legs in a second (Pike in "Menagerie," TOS; Jameson in "Too Short a Season," TNG).

There is also no doubt that in some cultures, both in our universe and in that of *Star Trek,* any disability is tantamount to a death sentence. This was originally true in our prehistory in terms of overall viability—a seriously handicapped infant would dangerously encumber first the mother, then the tribe.

The requirement for "lack of blemish" later became culturally embedded. The fire-breathing Spartans of ancient Greece examined each child before admitting it into citizenship. The mother of their famous lame bard, Tyrtaios, had to rear him in strict secrecy and fear for both their lives. The kings of the ancient Celts had to abdicate immediately if they received a disfiguring wound in battle, let alone lost a limb.

Similar strictures are equally true in both the Romulan and Klingon cultures. In "The Enemy" (TNG), Geordi's unwilling Romulan ally cannot comprehend how Geordi's parents let him live. In "Ethics" (TNG), Worf's determination to commit suicide after his accident tells us volumes about Klingon attitudes on physical imperfections. Such outlooks will obviously not be satisfied with prostheses. Only true reconstruction will suffice—the gift of medicine and genetic engineering.

So, why is genetic engineering oh-so-subtly demonized in *Star Trek*?

One of the reasons given is the Eugenics Wars. Presumably, in the *Star Trek* timeline, misguided efforts to generate humans with enhanced abilities resulted in an arrogant group that ended up fighting among themselves (and anyone caught in the crossfire) almost to extinction. The remnants escaped on the ship *Botany Bay,* under the leadership of Khan Singh. The Federation has overcompensated in a dangerous manner: genetically enhanced people are institutionalized, even if they are perfectly stable and even though they underwent the procedure as children, before the age of consent ("Statistical Probabilities," DS9).

However, the Eugenics Wars were neither the last nor the worst conflict on our planet. The Eugenics Wars supposedly occurred in the late twentieth century. DS9 tells us that the truly devastating World War III took place on Earth sometime in the twenty-second century, without any input from enhanced humans. The instigators were just the usual garden-variety villains, the same nonengineered kind that has bedeviled our planet ever since our species began. Or are we to believe that malevolent aliens have custom-produced the countless destroyers and bloodthirsty despots solely to prevent us from expanding into the galaxy?

Furthermore, Khan and his followers do not show any obvious special abilities. If I were a member of the Earth government, I'd have fired the head of the eugenics lab that produced that batch. The taxpayers obviously got little value for their money. The only shared characteristics of the enhanced brood were towering egos and a vast sense of entitlement, characteristics that have routinely appeared among humans without any input from genetic engineering.

The real fear, of course, is that genetic engineering will produce another de facto underclass. Such an outcome has repeatedly appeared in dystopian futures, from Aldous Huxley's *Brave New World* to Cordwainer Smith's Underpeople to the recent film *Gattaca.* Humans, and twentieth-century Westerners in particular, want to believe that we are all free not merely to try equally, but also to achieve equally.

Star Trek does, too. Captain Picard grouses about the genetic interference on Moab IV, which leads to people occupying niches specified at birth ("The Masterpiece Society," TNG). Eastern philosophies, with their ideas of kismet and karma, are more reconciled to such pigeonholing.

We abhor having our choices narrowed down. We are led to believe that we can do anything, if only we put our will to it. Nevertheless, most of us know that we won't get to realize even a fragment of our dreams. How many will lead fulfilled and happy lives? How many will do something that will be remembered? No wonder we get midlife crises. Better to put the blame on heredity or environment—or, if all else is accounted for, bad luck.

Nevertheless, the bitter truth is that a quadriplegic cannot be a ballerina, and a blind person cannot become an experimental scientist. And the irony is that genetic engineering may in fact be the only way of truly removing these limitations, rather than merely compensating for them with prostheses.

Already, transgenic technology is discovering how we can activate genes at the appropriate place and time. Specific cell types (skin and cartilage) can be grown to repair burns and breaks; the ability to grow and replace damaged organs is not far behind. Also, genetically engineered organisms have begun producing human gene products.

These solve three major medical and social problems. They bypass shortage of available organs as well as graft rejection, which arises because transplant donors aren't always fully compatible. They also prevent allergic reactions that can cause serious complications (comas, for example, when diabetics use nonhuman insulin).

Lastly, genetically engineered products eliminate the danger of fatal infections that can arise from using contaminated body parts or products. Two such notorious cases occurred relatively recently. Pathogenic prions in pituitaries and corneas harvested from corpses caused lethal outbreaks of spongiform encephalopathy (Creutzfeldt-Jakob disease) among humans in both Britain and the States. France, Japan, and the United States were rocked by the discovery that large numbers of hemophiliacs succumbed to AIDS caused by HIV lurking in preparations of blood-coagulating factors.

There's no doubt, of course, that genetic engineering carries some worrisome baggage. If it becomes commonplace, it will probably result in eradication of birth defects, particularly those that result in mental retardation or severe disabilities. Scientists and nonscientists alike worry that such practices may effectively be old-style eugenics draped in showy new clothes. They also worry that elimination of undesirable traits may lead in concurrent extinction of linked desirable ones.

Recall that most genetic diseases show up when both chromosomes carry a defective gene copy (homozygosity). Why have these diseases persisted for so long? The answer is, because carriers of a single copy of the defective gene (heterozygotes) enjoy hidden benefits. Heterozygotes for sickle-cell anemia are resistant to malaria. Heterozygotes for cystic fibrosis are resistant to cholera. Dyslexia seems genetically connected to mathematical ability. And families prone to depression contain unusually high numbers of creative people in their ranks.

Yet the argument of hidden benefits will weaken once the properties and interactions of the genetic products become fully known. Furthermore, we humans have already imposed such rapid and radical cultural changes on our bodies that it is impossible to determine what we would have looked like had we let natural selection truly take its course and allowed our weaker members to die before reproducing.

In fact, one last indirect benefit of genetic engineering may be that it could foster change in the human gene pool, instead of uniformity: it will separate tightly linked traits, on which natural selection cannot operate. Imagine, for example, that the gene for inspired writing is right next to the gene for baldness. Wouldn't you prefer to serenade your love object with both beautiful poetry and a full head of hair?

For another, gene engineering may indirectly replace the founder effect. Founder populations are defined as small, isolated pockets of a species. These act as experimental dishes, in which natural selection can choose the next viable variation in its theme. By our global colonizing and enthusiastic interbreeding, we have negated the founder effect. This means that we may have driven ourselves into an evolutionary cul-de-sac.

In support of this, our brains have remained essentially unchanged since the Paleolithic age. You'd be hard put to distinguish a Cro-Magnon skull from a contemporary one. After reading the Sumerian hymns to Inanna and the *Iliad,* I'd say that the contents of our brains haven't altered too much either. We still love and hate the same way. Many people suspect that most of our current problems can be traced to the unpalatable fact that while our technology belongs to A.D. 2000, our thinking remains rooted in 5000 B.C. Genetic engineering could reverse this stagnation.

The only other solution is to take to the stars—in effect, to force the progression of our evolution by compelling our adaptation to new extraterrestrial environments. Each starship will then effectively become a founder population both genetically and historically. The various subtly differentiated humanoid populations in *Star Trek* point either to the founder effect or to extensive dabbling in genetic engineering.

On the other hand, the cautionary tale of the skewed gender ratio in prenatal screening programs of widely different cultures strongly suggests that similar selections may be applied to whatever genetic trait is deemed deviant or socially undesirable. It is undoubtedly true that complex behavioral traits (or propensities toward them) are caused by multiple genes. However, once we know how genes interact, some multigene traits may become amenable to genetic engineering. This could destabilize society and lead to various forms of pernicious stratification.

Already, insurance companies can hardly be restrained from demanding genetic screening as an aid in denying coverage. As another example, gay people have welcomed the possibility that homosexuality may be genetically determined. Gay genes, if they exist, remove the burden of choice and, with it, any ground for moral disapproval. Still, if I were a gay activist, I'd be more worried if a gay gene did exist—because then it could be engineered into oblivion.

Although I definitely don't abjure scientists' responsibility to society, I consider such distortions social phenomena, not scientific ones. As I've repeatedly said before, we humans love classifications and dislike those too dissimilar from us. These mechanisms may have served human prototribes well at their emergence.

Today, the same attributes have become counterproductive, even dangerous. Although we are no longer gatherer-hunters in the savanna, we've kept our primordial xenophobia and intolerance, just as we've kept our appendix despite our inability to digest cellulose. What we've also kept and expanded is our inexorable capacity and desire for futzing with whatever is around us, like an eager child surrounded with toys.

We humans have experimented on ourselves in countless ways from the beginning, from decorative scarring to urban living. Contemporary genetic engineering is merely a change of scale and speed. Given the primary preoccupations and power structures of humans, it is unlikely that any strictures from any government will stem the tide for long. Ethical debate aside, the major reason that genetic engineering has not yet been used to manipulate humans is that not enough is understood of the genes and their products as an emergent system to result in reliable methods of alteration.

Nevertheless, if we judge both from recent debates and from the stance in *Star Trek,* there will be two domains of genetic engineering that we will (and should) traverse as carefully as we would walk through a minefield. These are human cloning and tailored humans.

THE SHEEP IN WOLF'S CLOTHING

The truth is that cloning occurs in our system routinely and fulfills a critical function. Our immune system produces clonal populations from a single progenitor cell whenever it produces antibodies or patrolling cells against a new threat. The short-circuiting of this mechanism is one of the major woes that beset people who have AIDS or are otherwise immunosuppressed (for example, by radiation or chemotherapy).

However, in the popular imagination, cloning implies a copy of an entire organism. Until it happened, cloning from adult mammalian cells was considered impossible. The reason is something that I've already mentioned: namely, adult cells are differentiated and hence incapable of reexpressing the full repertoire necessary for embryonic development.

This barrier prevented the creation of someone's identical copy until the scientists in Roslin Institute, Scotland, finally succeeded. As genetic material, they used the nucleus from a mammary gland cell, which they then used to replace the chromosomes of a donor egg whose own nucleus had previously been removed.

When Dolly got cloned in '96, we humans effectively became demigods in the field of biology (coming up next, universe building). We could not quite resurrect the dead—yet. Instead, we could do serial life extensions. And as with all new gods, we encountered immediate and stiff resistance from the older gods already in residence.

Seriously, though, I've listened carefully to the noise swirling around Dolly's creation. When I decode it into meaningful signal, it seems to boil down roughly into three kernels of concern.

The first is the old interdict against interfering with the work of the deity, which has been dogging science—and gene engineering in particular—all along. Similar stances labeled the Copernican heliocentric system heretical and forbade relieving women's labor pains, which had supposedly been ordained by the Old Testament.

The second is the sanctity of the unique human individual and the possible nefarious uses to which clones may be put. The third is the fear that this technique will increase stratification in an already very unequal world—again, a social concern.

Incidentally, no one particularly minds cloning in any other organism except humans. Worse yet, we rend our clothes over cloning but seem to care a lot less about stunting or destroying countless numbers of unique human individuals by war, malnutrition, disease, slavery, and illiteracy.

In the *Star Trek* universe, the Federation has not merely outlawed genetic engineering of adults. It has also forbidden human cloning. Yet I see a rather disturbing contradiction in its attitude.

Our heroes unquestioningly accept fission cloning when it is caused by technology based on physics. In "Second Chances" (TNG), the transporter splits Riker into William and Thomas. I can almost hear the *Star Trek* creators congratulating themselves in finding a way to have cloning without its attendant dilemmas ("A chance event—nothing we could do"). The *Enterprise* crew shrugs over Riker's duplication and takes it in stride. Will even gives Tom permission to court ex-flame Deanna Troi and—more importantly—gives him his (their) trombone.

However, the very same folks grow queasy when cloning is achieved by technology based on biology. Why, then, do they keep DNA cloning stocks, which they use to regenerate Dr. Pulaski in "Unnatural Selection" (TNG) and Picard et al. in "Rascals" (TNG)? In "Up the Long Ladder"

(TNG) they refuse to give the same DNA cloning stocks to a dying colony. If they had done so, the colonists would have ceased cloning themselves and reverted to traditional reproduction. To make matters worse, in the same episode Riker kills his cloned "copy," invoking his right to uniqueness.

I must have blinked and missed something there. It's not okay to create clones but it's okay to kill them? This is like outlawing abortion, only to send the resulting child to an orphanage—or to a war zone. If a clone is a full human, killing one is murder. Even Data, a completely artificial life-form, has full citizenship rights ("The Measure of a Man"). Conversely, if clones are considered inferior enough that they can be killed with impunity, it becomes unclear what the fuss over uniqueness is about.

The series has waffled endlessly on this, without reaching a conclusion. In two episodes (the previously mentioned "Up the Long Ladder," TNG, and "Whispers," DS9) a clone is killed with nary a ripple of moral indignation among the spectators. In marked contrast, in "A Man Alone" (DS9), someone is taken into custody for killing his own clone. Perhaps the critical division is whether the killing is done by a series regular or a walk-on extra—especially a villain, as is the case in the latter episode.

In terms of tampering, cloning is less intrusive than genetic engineering, which changes the content of the genome. Cloning is really a step further into artificial fertilization techniques, which attempt to overcome difficulties in either conception or implantation. The difference between cloning and other artificial fertilization methods is the method of producing the zygote. Whereas the latter consist of various ways of persuading the egg and sperm to meet and fuse, the former injects a preformed diploid nucleus into an egg. So in cloning, all the genetic material in the nucleus comes from one progenitor instead of two.

The specter of eugenics looms over in vitro fertilization as darkly as it does over genetic engineering. Genetic screenings at various stages are a given in artificial fertilization programs. These methods have already been utilized to abort any fetus that carries an undesirable trait.

For example, such programs produce abnormally high numbers of male zygotes in both developed and developing countries. This preference is so marked that parts of northern India and China now have a male population of 80 percent. Admittedly, this is a more humane alternative than getting rid of unwanted daughters by the more traditional methods—poisoning, exposure, battering, or starvation. In the future, a fetus may be aborted if the screening discovers "gene alleles" for homosexuality, low math ability, or poor hand-to-eye coordination.

It has been argued that clones may be created only to be used as organ repositories—or that the value of the original may decrease if there are clones around. That is theoretically possible, but only if the clones are denied full citizenship rights. Do parents value singlets more than identical twins—or more than the multiplets often conceived after hormonal fertility treatments?

People who are against cloning also maintain that the procedure is incompatible with free will and free choice. How so? None of us dictate our genome, pick the era and culture of our birth, or choose our parents. Furthermore, unless we firmly believe that everything about us is hardwired solely in our *nuclear* genes, someone's clone will be a lot more different than an identical twin. For one thing, s/he will be reared in a very different environment from that of the original. For another, the mitochondrial and cytoplasmic information of the clone will come from the egg into which the nuclear genetic material was injected.

Cloning also disturbs people's ideas of "natural order" because it decouples reproduction from sexual congress even more decisively than contraceptives or artificial insemination. It also decouples conception from pregnancy as much as surrogacy does. All these issues are tinderboxes, especially because they are tightly linked to women's status as humans in their own right, rather than as mere propagation vessels.

I have my own strong opinions on all these issues, but so do we all. The only thing that I will say is that people usually forget all about "natural order" when they fall ill or are about to die. They shriek against "natural order" if their children are born with something wrong. Hell, they jettison the concept without a backward glance when ecologists tell them to drive their cars a little less and occasionally take the train. We have interfered too much with nature, and hence we have forfeited the right to evoke it whenever—but only if—it's convenient.

However, if we still want to address natural-order issues, one point that people seem to selectively overlook when they condemn cloning is the desire for genetic descendants. And yet in other ways, the pendulum has swung almost all the way in favor of genetic continuity at all costs—the genetic continuity of the father in particular. This is obvious from the linguistic and legal contortions in the surrogacy issue, where the term *surrogate mother* often hides the fact that the surrogate is in fact the biological mother.

In most countries outside the States, childless people will most often adopt a niece or a nephew, ensuring at least partial genetic kinship. Even among the generally inclusive Americans, a recent survey showed much greater ambivalence toward adoption than people are willing to openly admit.

So what happens if someone cannot have genetic continuity in any other way, either because of infertility or because s/he cannot find a partner before her/his gametes atrophy? Cloning is an obvious way to overcome these hurdles. Additionally, it simplifies things by requiring only one parent. Cloned children would never find themselves in the midst of a custody fight.

On the third or fourth hand, it is conceivable that clones will be used as stand-ins for the original, with possible political or legal repercussions. The Klingons have already faced such a dilemma. In "Rightful Heir" (TNG), Worf discovers that the Kahless whom he encounters is not the legendary hero reborn but a clone of the original. Yet the Klingon High Council, for the sake of stability, proclaims the clone "real," realizing that, as far as faith goes, the origins of this Kahless are irrelevant.

Ethics or power issues aside, are there hidden biological problems in cloning?

Actually, there are a few. *Star Trek* has guessed one and shown it in the episode "Up the Long Ladder" (TNG) under the name *replicative fading*. Our cells accumulate mutations as we age. It is possible that our clones may be more susceptible to diseases such as cancer. They might also have problems with fertility or be more likely to produce descendants with genetic problems.

The reason for this is the age of our clones' gametes. As I've mentioned earlier, eggs and nurse cells that nourish sperm are born when we are born and age along with us. So unless the recapitulation of development resets the cellular clock, a six-year-old clone of a forty-year-old parent will have forty-year-old gametes. Dolly is about to be mated, so we'll have that answer come next lambing season.

If Dolly proves less than fruitful, we can circumvent this pitfall by putting away stock cells at birth, the way people store eggs and sperm prior to undergoing chemotherapy or radiation—and the way Federation members squirrel away their DNA blueprints. If we clone from such stock, the clones will be as good as new.

On the social side, the problem of unequal access to resources will unfortunately be harder to solve. As a former U.S. president said, life is unfair. The rich and the powerful have always had easier access to the desirable things. However, we know from watching the dramas of artificial fertilization that the couples who undergo these arduous procedures are usually not particularly rich, just committed—especially the women, who often endanger their lives during these processes.

So the people who end up desiring clones of themselves may not be the power hungry or the manipulative, but those who like the person they see in the mirror. This particular kind of cloning may ignite religious and political passions, but when all is said and done, it falls squarely into the domain of reproductive choice. In that respect, it's much less problematic than engineering humans for specific purposes.

However, the picture changes radically if people are cloned without their consent, against their wishes, or worse yet, for a destructive purpose. This is where people's nightmares about identical warrior drones come close to brushing reality. When cloning serves impersonal ends, it is as problematic as producing tailored humans.

MAN FOR WAR AND WOMAN FOR THE WARRIOR'S PLEASURE

If the motives for cloning can range from the understandable to the dubious, "customized" humans are difficult to defend. Beyond the usual hesitations involved in genetic engineering, there is no escaping the fact that such people would be tools. In keeping with historical precedents, each society will always shift any occupation that is dangerous, unpleasant, or deemed contemptible onto such constructed humans, keeping the prestigious, rewarding professions or occupations for "real" members.

Humans have turned animals into tools without hesitation. Dogs have been so extensively engineered that many breeds are no longer recognizable as wolf descendants. Domestic animals have been optimized for whatever particular function they must fulfill (milk yield, meat mass, speed) and for one more attribute: docility.

Of course, slavery by conquest, caste division, or birth circumstances has flourished in human societies without any interference from genetics. In the ancient world, slavery did not carry with it the stigma of inferiority, only of bad luck; slaves came in all colors and shapes. It was only later, particularly with the advent of lifelong serfdom, that it became necessary to justify slavery with pseudoscientific grounds of intrinsic inferiority of the exploited.

Selective breeding among humans has also been extensive. People considered undesirable genetically (or politically, which is sometimes synonymous) have been castrated or otherwise sterilized in many societies across the ages.

Also, from time immemorial, certain groups have tried to keep the reins of power by mating only among their own tight circle. Egyptian pharaohs and Inca emperors maintained the "purity" of their line through their sisters. And spouses in all the European royal houses at the beginning of this century were at most second cousins, thanks to the prolific output of Queen Victoria. Along with the purebred pedigree, she also bequeathed hemophilia, "the royal disease," to the all-important male scions.

In *Star Trek,* with the enthusiastic interbreeding among humanoids and the ostensible removal of all isms, there is no shadow of exclusionary mating groups. Moreover, we're left in no doubt that a society that condones slavery ("Accession," DS9) or tailors humans for slave tasks will never be accepted into the Federation.

Such engineering as *Star Trek* has chosen to illustrate gives us considerable insight into the series' preoccupations. In Cordwainer Smith's Norstrilia cycle, the half-human, half-animal Underpeople specialize in a wide spectrum of service tasks. In *Star Trek,* we see only two specializations, and these are gender-segregated in the most primitive manner imaginable: females bred for sex and males bred for slaughter.

Remember the sociobiological opinion that men are designed for a short, nasty life and women for a long, brutal one? It must be obvious by now that I take a dim view of sociobiology. However, I consider this phrase correct not in its biological but in its cultural manifestation—and the *Star Trek* stance justifies my conclusion.

TOS shows a relatively mild preview of "enhanced" women in "Mudd's Women." "The Perfect Mate" (TNG) portrays an even worse case, this one condoned by the Federation for the sake of peace. Kamala is an "empathic metamorph" who unconsciously molds her personality to meet the desires of men. In short, she is the perfect adolescent fantasy.

I already hear someone arguing that Kamala's characteristics sound genetic. However, the plot reveals that she has been bred or engineered to bond to a specific man, ending the feud between her race and his. Not to mince words, she is a war trophy. And since logic dictates that her entire race cannot be empathically metamorphic, those who are clearly constitute commodity items.

Before you label Picard and Co. hypocrites, reflect that similar stances abound in today's politics. Human rights go out the window when they get in the way of trade or political alliances—especially women's rights.

Kamala is destined to spend a long life chained to the needs of someone who is at best indifferent to her. On the other hand, the various soldier drones that we encounter in *Star Trek* are kept oiled and loaded, like the weapons they are. The moment they malfunction, they are discarded.

We first glimpse such constructs in the Angosian soldiers ("The Hunted," TNG). These are physically and mentally augmented warriors, who won the war they were bred for. In an obvious parallel to Vietnam, when peace descended, these soldiers were disruptive to the society that they had fought to maintain.

The observation that warriors can harm society and themselves during peace is as old as the *Book of Gilgamesh* (we'll revisit warriors in chapter 11). The new wrinkles in *Star Trek* are the enhancements—which may not be as far from the thoughts of the military as we'd like to think. The envisioned Jedi knight that I mentioned in chapter 5 is brother to the Angosian soldiers. The sensor-invisibility of Roga Danar in "The Hunted" is already theoretically achievable by technology (although the Stealth bomber has proved anything but stealthy), and chemically induced berserker rages are already with us courtesy of anabolic steroids and neural implants.

In her fascinating book *Blood Rites,* Barbara Ehrenreich postulates that war evolved not as a victorious gesture of Man the Predator but as a propitiating ritual of Man the Prey. Specifically, she suggests that war evolved out of the custom of human sacrifice. These sacrifices—a willing offering—were meant to appease the gods who, in their original animal incarnations, preyed on humanity's simian ancestors.

However, once we became hunters ourselves, hunting, "the sport of princes," served as a substitute for war. In "Captive Pursuit" (DS9) we meet Tosk, a lizardlike humanoid specifically created to be hunted. As in many cultures who ritually honor their animal prey, the hunters honor the Tosk if they make the hunt challenging—and the Tosk strive keenly for this perverse distinction.

This, of course, brings us to several burning questions: If the tailored humans are devoid of the capacity to choose, can they still be considered human? In the other direction, if they consciously embrace the task they have been built for (as both Kamala and Tosk do), should we respect their choices, disagreeable as they may be to us or our *Star Trek* heroes?

Such questions burst on us in full gale force when we see the apotheosis of tailored humanoid constructs—the Jem'Hadar, shock troopers of the Dominion (DS9).

The Jem'Hadar, an exaggerated version of hormonally bonded warrior ants, need no sleep, food, or sex ("To the Death," DS9). According to "The Abandoned" (DS9), they have been engineered to grow and age rapidly and to lack a critical enzyme that only their Vorta overseers can provide. This makes them dependent on an addictive substance (ketracel-white), and given their vocation, their lives are indeed nasty, brutish, and short.

Having the Jem'Hadar both inherently lacking an enzyme and addicted to its replacement is overkill. Either one would suffice to make them fanatically obedient. In "The Jem'Hadar" (DS9) we also discover that they share with Tosk (and with the alien in *Predator*) the ability to "phase"—that is, literally fade into the scenery.

Are the Jem'Hadar biologically possible? Given their purported capacities, I cannot envision any way that they can sustain themselves short of photosynthesis. Come to think of it, they do look slightly greenish. Alternatively, if ketracel-white not just hooks but also nourishes them, it can't be merely an exotic heroin substitute.

As for their cloaking abilities, there are terrestrial life-forms that can blend with their surroundings. (I listed a few in the shape-shifter section of chapter 3.) However, there are two caveats to the extraordinary camouflaging capacity of the Jem'Hadar. One is that they can change their refractive index (very unlikely). The other is that, even if they can perform this feat, their clothes and weapons should still be visible.

Star Trek has grudging admiration for the Jem'Hadar. In "Rocks and Shoals" (DS9), Captain Sisko explicitly treats them as honorable enemies, to the extent of endangering the lives of his own party. This highlights two points: awarding honor implies choice, in which case the Jem'Hadar are morally responsible for their actions; and soldiers, no matter what their behavior or their cause, are still considered more honorable than prostitutes in both our universe and that of *Star Trek*.

Yet when you reflect on it, warriors bring death and destruction, whereas prostitutes bring pleasure, no matter how dubious or fleeting. It's odd that we're so tolerant of violence but so stern about sex.

Star Trek may dither on the subject of engineered warriors. However, it draws the proverbial line in the sand (the crossing of which means war) when such foes fall below a certain size—when they're viruses or microbes.

DON'T DRINK THE WATER, DON'T BREATHE THE AIR

Biological warfare is widespread among plants and animals, especially those disadvantaged by size or lacking conventional armaments such as teeth and claws. Anyone with a claim to sophistication manufactures toxins either to discourage predators or to immobilize prey. Spiders, wasps, snails, scorpions, blowfish, toads, vipers . . . the list can continue endlessly. Nor do these products deal only death. Natural toxins have made powerful additions to our pharmacological arsenal.

Among humans, biowarfare probably started with peeing in the enemy clan's well. It then escalated to catapulting bodies of cholera victims into the enemy camps or sending blankets containing smallpox to competitors for resources.

Sometimes, I'm bemused to hear arguments solely and specifically against biological weapons, when the visible annual military budget of this country is half a trillion dollars and the deployment of a single nuclear warhead could start another ice age. After the collapse of the Soviet Union as a balancing superpower, the quantity, quality, and accessibility of conventional and nuclear weapons has escalated. Right now, the United States is the largest weapons seller on this planet.

On the other hand, biological weapons are powerful agents of terror, if only because they are subtle and insidious compared to the more conventional instruments found in the industrial war-fighting armory. Biological warfare is relatively cheap and easy, as it can be done in a garage—unlike purifying plutonium, which requires specialized facilities and access to uranium ore. This makes governments nervous. They prefer to have all means of mass destruction concentrated in their hands. Also, weapons of mass destruction are useless if your enemy is nameless or invisible.

The kitchen-sink aspect of biological weapons makes them almost impossible to monitor. One of the best-known cases of misguided zeal arose when ex–secretary of state Al Haig breathlessly announced to the world that the Soviets were spreading a deadly poison over Southeast Asia. Matt Meselson of Harvard went to investigate and discovered that the unspeakable weapon actually consisted of bee feces—which, in all fairness to those concerned, can cause allergic reactions.

Biological weapons, however, have certain distinct disadvantages. Their spread cannot be easily directed or contained. Spray the country next door and you might end up devastating your own. Microorganisms undergo rapid mutations, which means that they could end up doing something their creator had not envisioned.

Microorganisms are also fragile. Most viruses die if they remain outside their host for a few hours, and most microbes are susceptible to sunlight, oxygen, antibiotics, and detergents. The great plagues in history happened when sanitation and public health were at their lowest ebb, or when microorganisms suddenly had access to populations who had had no time to build immunity (smallpox, tuberculosis, and influenza in the Western Hemisphere; syphilis in its Eastern counterpart). Thus, the microscopic life-forms tend to wreak havoc without human intervention, although they have often played right into the hands of aspiring imperialists.

They seem to do the same in *Star Trek*. The races accused of dark designs tend to favor aggressive expansion—most notably the Cardassians, who are repeatedly suspected of manufacturing "metagenic weapons," the biological equivalents of the neutron bomb ("Chain of Command" and "Preemptive Strike," TNG). Just as in the case of the Russians, however, these rumors have never been substantiated.

In the mind of most contemporaries, biological warfare is synonymous with engineered viruses. Dark murmurings periodically circulate about the provenance of HIV and the Ebola virus. In August of '97, the usually staid *Journal of the American Medical Association* added to the artificial-militarization hysteria by devoting an entire issue to biological terrorism. The overall recommendation, not surprisingly, was an increased military budget.

Star Trek is head over heels in love with the concept of viruses even though it abhors the critters themselves. Engineered viruses have popped up repeatedly in the series, from the well-meant mistake of "Miri" (TOS) to entire contaminated races that act as virus reservoirs and therefore have to be kept in perpetual quarantine (the Tarellians in "Haven," TNG; the Ennis and Nol-Ennis in "Battle Lines," DS9).

Some of the more exotic viruses postulated in *Star Trek* may actually be possible. In "Babel" (DS9), the Bajoran resistance has manufactured a virus that attacks the language centers, causing aphasia, and eventually destroys the rest of the nervous system. Many viruses do attack our nervous system (herpes, meningitis), although they don't target the language centers specifically.

In "The Vengeance Factor" (TNG), the last survivor of a clan has been turned into a carrier of a virus specifically directed against clan enemies. Such a virus could work if the clans are completely inbred—which can happen after a really long war—and have totally different blood-specific antigens. The major such antigens specify blood type and rhesus compatibility. Viruses are already fine-tuned to recognize specific receptors without any human engineering. For example, HIV docks on a platform that only appears on T cells, the immune system security patrol.

Such viruses are unlikely to be developed intentionally. Genetic engineering may offend the religiously orthodox of all faiths, but, at least, it has not yet participated in the industry of war.

BEHOLD, I AM BECOME LIFE, THE CREATOR OF WORLDS

Like Janus, the Roman god of beginnings, genetic engineering has two faces—one promising, one terrifying. Whether we turn it into a plough or a sword is entirely up to us. I can only hope that the involvement of scientists in projects such as nerve gas production and the Tuskegee syphilis experiments has made us wiser.

And yet, people do expect miracles from genetic engineering and expect them right away. Skepticism instantly evaporates before dangers to life and health. Because my work is connected with the nervous system and dementia, I get mountains of mail from families with afflicted members asking me why research isn't progressing faster.

My answer is, tell the legislative branch to divert, oh, say, 1 percent of the budget for "nonlethal weapons" into research. One Stealth bomber is equivalent to one thousand well-endowed labs. And when Jeremy Rifkin comes to you with yet another horror story about gene splicing, listen to our side as well, before deciding that scientific decisions are best left to politicians and demagogues.

Star Trek may have stumbled in its scientific details, but it has depicted the dilemmas of genetic engineering accurately. Although scientific facts are neutral, science is only as good as the people who make the discoveries and determine the applications. Science is solidly embedded in culture and contemporary mores, regardless of the ivory tower mythology. Ideally, both the knowledge and the benefits that come from science are meant to be shared—not merely locally, but universally. Perhaps the universe of *Star Trek* has solved so many problems precisely because it has more or less followed that route.

SCENE 10.
SEND VIRUSES, GUNS, AND LATINUM

New Worlds and the Prime Directive

Life in late 1950s Greece was positively bucolic. I could have spent my entire time playing tag on streets practically empty of automobiles or hide-and-seek in courtyards shaded by orange trees and bougainvillea. Instead, when I was a four-year-old anklebiter, I taught myself to read. I had noticed that this activity fascinated my father to such an extent that it distracted him from paying attention to me. Two years later, my parents gave me full access to their library. I was never restricted to "books appropriate for children."

Their friends were horrified, of course. A child—and a girl, yet!—exposed to all these adult novels, art books brimming with nudes, histories of wars. What would happen? Trauma was imminent. My parents shrugged and said that if I came across something that I was too young to understand, I'd either ignore it, ask them to explain—or check it out in the encyclopedia.

My parents were right. The prophesied mental and emotional traumas never materialized. Reading, more than anything else, has made me the person I am today. However, I must also add that their library contained neither pornography nor insipid trash.

Whenever I consider *Star Trek*'s Prime Directive, I'm reminded of my parents' friends. They meant well and might have been right under different circumstances. But I can't help but think that they were patronizing busybodies.

In Starfleet, the imperative of the Prime Directive takes precedence over any and all other considerations. It basically states that Federation members shouldn't interfere culturally with a civilization that doesn't know about space travel. What that means is that they can't give technology, scientific knowledge, or support (military or civilian) to pre-warp societies. Starfleet members may not violate the Prime Directive, not even to save their own lives or the lives of others. "Better dead than culturally contaminated" seems to be the Federation motto, though they seem considerably laxer in the domain of biological contamination, which transcends warp capabilities.

Each time the Prime Directive gets mentioned, Peter, my significant other, retorts cynically, "Prime Directive, Shmime Directive. Out the window whenever Kirk gets an erection." Indeed, this much vaunted moral principle of *Star Trek* is the quintessence of standardless discretion. It is applied so haphazardly and arbitrarily that it might as well not be there at all. It's like a sign that says, "The speed limit will be enforced"—without posting it or mentioning that the speed limit is whatever makes Officer Jean-Luc uncomfortable.

In the series, the Prime Directive is followed only if it augments the drama of the plot or when there are no curvaceous females who ignite Captain Kirk's exploratory instincts. It can be sidestepped automatically if an antagonist has already tilted the balance ("Errand of Mercy," TOS; *First Contact,* ST8), or by a convenient onset of amnesia ("The Paradise Syndrome," TOS; "Thine Own Self," TNG). In short, the Prime Directive faithfully simulates the various "values" that nations argue about when their real quarrel is over resources.

Through the medium of books and films, human cultures have endlessly speculated over the details of a first contact with intelligent life from another planet. If we receive a signal, the decisions before us will be relatively easy. We won't be dealing with difficult questions of biological contamination, and we'll have time to consider a strategy for the eventual "encounter of the third kind." In fact, given the enormous distances that separate solar systems, a face-to-face meeting is unlikely, even if both sides possess advanced technology.

However, what if we (or they) conquer the light-years, as it has happened in *Star Trek*? In a situation of unequal first contact, is it possible to do no harm? What rules will govern an encounter in person? And if in our travels we discover Earth-like planets, should we colonize them—and how? These are the situations that push the Prime Directive dilemmas front and center.

FOR KING AND COUNTRY?

How did the need arise in the *Star Trek* universe for a rule such as the Prime Directive? Obviously, the Federation must have reviewed the outcomes of first contact among human cultures. The historical record of this activity is dismal, to put it mildly.

I have repeatedly mentioned that fear of the other served the small, isolated human proto-clans by improving cohesion and survival. However, this almost hardwired response became maladaptive when the isolated human groups started moving out of their circumscribed territories. Need combined with curiosity made rovers of us early on. Population pressures or dwindling resources led to a literal search for greener pastures. Naturally, nomadic groups immediately ran into other bands, who were disinclined to let the newcomers use their wells—or take a few of their women along as souvenirs.

Not all contacts between groups were disasters. In fact, interactions based on trade tended to be long-lasting, peaceable, and either neutral or benign. All the extended networks running across continents, down navigable rivers, and over mild seas were instrumental in disseminating not just trade goods but ideas as well.

Such interactions began early. Tin from Cornwall is found in ceremonial Minoan labryses (double axes) crafted around 2000 B.C.; Mycenaean pots have been unearthed in Bronze Age settlements around the Sea of Azov, at the far eastern corner of the Black Sea. Egyptian murals of the Middle Kingdom show traders of numerous nations, easily identifiable by dress, presenting their wares to the pharaohs' ministers.

After a quick survey of first-time encounters, it looks to me that the major determinant of peaceful interaction is "congruity"—namely, how much the two interacting cultures resemble each other. This property can be broken down into three independent factors.

The first factor is degree of tolerance for different opinions. Cultures that followed the banner of a jealous single God—the Old Testament Hebrews, the Spanish conquistadores, the first wave of Moslem expansion—tended to leave scorched earth behind them. In each of these three cases, entire cultures were extinguished in the wake of the expansion, like jungle fauna in the path of army ants. The concept of the Borg is not that radical, if seen from this angle.

The second factor is the level of emergency that prompted the migration. Groups that have little to lose tend to be more ruthless than those who are expanding in a leisurely fashion. The ancestors of the Polynesians initially crossed the Pacific archipelagos with scarcely a ripple, but they were not running from either starvation or oppression. When they faced each other later, the results were much bloodier—for example, when Maori raiders attacked the neighboring Chatham Islands, wiping out the local population, one of the most peaceful of Polynesian subgroups.

Such outcomes have to be borne in mind when we consider interstellar refugees who are fleeing an event, whether geological or political, that will forever prevent them from returning to their home planet (Khan's band in "Space Seed," TOS; the Skrreeans in "Sanctuary," DS9; the Maquis in TNG and DS9).

The third factor is disparity in technology. In a confrontation, rifles will invariably prevail against arrows or swords. The native Australians with their stone adzes didn't have the ghost of a chance against the English in the mid-nineteenth century; the Tasmanians, whom the English flushed out and hunted down systematically like coveys of partridges, were even more defenseless. Similarly, the Dominion Fleet—warp engines, engineered Jem'Hadar, and all—has no hope against the wormhole aliens, who can manipulate space and time at will ("The Sacrifice of Angels," DS9).

The Prime Directive seeks to compensate for disparities between cultures. The major discrepancy in the cultures that the Federation starships encounter is level of technology. The Federation is tolerant of other outlooks up to a point, and it doesn't have urgent internal problems of its own to solve until the rise of the Maquis (we'll get back to both these points in the next chapter). The *Enterprise* and the *Voyager* are primarily vessels of exploration, not conquest.

On the other hand, station Deep Space 9 is actually guarding a valuable resource (the Bajoran wormhole) in disputed territory. Therefore, it comes as no surprise that the DS9 universe is much more riven by strife than the others—and seems to spend less time agonizing over the Prime Directive. When you're fighting for your own territory, niceties of behavior justifiably tend to get lost in the scuffle. It's usually during times of peace and plenty that people have time to moralize.

Star Trek's Prime Directive is most certainly a peculiar animal that we should perhaps examine under a higher microscope setting.

DO UNTO OTHERS

How absolutely is the Prime Directive enforced by the Federation? I mentioned in the previous chapter that our systems of logic and morality haven't kept pace with our technology. All the systems of law in the West spring essentially from those of Bronze Age fishermen and shepherds from around the Mediterranean basin. The United States Constitution is an interesting partial exception, since it borrowed some of its concepts (for example, state autonomy) from the precepts of the Iroquois Confederation.

Systems of law can be stern or lenient. Think of the difference between Hammurabi's code of circa 1770 B.C., whose laws were fair but draconian ("an eye for an eye"), and that of the Jain religion, which insists that no life should be injured—not even an insect's. However, the crucial question that has always haunted human justice is, how absolute must the law be?

The sophists of classical Greece were the first moral relativists. In contrast, their opponent Socrates held the extreme absolutist position. In Plato's dialogues, he argued that, once the law is enacted, it is above the humans who wrote it. According to this interpretation, the law is the abstract equivalent of the deity.

This is not surprising, given that religion and law have been conflated during most historical epochs. However, the absoluteness or relativity of rules has never been resolved, either on today's Earth or in the *Star Trek* universe. The major reason, of course, is that unless you do believe that the truth has been handed to you on stone tablets, any system of justice can argue for its own validity. Secularists have trouble with the idea of absolute laws, and *Star Trek* is nothing if not secular.

Star Trek tends to ping-pong between the two positions, depending on who is accused of what. In fact, the inhabitants of Rubicun III are faulted for having an absolute solution for any infraction: death ("Justice," TNG). The Prime Directive is the single item upon which our heroes tend to assume a relatively rigid position—Captains Picard and Janeway, at least.

Nevertheless, there are some odd and troubling inconsistencies on both the small and large scale. For one thing, too often *Star Trek* treats general noninterference and the Prime Directive as though they're interchangeable. The former is as concrete and pragmatic as the latter is vague and moralistic.

When city-states, feudal territories, and later, nation-states dawned as entities, they evolved a practical modus vivendi. This dictated that each of these units could tyrannize its subjects at will, but would not interfere with how any other unit tyrannized its own members. This paradigm, of course, has traditionally been broken with impunity by both unsubtle and subtle coercion, such as war, use of superior technology, or economic embargoes.

Today, enforcement of noninterference has essentially been limited to whatever feeble moans the United Nations can emit and to how much heads of states are in debt to various corporations that have financed their party or election. On the global scale, though ecologists have tried to make people aware of the fragility and interdependence of our ecosystem, their success has been slow and limited. People are unwilling to make short-term sacrifices for long-term benefits, especially when they are led to believe that the two are not causally connected. The lukewarm or hostile responses to global warming are perfect illustrations of this all-too-human tendency.

In the gentler, kinder universe of the Federation (which we'll briefly describe as a paradigm in chapter 11), noninterference is strictly motivated by flawlessly rational ethical considerations. The heaviest stick to use on noncompliants is denial of Federation status, which translates to no Federation technology. And since all that traveling inevitably leads to contact with cultures of vastly divergent levels of technological development, the Prime Directive has been added as an additional prophylactic against undue interference.

Instances where noninterference and the Prime Directive get mixed up occur in the aforementioned "Justice" (TNG) and in "Captive Pursuit" (DS9), in which the station people debate about sheltering the hunted Tosk. They believe that such an action would violate the Prime Directive but that cannot be, since Tosk's culture obviously has star-faring technology. The Federation would interfere in their cultural affairs, which is not the same thing (our heroes never clear up the mistake). This bears an interesting resemblance to current debates over extraditions and political prisoners.

Star Trek is inconsistent even about cultural interference. For example, Sisko intervenes quite heavily when Worf's brother Kurn requests ritual death at his brother's hand, as is his due after he has been dishonored ("Sons of Mogh," DS9). Sisko has Worf arrested for attempted murder, though Worf's actions are completely in agreement with Klingon custom.

Picard does even worse when he throws the technological and moral weight of the Federation behind one side of an internal conflict on Rutia IV ("The High Ground," TNG). The fact that the adversaries of the ruling group are considered "terrorists" should be irrelevant to his decision. As a reader of Homer and Shakespeare, Picard should know that the dominant side always gets to call the shots—and the names.

On the other hand, Picard considers it an internal cultural matter when Kamala is handed around as a gift ("The Perfect Mate," TNG) or when Timicin of Kaelon II must die because he has reached the "Resolution" age of sixty ("Half a Life," TNG). This attitude prevails despite the fact that Timicin has scientific knowledge crucial for his planet's survival and, moreover, has requested asylum.

Even worse contradictions crop up when entire planetary civilizations are about to be destroyed because their planet or their sun has become unstable. In "For the World Is Hollow and I Have Touched the Sky" (TOS), Kirk and Co. break the Prime Directive to save a long-generation starship that is on a collision course. In "Pen Pals" (TNG), Data exchanges messages with a young girl who, like the Jodie Foster character in *Contact,* is a radio ham. From these exchanges, which explicitly violate the Prime Directive, the *Enterprise* crew discovers and eventually corrects the geological instability of her planet.

In stark contrast, at least twice Federation starships sit idly by and watch whole civilizations go up in smoke ("Homeward," TNG, and "Time and Again," VOY). They cannot correct the problem without giving themselves away. Their line of defense is that to either transport or warn the endangered civilizations would violate the Prime Directive! I call this a crime against humanity—the humanity of the people being destroyed, certainly; but equally so, of those watching it happen. And to say that these people are alien, not human, misses the point entirely.

All this hairsplitting, all these contradictions—and yet the Federation seems nonchalant about contamination at the level that counts: biology. Not only is this aspect more troublesome, but it also pertains to situations of both first contact and planetary colonization.

CAN YOU DIGEST RIGHT-HANDED PORRIDGE?

On the biological level, Starfleet personnel seem to violate the Prime Directive each time they land on a planet. This is true regardless of the local level of technology.

Whenever an away team travels, the transporter supposedly filters out harmful microorganisms from either the *Enterprise* or the planet. If it does not, the microorganisms carried by the crew will most likely wreak terminal havoc on life-forms of the new planet, just as the diseases of the Europeans wiped out the American Indians and Australian aborigines even more efficiently than their advanced weapons did.

The transporter biofilter is a step in the right direction, but isn't quite enough. To function correctly, the filter must recognize each and every life-form that is potentially harmful. Otherwise, it may get rid of something vital, such as the Trill symbiont—which explains the reluctance of joined Ambassador Odan to use the transporter ("The Host," TNG). How does the transporter distinguish between the various alternatives and make the correct choice? We're back to that annoying crutch, magic.

Still, let's assume that the transporter discharges its decontamination function perfectly. Recall from chapter 6 that symbiotic intestinal fauna is obligatory for efficient food processing. So if the transporter truly zaps all body flora and fauna, the away team will spend the first few days on each new planet crumbled up with debilitating nausea and diarrhea.

This sometimes happens to me when I switch water sources, from Athens to Cambridge. So you can imagine how it would be for a visitor from Bajor to ch'Rihan, the Romulan homeworld. The only way out of this that I can envision is that they've engineered nanites to take over the functions of intestinal bacteria.

Yet even if our heroes enjoy the benefits of intestinal nanites, let's suppose that they leave bodily wastes on the planet. Then they've left behind either bacteria (biological contamination) or nanites (technological contamination). Or do they run upstairs to the *Enterprise* loo each time their bladders bulge, multiplying the potential for accidental contamination severalfold?

There's actually a partial way out of this conundrum that *Star Trek* hasn't stumbled on. Cast your mind into the depths of the past. In chapter 1, I mentioned that all organic molecules have the property of chirality (asymmetry). More specifically, all organic molecules involved in Earth biochemistry are left-handed: when they're in solution, they rotate the plane of light in the counterclockwise direction.

So the entire biological paraphernalia on earth is intrinsically left-handed. This includes everything that can be used for food as well as the enzymes that process food macromolecules into smaller units that can be absorbed by the cells that line all digestive tracts.

The chances of an independently evolved alien carbon biochemistry choosing left-handed chirality are fifty-fifty. So if our heroes should chance on a planet with carbon-based life of chirality opposite of that from Earth, none of their microorganisms would affect the locals—but neither would they be able to absorb any native food. For left-handed planets, however, the list of vaccines needed prior to landing would exceed the length of my arm. The away team would also have to be quarantined extensively before being unleashed on the unsuspecting natives. So much for zipping in and out in an emergency.

Regardless of chirality, terrestrial bacteria and lichen can survive truly extreme conditions. Given all the exotic life-forms posited in *Star Trek* that can survive in near vacuum or hard radiation (examples occur in "The Immunity Syndrome," TOS, and "A Matter of Honor," TNG), such entities might make it intact to the planet surface despite stringent safety precautions.

Surprisingly, the entities that might not necessarily flourish in a planet with a biosphere sufficiently different from Earth are viruses, since they are obligatory parasites attuned to Terran hosts. On the other hand, if the native life-forms are similar enough to Terran ones, the paradigm of extreme virulence to suboptimal hosts that I explained in chapter 6 would apply—in which case our heroes would unleash a biological Armageddon on the hapless planet.

Larger creatures (as big as the predator in *Alien*) could also stow away in shuttle crafts, which seem to be decontaminated only upon return, not upon departure. Furthermore, shuttles are prone to crash landings. The number of episodes in *Star Trek* when that happens are too many to list; biological precautions will be the last thing on the shuttle crew's mind when they're trying to land safely. One only needs to look at the various ecological horror stories in which foreign newcomers completely swamped out native species—sparrows, starlings, and purple loosestrife in the Western Hemisphere; rats, cats, rabbits, and cane toads in Australia—to get a faint inkling of how chance additions might affect the biosphere of another planet.

The Federation seems rather nonchalant about such possibilities. All humanoid colonies in the series are shown surrounded by familiar flora and fauna. This goes beyond grumping at the special effects department. The unwelcome implication is that such settlements may have obliterated the local equivalents.

This is something space-faring races will have to face squarely when, unlike the Federation, they're not mockingbirds dipping into the nectar of different flowers. Civilizations that must leave their planet will most likely have no choice over their planetfall; nor will they have the luxury of debating whether they can spare local ecosystems, when they have nowhere else to go but back into space.

A small-scale preview of this is shown in "Resolutions" (VOY), in which Janeway and Chakotay must temporarily become planet-bound. Unlike the life of hardship of real homesteaders, their life looks like an interstellar version of the von Trapp family in Vermont. Worse yet, they bring tons of plant stocks from *Voyager,* which they leave behind when they depart. Does the Prime Directive only apply to sentients? What if Mars contains dormant microbes?

New planets would undoubtedly get their revenge, however, whether the newcomers have superior gadgets or not. Technology is useless when it's inappropriate. Robert Scott and his entire group died in 1912 when they attempted to reach the South Pole with horses. The medieval Norse settlements in Greenland disappeared under the onslaughts of the Arctic winter, despite their advanced Iron Age technology. The same would have happened to the Pilgrims in New England, accustomed to settled rural living and a less extreme climate: they would have starved without Indian assistance. As it was, the death rates in the Plymouth colony for the first two years were appalling. Other refugee or castaway colonies failed altogether, leaving no trace—and more importantly from the viewpoint of the Prime Directive, no influence on local cultures.

In *Star Trek* episodes, all Earth-like planets seem to have perfectly edible plants and nonthreatening animals. I can recall only one case where a planet harbored poisonous fruit ("The Way to Eden," TOS). In real life, I think that both temporary visitors and colonists would face enormous problems. Such a scenario is marvelously handled in Donald Kingsbury's novel *Courtship Rite.*

Let's now address a more specific concern. If the Federation wishes to observe a less advanced culture closely, they have to send representatives to the planet, in the time-honored way of extraterrestrial visitors of all ages. How will they perform their task undetected? Obviously, there are two ways. One is to generate a force field that renders them invisible, like the one-way mirrors used in interrogation and observation rooms. The other is to attempt to "pass" as natives.

Both of these methods carry associated dangers. Any technology, even that of the Federation, can blow a fuse or buckle under an earthquake or a sudden solar flare. This happens in "Who Watches the Watchers?" (TNG), in which the "duck blind" fails on Mintaka III, home to a Bronze Age proto-Vulcan race.

The attempt to "pass" can be jeopardized if the visitor has a sudden medical emergency. This occurs in "First Contact" (TNG), in which Will Riker is pegged as an alien on Malcor III. Despite his suitably altered exterior, medical technology unmasks him when he is taken unconscious to a local hospital.

Both cases court not merely cultural contamination but also biological disaster, because they involve medical emergencies. In "Who Watches the Watchers?" one of the Mintakans has to be beamed to the *Enterprise* sick bay. In "First Contact," Riker is treated at the Malcorian hospital. Worse yet, he has to bribe the nurse in the manner favored by Captain Kirk to secure his escape.

Dare we assume that Riker brought along a condom for this eventuality, when he wasn't even prepared for a blow to the head? Of course, he's also damned if he did, because that implies that such a possibility had crossed his mind. And even if he came equipped, hospitals throughout the ages have been notorious for causing unrelated infections if patients stay long enough—although the patients get theirs back by invariably putting their own bacteria into general circulation as well. In both these episodes there has been breaching of skin, which is often the prelude to contagion.

And speaking of exchange of bodily fluids, let's take a brief detour into the application of the Prime Directive by the least xenophobic Federation representative—Capt. James Tiberius Kirk. Just as Spock melds with any life-form, carbon, silicon, or energy, so does Kirk mate with all life-forms, human, humanoid, or other. He violates the Prime Directive routinely and lustily—but at least you can't accuse him of discrimination.

Like a self-respecting sea captain of old, Kirk acquires a woman at every port. Here's a list of just his truly exotic conquests: Kelinda from the Andromeda Galaxy in "By Any Other Name"; Sylvia, another transgalactic, in "Catspaw"; blue-haired Shahna the gladiator in "The Gamesters of Triskelion"; the sorceress Nona in "A Private Little War"; the androids Rayna Kapec in "Requiem for Methuselah" and Losira in "That Which Survives"; the sped-up Deela of Scalos in "Wink of an Eye." I also count at least seven human or humanoid women—including, of course, the devoted and accessible Ensign Rand.

Granted, one snowflake doesn't make a snowstorm. Nevertheless, this cavalier treatment shows how much more gung ho the first incarnation of *Star Trek* was, compared to the sedate, measured tones of its successors. There's a real reason for this—TOS aired after the advent of contraceptive pills but before the dawn of AIDS. Still, the subsequent

Star Trek series have been loath to totally abandon such a noble tradition and have hence put forward anemic Kirk descendants—Will Riker in TNG, Julian Bashir in DS9, and Ensigns Kim and Paris in VOY.

The women in the main cast are not allowed such shenanigans. They're generally either monogamous or celibate—with the refreshing exception of Major Kira (DS9), who has at least three notches on her bedpost. Nevertheless, in the interests of fair play, each member of the main cast in each series, regardless of gender or species, is allowed at least one short-lived fling with an exotic partner.

Still, old satyr Kirk's unbridled gusto has real joy in it, and in a backhanded way, this Starfleet captain awards full equality to the cultures that he visits. After all, he truly mourns when he loses these women—who must either be killed or renounce him, so that he can continue roving. He weeps for Miramanee in "The Paradise Syndrome," and he is so torn up over Rayna that Spock has to suppress his memories of her in "Requiem for Methuselah." You may lust for someone you consider inferior, but you don't grieve for them unless you consider them your peer.

This egalitarian if politically incorrect attitude of Kirk's brings us to the most pernicious aspects of the Prime Directive—its condescension and one-sided judgments.

DADDY KNOWS BEST

In Greek mythology, when the Titan Prometheus stole the fire of the gods and gave it to humanity, the gods shackled him to Mount Caucasus and sent a vulture to devour his liver. Sometimes I wonder if the Prime Directive, enforced only on the cultural level, does not smack of a wish to retain prerogatives similar to the gods' desire to hang on to their fire.

What the Prime Directive effectively says is that technology should not be given to societies that cannot use it wisely. The perennial question, of course, is—who decides? To give an obvious example, who deemed the Klingons mature enough to give them warp technology? Between their endless civil wars, their unstable alliances, and their lousy tempers, they endanger themselves and others constantly. And given their contempt for all nonwarrior occupations (such as science), as well as their lack of large-scale cooperation (necessary for development of technology), I very much doubt that they discovered warp technology themselves.

The equation of various cultural stages to biological ages is facile and often incorrect. Which aspect of the culture is the deciding factor? Technology? Morality? Philosophy? Cultures with low levels of technology can be very sophisticated otherwise, and their low-key technology is often (though not always) carefully calibrated to their environment—such as the dry-agriculture methods of the American Southwest.

There is something paternalistic in the Prime Directive, as if the more advanced societies are jealous of their privileges, rather than anxious to safeguard the cultures whose inferior technology makes them vulnerable. It resembles the customs that "guard" the purity of unmarried girls. This keeps the young female minds conveniently blank and malleable, thereby perpetuating their thralldom.

When our heroes are on the receiving end of such high-handedness, they don't like it ("Q Who?" TNG; "Prime Factors," VOY). They correctly perceive that they are being treated condescendingly. I would have rebelled if my parents hadn't let me loose on the library. I bet, too, that the people of Earth would fume if they found out that the reason that SETI has been so silent is that those civilizations eavesdropping on us have deemed us too primitive, too "childlike."

Such arrogance becomes unbearable when the Federation acts as judge, jury, and executioner for entire civilizations, as I described earlier. Under such circumstances, I would agree wholeheartedly with the Talmud and with Nikolai Rozhenko ("Homeward," TNG) that to save even a single life is a mitzvah, cultural contamination be damned.

Just as it confuses cultural interference with the Prime Directive, the Federation also tends to conflate two very different exports: the products of high technology and high technology itself. Exposing a less technologically advanced culture to products that it cannot produce itself is invariably disastrous, because it builds dependency and/or because the prestige of the new import may displace a better native resource.

The Opium Wars of 1839 and 1856 between China and England are a prime example of such artificial dependency. The English importation of opium into China was an extremely profitable enterprise. Once they had enough Chinese hooked on the drug, the English first blackmailed, then strongarmed the Chinese government into relinquishing all efforts to combat addiction. *Star Trek* shows a case almost identical to the Opium Wars in "Symbiosis" (TNG), which should probably have been titled "Procurers for the Nation."

Another example is the peddling of maternal milk substitutes to third-world countries, a practice that the World Health Organization tried to stop officially in 1981. These infant formulas led to widespread infant malnutrition as well as disease: their reconstruction required water, which is often contaminated in poor countries, and their use prevented access to the natural extra nutrients and antibodies of maternal milk.

Exporting technological knowledge is a very different story and may actually benefit the recipient culture—as long as it's evenly distributed. Governments know the leveling effects of technology all too well and have traditionally put heavy restrictions on new technology, often ennobling the desire for military or financial dominance by renaming it national security. The Chinese were as jealous of their silk monopoly and the Byzantine Greeks as chary about sharing the secret ingredients of "liquid fire" (an incendiary substance that burnt upon contact with water) as the United States is now about its cryptographic software.

In many historical instances, human cultures adapted quickly and well to new technology. American Indians took to horses like ducks to water. In fact, the Great Plains mounted cultures (the Cheyenne, Crow, Lakota) were the ones that withstood the U.S. cavalry the longest. If they had remained untouched by the new technology, they might have vanished altogether.

As an equivalent case, the inventive Iotians in "A Piece of the Action" (TOS) have re-created an entire culture and its associated technology from a single Federation item—a book. I would argue that these people are intelligent and dexterous enough that they will not be harmed from extraneous technology unless they are literally handed an atom bomb.

The slipperiness of the Prime Directive and the difficulty of enforcing it clearly show that it is dispensable. In fact, in TOS it is made obvious that the Federation did not always include the Prime Directive among its moral tenets—and that the outcome of accidental contact wasn't always disastrous. Four TOS episodes act as cautionary tales to those who would gainsay the application of restraint ("Bread and Circuses," "A Piece of the Action," "Patterns of Force," "The Omega Glory"). In each of these, inappropriate interference by Federation starships turns the affected societies into either static tyrannies or devastated war zones. Yet in two other episodes ("The Apple" and "For the World Is Hollow and I Have Touched the Sky"), Kirk effectively overthrows a local god, to the benefit of all concerned.

Several additional *Star Trek* episodes show interactions in which an unplanned unveiling of the existence of the Federation does not unleash cataclysms. One such instance is "A Private Little War" (TOS), in which Kirk is friendly with the leader of a local clan. These people know of the Federation's existence but haven't allowed this knowledge to alter their way of life—though in the end, advanced technology indeed destroys them.

Too, in both "Who Watches the Watchers?" and "First Contact" (TNG), Captain Picard is forced to reveal the existence of the Federation. Although this has certain concrete repercussions, they mostly occur on the personal level. Neither society is permanently destabilized, and both make choices as to how they wish to treat the new knowledge.

Furthermore, in positing that a single Federation starship can derail a whole society, our heroes think a bit too much of themselves and their toys. Castaways, especially isolated ones without additional backing, can't overturn centuries of local customs. The stupefying success of Cortés in Mexico came about not only because he had vastly superior technology (guns and horses) but also because the Aztecs had treated their neighbors so abominably that the Spaniards found themselves at the vanguard of local armies. Something similar happens in "The Cloud Minders" (TOS), in which Kirk and Co. find themselves heading a revolution of the disenfranchised miners on Ardana.

The last time that we see our heroes break the Prime Directive is, of course, *First Contact* (ST8), where they end up helping Zefram Cochrane achieve the first warp flight. Again, they are forgiven for their trespass, since the end clearly justifies the means. Why can't they be equally reasonable the rest of the time and weigh each case on its merits?

So I think that, although the moral restraint of the Prime Directive speaks well for the Federation's intentions, civilizations can generally take care of themselves if they are approached peacefully and in good faith. This means that the Prime Directive is effectively redundant. Those who enact such laws are likely to be benevolent and principled to begin with. Those who aren't won't be stopped by such considerations.

Furthermore, I would argue that knowing that a superior civilization exists would spur the less advanced culture on in its efforts to reach technological maturity—and hence gain both self-respect and independence. My father and I became happier people and fast friends once I sank my teeth and mind into my parents' books.

Redundant as it is, the Prime Directive exists to make the universe as safe as possible for budding civilizations. What about those who don't bother with such niceties?

SCHOOLYARD BULLIES AND SISTERS OF MERCY

In contrast to the Federation policy, the Prime Directive does not appear to be widespread in other galactic races or cultures. This is independent of whether they're peace-loving benefactors or leering conquerors.

If a nation wishes to exploit its less advanced neighbor, there are several ways to do so. War is the obvious first alternative, but it does create havoc and produce casualties. Unequal trade is the second approach—much tidier, but it leaves something to be desired, since it still requires production of the trade items. The best way, however, is to awe the other side with superior "knowledge," so that they just worship you for that alone and keep you supplied with luxuries with no effort from your side. Or, if you are ethical, you can make sure that they don't stray too far from the path of righteousness by supplying them with "divine laws." As Arthur C. Clarke said, any technology that is advanced enough will be seen as magic.

Star Trek shows all these variations. As examples of the first two methods, there's no doubt that neither the Klingons nor the Ferengi feel bound by the noblesse oblige of the Directive. The former are totally consumed with the idea of conquest. Hence, they supply weapons to anyone who asks ("A Private Little War," TOS) and try to attain superiority by means fair or foul (*The Search for Spock,* ST3). Conversely, the latter are just as consumed with the idea of profit and therefore do not hesitate to set themselves up as local gods and rob the awed locals blind ("False Profits," VOY).

The third approach is primarily exemplified by good guys, though Q is not above playing God just for the fun of it. The benevolent aliens in both "The Chase" (TNG) and "Tattoo" (VOY) respectively gave humans life and language. The collective memory and disjointed artifacts that the aliens left behind in "Tattoo" are eerily reminiscent of the cargo cults that sprang up throughout Oceania, which started in the nineteenth century and received new impetus during World War II. Contact between Europeans and people with Stone Age technology resulted in messianic cults that prophesied "the return of the cargo"—and exhibited canned noodles as marks of status.

The Federation, by instituting the Prime Directive, has set its behavior against that of all gods—pagan, Hebrew, Christian, Q, the Prophets, you name it. None of these can resist manipulating their constituency.

However, as the early Christians, the Albigensians, and other completely pacific sects learned to their cost, turning the other cheek didn't spare you in the arena. By being alone in positing and obeying the Prime Directive, the Federation has put itself at a dangerous disadvantage. It's a fine gesture to be peaceful and mean well, as long as your actions are reciprocated. By being the only one that acts as ethically as possible, the Federation endangers its territory and the civilizations under its protection.

This behavior falls under a classic problem of game theory known as the Prisoner's Dilemma. The scenario unfolds as follows: Two people are arrested and are interrogated separately. Each can choose independently to deny or to confess the deed. If neither confesses (cooperation), they go free; if both confess, they receive relatively light sentences. On the other hand, if only one confesses (defection), he goes free and his companion receives a heavy sentence.

You can see that this situation can occur not only in real-world or TV police dramas, but in politics, ethics, and ecosystems as well. If you defect every time, you end up with no allies. If you cooperate every time, you end up cheated or imprisoned. Those who have studied the Prisoner's Dilemma argue that the best policy is to cooperate the first time, then modulate the response according to your partner's action in each turn.

So if the Federation decides that it will be the guy with the white hat no matter what, its chances of long-term survival are close to zero. This outcome, which may outrage our idealism but justifies our cynicism, is actually shown in the mirror universe. There everyone wears not just black hats but black leather, and the usual greeting is a stab in the back.

The *Enterprise* crew accidentally enters this world in "Mirror, Mirror" (TOS). Kirk's well-intentioned preaching of the gospel of universal brotherhood causes the Federation to become excessively pacific. When the Terrans later return to that universe ("Crossover," "Through the Looking Glass," and "Shattered Mirror," DS9), they discover that Kirk's urging not to give in to the Dark Side of the Force has cost them everything. Because the mirror Spock heeded Kirk's words, Terrans and Vulcans are now despised slaves to races that were not hindered by such ethical burdens as the Prime Directive.

Finally, what will happen if two races meet that are so unequal that one deems the other too low on the sentience scale to arouse any ethical dilemmas? The dominant one may use the other as experimental animals—or swat them like flies. *Star Trek* has shown several such examples, in which highly advanced aliens toy casually with the lives of starship crews ("Where Silence Has Lease," "Frame of Mind," and "Schisms," TNG; "Scientific Method," VOY). We don't really consider the emotions of ants when we step on their nests. What will we look like to beings who are to us as we are to amoebas? No matter how you look at it, the Prime Directive can only be applied in degrees.

SHARE YOUR TOYS AND PLAY NICE

So I seem to have reached another of my many counterintuitive conclusions. Although I must applaud the Federation for adopting the Prime Directive, it looks as if this moral imperative is either irrelevant or dangerous. Given the technology that the Federation commands, it would have been easier to apply the neural mind-wipers used in *Men in Black* (and in several *Star Trek* episodes) rather than go through the physical, mental, and ethical contortions that the Prime Directive demands.

Biological contamination is a much harder problem to combat than its cultural counterpart. The coordinators of the Mars expeditions took some elementary precautions (irradiation and isolation of the landers and rovers prior to launching), after the possibility was raised that the planet might harbor fossils or descendants of the non-Earth bacteria discovered embedded in Martian asteroids found in the Antarctic.

No matter how hard we try, it may be impossible to travel away from our world without leaving traces of our passage. The strongest argument in favor of *Star Trek*'s Prime Directive may be not to safeguard a robust advanced civilization, but to ensure that alien life is recognized as such, and its fragile signal is not overwhelmed by our exuberant noise.

SCENE II.
IS EVERY DAY A GOOD DAY TO DIE?

Marooned in Monochromatic Societies

Star Trek's starship *Enterprise* hasn't been the only vessel with a five-year mission. In 1831, a British survey ship, the H.M.S. *Beagle,* sailed with a tiny budget and practically no cannons on board. Its five-year mission was to chart the treacherous waters of South America and the Eastern Pacific, so that British merchant ships would have access to alternative trade routes. Along as ship's naturalist came a twenty-one-year-old Cambridge graduate with average grades, who intended to settle into the comfortable life of a clergyman. His name was Charles Darwin.

The explorations that changed the history of science, and indirectly the world, were undertaken by unprepossessing nonmilitary vessels—the *Beagle* then; the Alvins, Voyagers, Vikings, Mariners, *Sojourner*s now. A big budget helps, but the ironclad prerequisite is a burning desire to know. What promotes or suppresses scientific discoveries and their applications is the worldview of the society in which they are embedded. The character of the society will determine whether its members will turn a piece of Earth into a garden or a waste, if they'll go to the stars as explorers, as conquerors—or not at all.

Humans love thinking of alternative societies, whether utopian, dystopian, or merely different. Witness the endless fascination of travelogues through the ages. Such projections form the nucleus of most serious science fiction writing and, therefore, could not possibly have been ignored in *Star Trek*.

Star Trek has examined social questions primarily through four different lenses: mirror universes where moral values are reversed ("Mirror, Mirror," TOS; "Crossover," "Through the Looking Glass," "Shattered Mirror," DS9); small, isolated human colonies ("Up the Long Ladder," TNG); societies that take one character aspect to its extreme end point (all episodes centered on Vulcans, Klingons, Ferengi, Kazon); and the rare matriarchy ("Angel One," TNG; "Favorite Son," VOY). All these are measured against the "ideal" world of the Federation, which takes space exploration as a given and has eradicated all Four Horsemen—poverty, disease, inequality, and war.

Being in most respects solidly middlebrow, *Star Trek* also suffers the universal ambivalence about whether to treat women as first-class citizens or restrict them to traditional feminine roles. Whenever women appear dominant, ominous music swells. The apogee of evil in *Star Trek* is not the reverse universe in "Mirror, Mirror" (TOS and DS9), which unfolds rather like a cross between an S&M fantasy and a Dungeons & Dragons game; instead, the most fearsome configuration is the combination of matriarchy and collective organization exhibited by the Borg.

Societal patterns may be partly dictated by our particular ancestry. The clan groupings of primates are very different from the strict canine pyramids or the coequal feline "wheel hubs" in which every group member is equidistant in power and influence from the leader. Furthermore, the details of primate societies differ among even closely related species: bonobos, or pygmy chimpanzees *(Pan paniscus)*, enjoy greater equality and flexibility than chimpanzees *(Pan troglodytes)*.

We humans have gone far from our origins and have experimented with all kinds of social configurations. On earth, there certainly have been (and still exist) societies and social groups obsessed with particular ideas—primarily those that follow rigid beliefs of whatever stripe (the Hasidim, the Mormons, the Saudis, the Red Guards). However, some ideas are more equal than others; certain types of social organizations are decidedly more conducive to star-traveling. In both our Earth and in the *Star Trek* universe, two patterns in particular will result in unstable, eventually nonviable configurations: the one-note societies and those that have limited genetic material to draw from.

ONE-INSTRUMENT ORCHESTRAS

Star Trek has often explored tensions between very different systems by juxtaposing extremes. Sometimes, these cohabit a single person, as is the case with the various humanoid hybrids. Other times, the roles are given to specific crew members. *Star Trek,* aspiring to universality and mythic status, has made each of its main characters a carefully chosen collection of few traits. In that, it follows the path of old epics, which gave heroes a constantly repeated sobriquet—Erik the Red, Ethelred the Unready, Bright-Eyed Athena—to distinguish the characters and give a mnemonic device to both the bards and their audience.

The various *Star Trek* series reflect the historical and psychological preoccupations of American culture at the time of their creation. TOS is Freudian and has apportioned the superego/ego/id roles to Spock/Kirk/McCoy, respectively. Several of its episodes show two opposing superpowers ("Balance of Terror," "Errand of Mercy") or allude to the Vietnam War ("A Private Little War").

The more polyphonic cast of TNG has chosen to divide along the fault lines of Jungian archetypes—or to personify the major arcana in tarot cards: Picard, the Magician; Riker, the Charioteer; Worf, the Paladin; Crusher, the High Priestess; Troi, the Anima; Data, the Holy Fool. TNG is also concerned with how to wisely use what we readily recognize as "peace dividends."

DS9 is preoccupied with multiculturalism: the station crew has undergone a fragmentation similar to that of former Yugoslavia. Each member of the main cast practically represents their race or nation. DS9 is also preoccupied with internal dissension (the Maquis episodes as well as the ones that deal with Bajoran religion).

VOY seems to represent the atomized state of today's society. There's an odd feeling that everyone in that ship is disconnected and adrift. There is also the not-quite-melting pot of Federation-*Voyager* and Maquis-*Voyager* crew members, at about the same time that all Americans have suddenly become hyphenated according to ethnicity.

This isolation of character components into easily identifiable "types" allows the series to pursue such attributes to their (il)logical conclusion. It also lets our heroes engage in exchanges eerily reminiscent of the dialogues of Plato and the classical Greek dramas. In those, the two voices usually represent diametrically opposed views, both of which can nevertheless be right. Whenever I hear Worf and Troi argue, for example, I am reminded of Creon and Antigone in Sophocles' play *Antigone.* In both pairs, the former argues for the letter of codified law, the latter for adherence to a moral code that springs from an innate sense of "rightness."

Another way that *Star Trek* illustrates extremes is through the lenses of one-note societies. There can be no doubt that different life-forms will have radically different societal patterns; even on Earth, the variety of animal and human societies is staggering. However, since the vast majority of *Star Trek* societies are humanoid, their choices are more limited: they must follow human patterns.

There is a precedent for single-note societies even among humans. In older days, people with very decided opinions about society or religion could withdraw from the fray and start anew—and those within their sphere of influence could be persuaded to obey the leader's vision by either brute force or moral blackmail.

That's how we got the Calvinist regime in early-Renaissance Geneva—in which eavesdropping on neighbors was a cardinal civic virtue—or today's isolationist communities, whether they are the Amish in Pennsylvania or the Taliban in Afghanistan. Such groups want to set up an absolute, "pure," self-contained system. However, the resulting systems are inherently unstable even when open; they are decidedly so when they extend to encompass an entire planet.

Dysfunctional social arrangements may limp along for a surprisingly long time. Examples abound even today, and they are independent of technology levels—from the Amazonian Yanomamo, who encourage perpetual war raids by systematically killing their women, to the corruption and inefficiency of dictatorships, to the outrageous shortsightedness and injustices of nations run by fundamentalist religious fanatics. However, it is unlikely that such societies will ever take to the stars. Neither science nor exploration thrives in surroundings that are obsessed with control. The military space endeavors of both the United States and the Soviet Union were prestige gestures, since they had no direct military value; today, all international space programs are civilian, including NASA.

Civilian government and centralized government are not mutually exclusive. In the increasingly libertarian twentieth-century United States, centralized government has been condemned as "evil" by conservative Congress members, who would prefer to abolish it altogether. However, those who think that privatization of everything will solve problems are in for a rude awakening. Large-scale undertakings almost require centralized authority—even if that authority is simply a standardized set of metrics or protocols, the creation of the Internet being the most accessible example.

Otherwise, stratifications will increase and states will fall into the bickering characteristic of both American Indian nations and European feudal baronies. On the other hand, too heavy-handed a central policy can lead to errors of historic proportions. It was such a "unified" policy that led the Chinese to dismantle their navy in 1433, leaving all of the Far East wide open to the Europeans. The mandarins decided that they should solve all internal problems first. Not surprisingly, they ended up solving none because they couldn't agree on which problems merited attention—an instructive analogy to the gutting of the U.S. space program by Congress in favor of vaguely defined "social programs" that never reach those who need them.

Almost invariably, entire planets on *Star Trek* are presented as a single social and cultural block, although their groupings almost always conform to the clan pattern—perhaps a realistic assessment of the long-term adaptive value of the nation-state. Whenever the series breaks this mold, the results are notable: one of the best is "The High Ground" (TNG), which grapples with the ever-relevant question of what distinguishes a terrorist from a freedom fighter. This episode is rare not only because it shows a fragmented society, but also because it gives equal time to both sides of an argument. The end, though, is depressingly predictable, as the *Enterprise* opts to back the dominant side—which purports to represent law and order.

Some of the societies shown in *Star Trek* are nuanced and complex. The Romulans, Cardassians, and Bajorans not only are believable societies, with both warts and beauty spots, but have also given us the most intriguing characters: the complicated, humane Romulan commander in "Balance of Terror" (TOS); the defiant, divided Ensign Ro Laren in "Preemptive Strike" (TNG); the Bajoran resistance fighter Kira Nerys, now second-in-command to Captain Sisko (DS9); and Elim Garak, ex-member of the Cardassian Obsidian Order (DS9), as ambiguous and cunning as Odysseus (he gets to deliver the best lines by far).

Three major *Star Trek* space-faring societies, however, serve as interesting "primary color" portrayals of some of the deadly sins: the Klingons (anger), Vulcans (pride), and Ferengi (greed). Occasional minor societies serve to make rather heavy-handed moral points—usually a case for tolerance ("Justice" and "The Outcast," TNG; "Resistance," VOY) or a plea for diversity ("The Masterpiece Society," TNG). As well, the mirror universe society in DS9 combines the worst characteristics of both Klingons and Ferengi.

These monochromatic cultures are effectively broad cartoons. Klingons suffer from terminal testosterone poisoning, Vulcans suppress emotions to such an extent that it impairs their judgment, and Ferengi seek profit to the exclusion of any other consideration. The first two are what I earlier called superego and id societies—the Vulcans dough without leavening and the Klingons yeast full of bubbles.

Let's check out the Klingons first, perennial favorites like the Mortal Kombat cutouts that they are (the Kazon of VOY are poor-quality Klingon copies). Here is a society that we are told is made up exclusively of warriors. If no external enemies exist, they kill each other—or playfully butt head ridges, giving themselves boxers' dementia. The closest equivalent to this on Earth is either a horde like Genghis Khan's or a prison—both "open" systems totally dependent on nonmembers for sustenance.

Whenever they appear in terrestrial societies, full-time warriors are destabilizing presences and obligatory parasites. Like male lions, they are given free sustenance solely to protect the rest of their group from others like themselves. In large-scale stratified societies (such as feudal Europe and shogunal Japan), they rely on slaves, peasants, artisans, and merchants. In smaller groups (the Plains Indians, the Masai), they rely—again like the lions—on the labor and products of their women. Since they depend entirely on others, warriors are by definition unable to be a complete society by themselves.

The Klingon society as presented completely lacks both stability and an economic basis. If its members additionally feel ashamed to grow old, there won't be much chance for maturing either individually or collectively. No wonder they resemble bad-tempered children. In this respect, what separates the Klingons from the Jem'Hadar is merely that the former are self-willed. People with such an outlook would have annihilated themselves before coming even close to achieving space flight.

To do them justice, Klingons have dash and swagger—and favor leather and metal, which can cover a multitude of sins. Like heroes of the Homeric epics and Norse sagas, they're obsessed with the right gesture: style eventually acquires its own substance. Quite appropriately, they produce Wagnerian-sounding operas.

And yet, how heroic are the Klingons, when dishonor lurks behind their every unorthodox action? Everyone speaks admiringly of the three hundred Spartans who stood against Xerxes' much larger Persian army at Thermopylae. Yet the Spartans had no choice: their culture forbade retreat or surrender.

Much braver, and almost unknown to history, were seven hundred soldiers from Thespiae who stood at the Spartans' side. These came from a small mercantile city-state and could honorably have left at any time. They still decided to remain. Therein lies the greatest bravery—just like Quark, who comes from a decidedly unheroic culture, yet takes on a Klingon adversary twice his size in "The House of Quark" (DS9).

At the extreme opposite corner from the Klingons are the Vulcans, supreme examples of self-control—or so they like to think. Vulcan society, by its strict adherence to logic, has created major problems for itself. For one, the Vulcan suppression of emotions may not only be biologically impossible (as I discussed in chapter 5) but also socially counteradaptive. Such a behavior pattern allows no room for highly valuable "hunches," which are critical not only in moments of danger but also in scientific insights.

As well, the Vulcan lack of body language decreases the information content of their spoken words—Vulcan vocal delivery is equivalent to reading E-mail, a notoriously poor medium for nuances. If ever there was a "creaky" society, the Vulcan one decidedly qualifies for the adjective.

With their total contempt for intuitive leaps and emotional nuances, Vulcans would make outstanding accountants but poor scientists and even worse leaders. We actually see this failure to grasp the larger framework whenever they are in charge of a mission (Spock in "The *Galileo* Seven," TOS; Tuvok in "Rise," VOY). Furthermore, since Vulcans are not allowed to explore and hence modulate their emotions, they erupt in juvenile rages whenever their control fails ("Amok Time," TOS; "Sarek," TNG; "Blood Fever," VOY).

Finally, Vulcans can't even be good shipboard comrades: for people priding themselves on their moderation, they are amazingly arrogant and boring. The automatic assumption of Spock that he's bringing the light to the benighted Romulans in "Unification" (TNG) is a case in point. The Vulcan sense of humor is as well developed as Data's. The practical nonexistence of Vulcan-centered *Star Trek* episodes after TOS speaks volumes about the dramatic potential of such a society.

Let's now proceed to the Ferengi. Their crass capitalism leaves no room for kin altruism or for the win-win variation of the Prisoner's

Dilemma, which I described in the previous chapter. People whose loyalty to profit supersedes all other considerations will end up with no allies. The Federation, of course, has removed the temptation of profit by the expedient of infinite resources.

Whereas variations of warrior societies have existed on Earth, the closest equivalents that we have to Ferengi societies are the Wall Street feeding frenzies that erupted in the eighties in the United States—and, ironically, in several of the former Soviet Union republics. The conditions of the latter speak for themselves regarding the long-term viability of such a system.

The Ferengi make adroit negotiators but seem to contradict themselves by making their women slaves. In "Family Business" and "Rules of Acquisition" (DS9) we find out that Ferengi women are property. By law, they are also naked, housebound, illiterate, and totally disenfranchised.

One might argue that the Ferengi men don't want competitors if they can possibly help it—a point that comes up repeatedly in Earth gender politics, from clubs to unions to governments. On the other hand, if profit is the Ferengi sole motive, why deny themselves the brainpower of half their population?

Neither Klingons nor Ferengi could possibly have invented warp technology on their own. The former apparently got it from the Romulans. The latter, not surprisingly, bought it ("Little Green Men," DS9). Ironically, both may have grown both more stable and more set in their extreme characteristics by expanding into space. Once they are in contact with other cultures, they can buy or take what they need.

The monochromatic societies ring hollow for an additional reason: there is no doubt that, just like the Klingon language, they're made up as *Star Trek* goes along. In each Klingon episode, we're introduced to a new ritual; in each Ferengi episode, we hear of a new Rule of Acquisition.

The three races I have just showcased may be as flat as the cardboard villages that Potemkin set up in the tour path of Catherine the Great, but they're still clearly in favor of technology. In fact, they represent an interesting example of Toffler's dictum that the three ways to power are, in order of increasing sophistication, force (Klingons), wealth (Ferengi), and information (Vulcans). In that respect, the Federation represents the synthesis of all into a harmonious whole.

What happens, though, when there's serious system failure—if resources run out, if technology fails? Worst of all, what happens if a planet gets isolated or a starship crashes?

UP THE PROVERBIAL CREEK WITHOUT A PADDLE

The word *society* means one thing if one wishes to define it historically or culturally and something rather different if one wishes to define it biologically. If humans attain true space travel, entire starship complements may get marooned. If the environment is even borderline hostile, such castaway colonies will not survive. Obvious counterparts are the doomed medieval Norse outposts in Greenland, which vanished even though they possessed iron implements and agriculture; and the inhabitants of Easter Island, who were first reduced to cannibalism and then disappeared altogether. This happened because, when they were deprived of trade, they destroyed their small, fragile ecosystem.

If they succeed in maintaining a foothold, castaways may eventually disappear due to genetic inbreeding. And even if they don't, their settlements won't resemble the Luddite heavens of "Journey's End" (TNG) or "Paradise" (DS9).

Whenever a group falls below a certain number, increasing homozygosity (genetic sameness) brings out deleterious or lethal traits. Humans, despite their hardwired xenophobia, have always tried to outbreed—hence the eternal allure of the dark, handsome stranger and the prevalence of all those semimortal mythological heroes sired by visiting "gods."

This requirement for genetic diversity is why Captain Kirk ("Wink of an Eye," TOS) and Ensign Kim ("Favorite Son," VOY) will never be able to regenerate races desperate for males, no matter how enthusiastically they impregnate. Equally doomed are the Boraalan villagers that Nikolai humanely saves in "Homeward" (TNG) and the two isolated whales in *The*

Voyage Home (ST4). The whales' problem is exacerbated by their long gestation period. For societies faced with the threat of genetic extinction, cloning from the initial varied stock may in fact be the only solution, contrary to the (ex)postulations of "Up the Long Ladder" (TNG).

Cloning, however, requires sophisticated technology—and dramatic loss of it will inevitably result from a difficult migration or a crash landing. The American Indians abandoned the wheel during their slow travels across the Bering Strait and down the Central American isthmus. The Australians and Tasmanians were the same stock, and both had advanced Stone Age technology. However, after ten thousand years of living in Tasmania, its inhabitants had lost practically everything: fire, agriculture, boats, bows and arrows, nets, spears, and all stone tools.

The only cultures that can afford to romanticize "return to nature" are those whose technology allows them to control nature—such as the contemporary campers who "rough it" with flash-frozen rations, Gore-Tex tents, and thermal underwear. In *Star Trek,* such are the Organians in "Errand of Mercy" (TOS), the Cytherians in "The Nth Degree" (TNG), and the Inheritors in "Tattoo" (VOY).

Getting truly marooned is not romantic. Most commonly, it's a death sentence; otherwise, it's a brutal struggle for survival. If isolated planetary colonists manage to survive, they will undergo large genetic drift. If they're isolated long enough to deviate significantly, they will eventually become a new species.

Therefore, even if we accept the bogus premise of common ancestry from "The Chase" (TNG), a downed starship on a planet beyond the easy reach of warp engines will create a subpopulation that will eventually not interbreed with other humans. C. J. Cherryh shows such a divergent group in her book *Forty Thousand in Gehenna.* Thus, if enough time has elapsed, it may be useless for Picard to offer the Bringloidi as breeding stock to the cloning-prone Mariposans in "Up the Long Ladder" (TNG).

Another method to combat a shrinking genetic pool is to recruit new members, which is the preferred method of the Borg. Borg are actually the second-best society for star-traveling after the Federation. They are technophilic, efficient, coordinated, and free from internal strife. They are not short-circuited by Klingon belligerence or Ferengi greed. The Borg weaknesses are their zero tolerance for deviation and their total dependence on their queens, the nexuses in the webs within Borg Cubes.

The Borg queens exert a horrified fascination on the *Star Trek* audience. This brings me to a subject that concerns me—the position of women in *Star Trek* societies.

HOW THE OTHER HALF LIVES

Star Trek is still not quite sure how to handle the hot potato of women as full humans. The series tries conscientiously, but I get the sense it would be happier if all women were from Betazed, sensitive empaths who can soothe fevered brows and psyches with the right word.

When *Star Trek* wades into matriarchal waters, some myopia becomes evident. Whereas the Ferengi attitude toward women is tolerated—in fact, is considered amusing—by Federation and non-Federation societies alike, an equivalent female attitude is cause for stern injunctions.

In "Angel One" (TNG) and "Favorite Son" (VOY) we meet two overtly antimale societies that are worse caricatures than the Klingons or the Ferengi. In the former episode, a Federation ship has violated the Prime Directive and destabilized the local society. Yet when the native women governors try to contain the alien men, Riker tells them they "are fighting evolution." This male fear of a viable matriarchal culture brings to mind two seminal science fiction stories: Joanna Russ's "When It Changed" and Alice Sheldon's (pen name James Tiptree) "Houston, Houston, Do You Read?"

In "Favorite Son" (VOY) a female society is shown to literally squeeze their rare men dry to harvest their Y chromosomes. Bear in mind that these women have developed extremely advanced genetic engineering and hence should know that a simple sperm centrifugation would be more than sufficient for the purpose.

Star Trek has taken care of the other major specter, racism, by several methods: the cast is multihued; the characters whom they embody come from different planets and races; xenophobia is kept to a minimum by the miraculous interbreeding ability of the *Star Trek* humanoids. As proof, Kirk kisses Uhura in "Plato's Stepchildren (TOS)—reportedly the first interracial kiss on American TV, and a brave act in 1968.

The series also implies that, at least within the Federation, classism, ageism, and homophobia are extinct, although they say so rather than show it. In fact, the two episodes of TNG that deal with homosexuality ("The Outcast" and "The Host") are among the clumsiest in *Star Trek*—though "Rejoined" (DS9) partially redeems the series on that count.

So if other isms have ostensibly been settled, why are gender wars still around in the twenty-fourth century? After all, Federation technology has cut the thick umbilical cord between women and reproduction; also, resources are ample and free, leaving everyone presumably free to explore inclinations and fulfill desires.

The debates on women's status are inextricably linked to how much of our societal formations derive from biology. This is another nature-versus-nurture debate. Many anthropologists (Desmond Morris and, more recently, the sociobiologists) have developed what are called Tarzanist theories, in which both male dominance and the propensity for violence are considered innate. Just like the putative causes of female inferiority that I listed in chapter 5, these male characteristics are assumed to arise from roots that change according to scientific fashion—our simian ancestry, our hormones (testosterone versus estrogen), even our chromosomes.

Our eyes and other senses tell us unequivocally that humans are sexually dimorphic. Also, there can be no doubt that, since many hormones are neurotransmitters, they are involved in brain chemistry. However, I hope that all the previous chapters have given some inkling of how complicated and unpredictable the resulting system is.

Whenever people have studied their fellow humans seriously and without an overwhelming number of preconceived notions, they discover that behavioral differences within the genders are broader than those between genders. This becomes even truer when the studies are cross-cultural: they show that most gender behavior is culturally determined. As random examples, Pueblo Indian women do all the building; Japanese women traditionally take care of the household finances. In several cultures (Scythians and Sarmatians, Dahomeans), women have even participated in wars as warriors, not camp followers. The sole universal labor division is care of infants dependent on maternal milk—not a permanent occupation, you must agree, unless you subscribe to the barefoot-and-pregnant credo.

The "biology is destiny" argument is as old and tired as the hills. It is particularly pernicious when it promotes "separate but equal" roles. Everyone knows that different almost invariably implies inferior. Power is heady stuff. To be assured that you're God's image and thereby gain the automatic right to order half of humanity around, regardless of your personal attributes, must be exciting indeed.

As I mentioned in chapter 9, when people invoke "natural order" (or divine laws or any related immutable truth), they usually wish to maintain the status quo. We have come a long way from our biological beginnings and have violated "natural order" so extensively that I think we've given up the right to use it as an argument altogether.

On the other hand, let's for the moment assume that we should follow "natural order." Then we should do away with male-headed families and clans. In practically all mammalian species, and certainly so in primates, the natural, stable unit is a mother and her subadult children. Groups, whether of lions, elephants, or bonobo chimpanzees, are made up of biological or adoptive sisters and their progeny. Several mammals have demonstrable female equality or even dominance—some rodents, wolves, elephants. Female equality also appears in primates: in lemurs and gibbons but, most notably, in bonobo chimpanzees, which are the closest relatives of humans.

Males are needed for procreation, of course. However, as every farmer and lioness pride knows, intact males (bulls, stallions, roosters, male lions) are a drain on energy and resources and are at best kept to an absolute minimum. Traditionally, human sacrifices were not the virgins of myth, but adolescent boys—still the major sacrifices in war. With fertility low, women could not be spared for appeasing deities. That became fashionable much later, when humans had gone way past the subsistence level.

So the Taresians of "Favorite Son" (VOY) may be onto something archetypal, after all. In fairness, however, I must add that once fertilization technology advances sufficiently, the genders can do without each other. If cloning and artificial wombs become acceptable and reliable, we may yet see gender divisions and imbalances that make the Islamic segregations seem mild by comparison.

For those enamored of the concept of alpha males, it may come as a sobering realization that for each alpha there are, of necessity, dozens of dead epsilons. Also, excessive testosterone is bad for the brain: mice with testosterone implants can't learn how to navigate mazes, and humans who pop steroids become psychotic.

Furthermore, in groups that do have alpha males (such as baboons), these paragons of masculinity have to constantly fight both internal usurpers and external enemies. In *Star Trek,* the teers of Capella IV are a good example of this ("Friday's Child," TOS). Ironically for those who invoke "natural order," humans are the only primates whose alpha males direct wars from the safety of their bunkers.

Finally, the human genders did not begin their civilization trajectory as a dominant/submissive dyad. To reach the complex social arrangements of today, they had to go through the gatherer/hunter stage, which dictated egalitarian arrangements with little room for stratification and specialization. Originally, hunting involved "driving" the prey, an activity that required the participation of the entire band. This style of hunting is still widely employed by primate groups. Only when climate fluctuations reduced the animal herds did hunting demand specialization and high mobility, thereby separating the occupations—and status—of the two genders.

So if we wish to invoke innate ape "values," there are few of those. The only universal among primate groups is reluctance of mothers to mate with their sons. Otherwise, they engage in many practices that we consider repugnant—theft, infidelity, murder, sibling incest, infanticide. It looks as if the prelapsarian world was a far cry from Eden. It also looks as if most of our moral values are culturally acquired and maintained, in which case they are indeed relative.

To give *Star Trek* credit, in addition to the "lunatic" fringe, it has shown several other matriarchal societies, which are deemed acceptable because they practice "discreet" versions of matriarchy: the Bajorans, the Cardassians, the Vulcans.

In Bajor, the husband and children assume the last name of the wife—Tora Ziyal is the daughter of Tora Naprem ("Indiscretion," DS9). In all three societies, women attain the highest positions: in Cardassia, Korinas is a high-ranking official of the dreaded Obsidian Order ("Defiant," DS9) and women dominate the sciences ("Destiny," DS9). T'Pau of Vulcan has authority that exceeds that of the Federation Council ("Amok Time," TOS). The two kais of Bajor, both women, can determine the fate of their entire planet ("In the Hands of the Prophets," DS9).

In marked contrast, both Ferengi and Klingons have poor suffrage records. This is odd, because societies of men who must travel (sailors, merchants, warriors) have to allow women leeway to manage affairs in their absence. It's a historical fact that women gain status and privileges when men are off to war, whether we're talking of the Spartans, the Crusaders, or the Klingons prior to the Khitomer Accords.

From the female viewpoint, the Ferengi are beyond the pale; the Klingons are more ambiguous. For one, they flip-flop about allowing women to participate in the High Council. Gorkon's daughter Azetbur is on the Council (*The Undiscovered Country,* ST6), K'Ehleyr is tapped for membership in "Reunion" (TNG), but Lursa and B'Etor of the House of Duras are excluded because of their gender ("Redemption," TNG).

On the other hand, Klingon women are obviously expected to shed their blood for the Empire. Both the *Pagh* ("A Matter of Honor," TNG) and the *Rotarran* ("Soldiers of the Empire," DS9) have women crew and officers. Perhaps the Klingon women should adopt and adapt the original American battle cry: *No conscription without representation!*

It seems overall that the Klingons follow the Earth custom of designating and treating women as honorary men if either the women or the circumstances are unusual ("The House of Quark," DS9). On our own Earth, this allows family names to be carried forward in China, or daughters to take up arms to defend their families. The latter, often called by the romantic name "shield maidens," occur in many cultures, from the Balkans to the Great Plains.

I'm personally familiar with this stance, because that's how I'm treated in Greece: my father's status, as well as my education and occupation, confer special privileges on me. In social gatherings, I get to sit with the men and talk about science and politics, while the women serve us and withdraw to the kitchen. I can never decide whether to take it as an insult or a compliment.

What about the paragon of the Alpha Quadrant and the universe in general—the United Federation of Planets?

The Federation tries to treat its women as equals. Its women are not constricted within traditionally submissive frameworks. The Federation is obviously aware that overspecialization and waste of human resources can doom a species or a starship.

However, though *Star Trek* is bold enough to violate several physical and biological laws, social prejudices are another matter. Ensign Kim gets a crush on Seven of Nine in "Revulsion" (VOY), but when she forthrightly offers him sex, he is horrified—he didn't get to make the first move! Human and humanoid females are still expected to abide by traditional cultural rules.

Roddenberry's original vision of having a woman as the original second-in-command of the *Enterprise* was apparently way ahead of its time in 1966. The projected first episode, "The Cage," got subsumed into "The Menagerie" (TOS). And Captain Pike's haughty and capable Number One, played in "The Cage" by Majel Barrett, got demoted to lovesick Nurse Chapel on the *Enterprise*.

Women's numbers and positions within the *Star Trek* main casts precisely bear out the famous "one-third rule." This posits that men become uncomfortable when women make up more than a third of a group or talk more than a third of the time.

TOS has only one woman on the bridge out of seven, with no power whatsoever: Lieutenant Uhura, communications. In TNG, we get two out of eight, both helpmate roles—Counselor Deanna Troi and Dr. Beverly Crusher. The intriguing Security Officer Tasha Yar got dispatched in the first season to be replaced by . . . Wesley Crusher!

DS9 is back down to one and a half out of nine, but at least Major Kira Nerys is second-in-command of the station; the half is Science Officer Jadzia Dax, because she's a Trill. In VOY it's still two out of eight—heavyweights this round, Captain Kathryn Janeway and Chief Engineer B'Elanna Torres. With the addition of Seven of Nine in "Scorpion," women finally just reach the one-third point, after thirty years in our world and three centuries in the *Star Trek* timeline.

Moreover, *Star Trek* displays the Hollywood penchant for dead or weak mothers: Lwaxana Troi (TNG, DS9) is portrayed as every child's guilty nightmare, though in "Ménage à Troi" (TNG) she shows herself a devoted mother. Spock's mother, Amanda, is entirely subsumed by his father, Sarek ("Journey to Babel," TOS). Poor Jennifer Sisko gets killed twice in DS9 (in "Emissary" and in the mirror universe in "Shattered Mirror"). K'Ehleyr is dispatched the moment she produces Alexander ("Reunion," TNG); ditto Juliana Tainer, after she and Soong create Data ("Inheritance," TNG). I can see why women avoid marriage in *Star Trek:* it's the surest way to get killed. Does this mean we're about to lose Dax, to whom Worf just pledged his troth in "You Are Cordially Invited" (DS9)?

Individually and collectively, the men in the series are obsessed with their fathers. In "Birthright" (TNG), Worf perorates that for Klingons "nothing is more important than receiving a revelation about your father." We know almost more than we need to about Mogh, Worf's father—but I can't recall his mother even being named. Yet the fathers seem to cause nothing but trouble: Mogh has managed to permanently dishonor his sons ("Sins of the Father," TNG); Kyle Riker pushes Will to the breaking point with his competitiveness ("The Icarus Factor," TNG), and Sarek does the same to Spock with his disapproval ("Journey to Babel," TOS).

In fact, I'm also guilty of suppressing my mother's contributions. From reading this book, you know by now that from my engineer father, the dreamer, I inherited my love for science and my habit of avid reading. All you know of my mother is that she cooks well; I haven't told you that she's a warrior, who bequeathed me her gift for languages, her lovely singing voice, and her fierce determination.

I think that the easiest solution to many problems is to opt for matrilinealism at least, if not for outright matriarchy. If people trace their line through their mothers, the stigma of bastardy will vanish. The recurrent problem of civilization, as prevalent today as in ancient Babylonia, is not how to satisfy women's demands; instead, it is how to define male roles that satisfy male egos. Women have no time to wreak havoc: they have too much work, too little power, and too many people forbidding them to act or think.

I personally believe that our societal problems will persist as long as women are not treated as fully human. Women are not better than men, nor are they different in any way that truly matters; they are as eager to soar, and as entitled. The various attempts to improve women's status, ever subject to setbacks and backlashes, are our marks of successful struggle against the old stereotypes. If we cannot solve this thorny and persistent problem, we'll still survive—we have thus far. However, I doubt that we'll ever truly thrive, no matter what technological levels we achieve.

So now that we've checked out all other *Star Trek* societies, let's investigate the paradigm against which all else is measured: the United Federation of Planets.

THE JEWEL IN THE CROWN

Of all the major *Star Trek* races, only the Terrans and Vulcans belong to the Federation. Our glimpses of Vulcans in their native surroundings are limited and usually occur during crises. I can recall seeing Vulcan twice: in "Amok Time" (TOS) and in *The Search for Spock* (ST3). But we can extrapolate a good deal about the Federation by seeing how things are run on the Starfleet starships, and from the occasional visits of our heroes to Earth.

The Federation, aided by a few centuries of internal peace and superior technology, seems to have wiped out all the woes that still bedevil the world today. Their medicine and biotechnology have conquered hunger and diseases. Their maturity and diplomatic skill have put an end to conflicts and environmental depredation.

Even more unbelievably, the Federation has managed to wipe out social inequalities and has apparently done away with one of the greatest stratification indicators: money or, more correctly, the power that money can buy. People just walk to the nearest replicator and presto!—the object they request materializes, whether it's Picard's Earl Grey tea or Jadzia's party gown. They also receive free education and medical care. This makes the Federation—dare I utter the dreaded word?—a socialist entity.

The lifestyle of the Federation is so desirable and its treatment of others so benign that every race in the Alpha Quadrant clamors to join the club. The Federation has a strict hands-off policy regarding internal affairs, though it frowns mightily on Bad Stuff—such as involuntary banishment ("The Hunted," TNG) or the reconstitution of the Bajoran D'jarras, which are the equivalent of Terran castes ("Accession," DS9). On the other hand, the Federation has surprisingly little to say about the status of Ferengi women—about as much as the United States has to say regarding the plight of women under fundamentalist religious rule or in countries that practice female infanticide or genital mutilation.

I'd say that in its outlook the Federation most definitely resembles the Roman Empire. Its other obvious prototype is the benign side of the United States. The Federation appears generous, optimistic, open-minded, tolerant, adventurous, honorable—like a Texan on holiday, with dashes of John Kenneth Galbraith and Richard Feynman thrown in. The Federation believes in both individual freedom and collective harmony. It supports cooperation as well as self-determination. It doesn't care what gods you worship, as long as you pay your taxes—in the form of service to the Federation.

Like any living organism, the Federation has also undergone some evolution from TOS to VOY, from confident adolescence to wary adulthood. In TOS it's freewheeling, insouciant, very much a cowboy. In TNG it has matured into mellowness and contemplation. In DS9 we see cracks appear and spread. And in VOY the Federation is actually the outsider, fighting in enemy territory. Several crossover episodes, in which cast members from different series mingle, clearly show that a casual and routine action in TOS might easily merit a court-martial in the later epochs ("Relics," TNG; "Trials and Tribble-ations," DS9; "Flashback," VOY; *Generations*, ST7).

The Federation starships combine the best of two worlds: although they fully enjoy the benefits of advanced technology, they function as villages where everyone knows everyone else. They have retained the nuclear family, at least in name; we even see one evolving—that of botanist Keiko Ishikawa and engineer Miles O'Brien, which starts in "Data's Day" (TNG) and is running through TNG and DS9 (I'm curious to see how the second nuclear family will fare—Dax and Worf).

However, everyone works full-time, including women, and their duties often take them away from their families. This strongly implies that in some respects they have reverted back to a semicommunal pattern where the entire ship or station acts as an extended family. Either that, or they've settled the seemingly intractable problem of day care, which is apparently more complex than sending a planetary rover to Mars.

The Federation mixture sounds like an unbeatable combination: benevolent paternalism, endless resources, high-minded moral values, plus both the ability and the willingness to explore. The Federation doesn't just love and encourage science and technology; it considers starfaring an integral part of its culture. All is sweetness and light. Or is it? There are several snakes hidden under all that luscious fruit.

For one, it is unclear how civilian-friendly the Federation really is. Starfleet, despite all its trumpetings about being an exploratory branch, is clearly organized in military fashion—uniforms, court-martials, chains of command, the full menu. All the starship crews, including the scientists, doctors, and engineers, are military personnel. To put it baldly, all our heroes are career soldiers. Furthermore, given its official brief, Starfleet has effectively monopolized all desirable professional outlets: science, engineering and technology, defense, diplomacy. Non-Starfleet members can be neither wizards nor warriors, only peasants—or playboys.

Within the nominally classless starships, the upper ranks fraternize exclusively among themselves (we get rare glimpses of the lower ranks in "Lower Decks," TNG, and "Soldiers of the Empire," DS9). I have never seen the crew evaluating the officers, who can order them to their deaths. Bona fide civilians appear only in the episodes when main characters travel back in time, to invariably land in the midst of some riot or impending catastrophe—showcasing, once again, that civilians are bumblers who must be saved from themselves by military intervention ("The City on the Edge of Forever," TOS; "Time's Arrow," TNG; "Past Tense," DS9; "Future's End," VOY).

Granted, all ships through the ages needed to vest authority in the captain. After all, someone must be able to coordinate the crew in emergencies. Nevertheless, I for one felt a chill when I realized that the Federation Council is much closer to the Joint Chiefs of Staff than to a parliament.

I lived my teenage years under the Greek military junta and would wish the experience only on people I heartily loathe. The Greek colonels actually were a relatively benign version of the beast compared to, say, Pol Pot or Pinochet. Civilian rule can be messy and corrupt, whereas trains of fascist nations tend to run on time. Yet I can't think of one instance where people gave unbounded powers to the police and the military and didn't regret their decision. As I said earlier, power does odd things to people's minds. Besides, a hierarchical organization such as the Federation Council makes the whole governing structure vulnerable to instant takeover, as is shown in "Conspiracy" (TNG) and "Homefront"/"Paradise Lost" (DS9).

I can hear arguments that details of organization don't matter, as long as the majority is happy. Even if this were true, what happens when enough people become unhappy? It's a cinch to be benevolent when you're not opposed.

In fact, the Federation, just like the Roman Empire and the United

States, does not like to be defied. When someone dissents significantly, the Federation Council acts like a jilted suitor—it starts stalking the one who spurned it, with intent to kill.

The first time this happens, the wrath of our heroes is played for laughs ("Errand of Mercy," TOS). The next time, it's deadly serious ("The High Ground," TNG). The usually discerning Picard joins one side of an internal conflict not because they're right, but because the other side dared to kidnap a sacrosanct member of his ship. The detached, Olympian Federation people suddenly can't stand to lose face. In a heartbeat, they are willing to interfere in the internal affairs of others, even scuttle the Prime Directive. Not an eye for an eye, but an eye for a tooth.

But if the Federation erupts like a volcano when outsiders challenge its standing, that fit of pique is a small bubbling teapot compared with the fury that's unleashed when the defiance comes from within—from the hapless Valeris in *The Undiscovered Country* (ST6), who distrusts the outcome of the Khitomer Accords; from Ensign Ro Laren in "Preemptive Strike" (TNG), who wants to keep not just her Bajoran earring, but also her opinions; and most significantly, from the Maquis.

The Maquis arc begins in "Preemptive Strike" (TNG) and continues in DS9, giving us some of the most memorable *Star Trek* episodes ("The Maquis," "Defiant," "For the Cause," "For the Uniform," "Blaze of Glory"). Given the promise of the Maquis angle, one of my major disappointments with VOY is that it has made no dramatic use of the intrinsic conflicts between the Federation and Maquis crew members.

Who are these people and why is the Federation so mad at them? The Maquis are a ragged band of Humans, Bajorans, and members of other races who live in the demilitarized zone between Federation and Cardassian space. Their location makes them convenient pawns in the chess game between the two powers—but inconvenient presences when they complain about their treatment at the hands of both. Think of the Roma, the Kurds, or any other group that is at the mercy of "larger geopolitical concerns" and you have a fairly good picture of the Maquis.

However, the main reason that the Federation is miffed at the Maquis and often treats them as terrorists is (hold on to your seats) that they voluntarily left the Federation! Why is their departure so important to the Federation? After all, they have neither power nor influence. This reminds me of the shenanigans in the harems of the Ottoman sultans. Of the thousands of concubines, most never even got to see the Grand Turk, let alone share his bed. Nevertheless, if one tried to leave, she was executed: property is not supposed to inconvenience its owner.

If the Federation is as close as can be to paradise, this is disquieting behavior. In "For the Uniform" (DS9) Sisko chemically poisons an entire planet because it shelters the group of Michael Eddington, an ex-Starfleet officer who has become a Maquis leader. This from the same people who chant the mantra of noninterference and the Prime Directive. The Maquis, on their side, are no angels—but terrorism is the last weapon left to the dispossessed.

Still, excessive self-regard and touchy ego notwithstanding, the Federation is indeed the best there is. When we venture into the other Quadrants, the available choices are noticeably poorer: the Klingons and Ferengi (Beta Quadrant), the Dominion (Gamma Quadrant), the Kazon (Delta Quadrant)—and hovering everywhere and nowhere, the Borg.

In particular, the Federation exhibits all the attributes that a culture must have to stably expand beyond just its planet: it has large resources that it tries to use wisely; it enjoys acquiring knowledge for its own sake; its members have some freedom of movement and balance autonomy with cooperation; the women are specifically not tied solely to reproduction; and in their individual occupations, all Federation citizens avoid overspecialization, so that their exploration vessels have built-in redundancies and fail-safes.

As imagined, *Star Trek*'s Federation is possible, viable—perhaps even necessary, if we want to escape our planetary envelope.

PER ARDUA AD ASTRA

So what kind of society will travel along the celestial corridors? I think one that will look much like the Federation, but perhaps lacking its monolithic and military aspects. Development of the relevant technology requires a tolerant, secular society—also one that does not spend half of its gross national product on instruments of war. Large-minded, enlightened self-interest combined with a thirst for knowledge is the best combination that I can think of. I envision the star-farers as the right mixture of Vulcan, Klingon, and Ferengi, with a healthy Terran topping, using science and technology as their lingua franca.

Perhaps I come across as an idealist wearing rosy-tinted glasses. Explorers have set out with various motives—desire for power, riches, fame. But it seems to me that all who were willing to leave their secure lives to pursue a will-o'-the-wisp shared one attribute: like scientists of all times, like Darwin on the *Beagle,* they were burning with curiosity to discover what lay beyond the horizon. The societies that nurture this spirit of inquiry are the ones that will send out starships. And the starships that will make the best scoutships will not contain solely warriors or merchants, but a well-balanced cross-section of the culture that sent them—just like the *Enterprise.*

CODA: THE INFINITE FRONTIER

A younger science than physics, biology is more linear and less exotic than its older sibling. Whereas physics is elegant and symmetric, biology is lunging and ungainly, bound to the material and macroscopic. Its predictions are more specific, its theories less sweeping. And yet, in the end, the exploration of life is the frontier that matters the most. Life gives meaning to all elegant theories and contraptions, life is where the worlds of cosmology and ethics intersect.

Our exploration of *Star Trek* biology has taken us through wide and distant fields—from the underpinnings of life to the purposeful chaos of our brains; from the precise minuets of our genes to the tangled webs of our societies.

How much of *Star Trek* biology is feasible? I have to say that human immortality, psionic powers, the transporter, and the universal translator are unlikely, if not impossible. On the other hand, I do envision human genetic engineering and cloning, organ and limb regeneration, intelligent robots, and immersive virtual reality—quite possibly in the near future.

Furthermore, the limitations I've discussed in this book only apply to Earth biology. Even within the confines of our own planet, isolated ecosystems have yielded extraordinary life-forms—the marsupials of Australia; the flowerlike tube worms near the hot vents of the ocean depths; the bacteriophage particles that are uncannily similar to the planetary landers. It is certain that when we finally go into space, whatever we meet will exceed our wildest imaginings.

Going beyond strictly scientific matters, I think that the accuracy of scientific details in *Star Trek* is almost irrelevant. Of course, it puzzles me that a show that pays millions to principal actors and for special effects cannot hire a few grad students to vet their scripts for glaring factual errors (I bet they could even get them for free, they'd be that thrilled to participate). Nevertheless, much more vital is *Star Trek*'s stance toward science and the correctness of the scientific principles that it showcases. On the latter two counts, the series has been spectacularly successful and damaging at the same time.

The most crucial positive elements of *Star Trek* are its overall favorable attitude toward science and its strong endorsement of exploration. Equally important (despite frequent lapses) is that the *Enterprise* is meant to be a large equivalent to Cousteau's *Calypso*, not a space Stealth bomber. However, some negative elements are so strong that they almost short-circuit the bright promise of the show.

I cannot be too harsh on *Star Trek*, because it's science fiction—and TV science fiction, at that. Yet by choosing to highlight science, *Star Trek* has also taken on the responsibility of portraying scientific concepts and approaches accurately. Each time *Star Trek* mangles an important scientific concept (such as evolution or black-hole event horizons), it misleads a disproportionately large number of people.

The other trouble with *Star Trek* is its reluctance to showcase truly imaginative or controversial ideas and viewpoints. Of course, the accepted wisdom of media executives who increasingly rely on repeating well-worn concepts is that controversial positions sink ratings. So *Star Trek* often ignores the agonies and ecstasies of real science and the excitement of true or projected scientific discoveries, replacing them with pseudoscientific arcana more appropriate for series like *The X-Files*. Exciting ideas briefly appear on *Star Trek*, only to sink without a trace (silicon life-forms beyond robots, parallel universes). This almost pathological timidity of *Star Trek*, which enjoys the good fortune of a dedicated following and so could easily afford to cut loose, does not bode well for its descendants or its genre.

On the other hand, technobabble and all, *Star Trek* fulfills an important role. It shows and endorses the value of science and technology—the only popular TV series to do so, at a time when science has lost both appeal and prestige. With the increasing depth of each scientific field, and the burgeoning of specialized jargon, it is distressingly easy for us scientists to isolate ourselves within our small niches and forget to share the wonders of our discoveries with our fellow passengers on the starship Earth. Despite its errors, *Star Trek*'s greatest contribution is that it has made us dream of possibilities, and that it has made that dream accessible to people both inside and outside science.

Scientific understanding does not strip away the mystery and grandeur of the universe; the intricate patterns only become lovelier as more and more of them appear and come into focus. The sense of excitement and fulfillment that accompanies even the smallest scientific discovery is so great that it can only be communicated in embarrassingly emotional terms, even by Mr. Spock and Commander Data. In the end, these glimpses of the whole, not fame or riches, are the real reason why the scientists never go into the suspended-animation cocoons, but stay at the starship chart tables and observation posts, watching the great galaxy wheels slowly turn, the stars ignite and darken.

Star Trek's greatest legacy is the communication of the urge to explore, to comprehend, with its accompanying excitement and wonder. Whatever else we find out there, beyond the shelter of our atmosphere, we may discover that thirst for knowledge is the one characteristic common to all intelligent life we encounter in our travels. It is with the hope of such an encounter that people throng around the Voyager and *Sojourner* transmissions. And even now, contained in the sphere of expanding radio and television transmissions speeding away from Earth, *Star Trek* may be acting as our ambassador.

SELECTED BIBLIOGRAPHY

This is a very partial list. I lean toward books that combine scientific accuracy with stylistic verve.

Alvarez, Walter. *T. Rex and the Crater of Doom.* Princeton, N.J.: Princeton University Press, 1997.

Calvin, William, and George Ojemann. *Conversations with Neil's Brain.* Reading, Mass.: Addison-Wesley Publishing Co., 1995.

Dawkins, Richard. *The Selfish Gene.* New York: Oxford University Press, 1989.

Dennett, Daniel. *Kinds of Minds.* New York: HarperCollins, 1996.

Diamond, Jared. *Guns, Germs and Steel: The Fates of Human Societies.* New York: W. W. Norton & Co, 1997.

Dowling, John. *Neurons and Networks: An Introduction to Neuroscience.* Cambridge, Mass.: Belknap Press, 1992.

Drexler, Eric. *Engines of Creation.* New York: Anchor Books, 1986.

Ehrenreich, Barbara. *Blood Rites: Origins and History of the Passions of War.* New York: Henry Holt & Co., 1997.

Gardner, James. *The New Ambidextrous Universe: Symmetry and Asymmetry, from Mirror Reflections to Superstrings.* New York: W. H. Freeman & Co., 1991.

Gleick, James. *Chaos: Making a New Science.* New York: Penguin Books, 1987.

Gosden, Roger. *Cheating Time: Science, Sex, and Aging.* New York: W. H. Freeman & Co., 1996.

Gould, Stephen Jay. *The Mismeasure of Man.* New York: W. W. Norton, 1996.

Hanley, Richard. *The Metaphysics of Star Trek.* New York: Basic Books, 1997.

Hawking, Stephen. *A Brief History of Time: From the Big Bang to Black Holes.* New York: Bantam, 1988.

Hazen, Robert, with Maxine Singer. *Why Aren't Black Holes Black? The Unanswered Questions at the Frontiers of Science.* New York: Anchor Books, 1997.

Hendrickson, James, Donald Cram, and George Hammond. *Organic Chemistry.* New York: McGraw-Hill, 1970.

Jaynes, Julian. *The Origin of Consciousness in the Breakdown of the Bicameral Mind.* New York: Houghton Mifflin Co., 1990.

Kaku, Michio. *Visions: How Science Will Revolutionize the 21st Century.* New York: Anchor Books, 1997.

Konner, Melvin. *Why the Reckless Survive: And Other Secrets of Human Nature.* New York: Viking, 1990.

Krauss, Lawrence. *The Physics of Star Trek.* New York: Basic Books, 1995.

Lehninger, Albert. *Principles of Biochemistry.* New York: Worth Publishing, 1994.

Luria, Salvatore, James Darnell, David Baltimore, and Allan Campbell. *General Virology.* New York: John Wiley & Sons, 1978.

Mayr, Ernst. *This Is Biology: The Science of the Living World.* Cambridge, Mass.: Belknap Press, 1997.

Okuda, Michael, Denise Okuda, Debbie Mirek, and Doug Drexler. *The Star Trek Encyclopedia: A Reference Guide to the Future.* New York: Pocket Books, 1994.

Regis, Ed. *Great Mambo Chicken and the Transhuman Condition: Science Slightly Over the Edge.* Reading, Mass.: Addison-Wesley Publishing Co., 1991.

Restak, Richard. *The Mind.* New York: Doubleday, 1988.

Sagan, Carl. *Pale Blue Dot: A Vision of the Human Future in Space.* New York: Random House, 1994.

Sagan, Carl, and Ann Druyan. *Shadows of Our Forgotten Ancestors: A Search for Who We Are.* New York: Ballantine Books, 1992.

Tenner, Edward. *Why Things Bite Back: Technology and the Revenge of Unintended Consequences.* New York: Knopf, 1996.

Trefil, James. *Are We Unique? A Scientist Explores the Unparalleled Intelligence of the Human Mind.* New York: John Wiley & Sons, 1997.

Watson, James, Nancy Hopkins, Jeff Roberts, Joan Steitz, and Alan Weiner. *Molecular Biology of the Gene.* Menlo Park: Benjamin/Cummings, 1987.

Wilson, Edward. *Sociobiology: The New Synthesis.* Cambridge: Harvard University Press, 1975.

INDEX